THE BOOK OF REVELATION

Treasures of One God

&

The New Birth

Louis Bradley Holub, Jr.

LOUIS BRADLEY HOLUB, JR.

THE BOOK OF REVELATION

Treasures of One God & The New Birth

Unveiling the Identity of Jesus Christ and His Glorious Bride, The Church

A Comprehensive Study

Unless otherwise noted, all Scripture quotations in this book are taken from the *King James Version* of The Holy Bible.

The Holy Bible, King James Version. Cambridge Edition: 1769; *King James Bible Online*, 2022. www.kingjamesbibleonline.org.

CONTACT ADDRESS:
Louis Holub
louisholub@hotmail.com   936-662-0950

Ordering Information:
Quantity sales. Special discounts are available on quantity purchases by churches, associations, and others. For details, please contact the author at the information above.

Treasures of Revelation/Louis Bradley Holub, Jr.—1st ed.
ISBN: 978-1-7373567-4-5

Printed in The United States of America

CONTENTS

DEDICATION

I dedicate this book to my two amazing daughters, Paige and Olivia.
You girls are the crowning jewels of my life!
May you continue to walk faithfully in the steps of our gracious Lord,
always resting in the comfort of His tender mercies.
Pray, fast, study your Bible, cherish this Great Salvation
and pass it on to your children.
God be with you always.
I love you.

FOREWORD

As I read *Treasures of Revelation*, I was impressed by the scriptural insight and thought put into this work. Surely the Lord was impressing Bro. Louis Holub as he compiled these wonderfully inspired pages!

Goethe once said, "It is easier to perceive error than to perceive truth; for the former lies on the surface and is easily seen, while the latter lies in the depths, where few are willing to search."

I've known Brother Holub for many years and have enjoyed our many Bible discussions. I wish this book had been available years ago when I first started my ministry in the Lord. It would have made the book of Revelation much more readable and understandable. There is so much more which might have been discovered had we had this labor of love available then.

I would admonish all to read with an open mind and heart and allow your spiritual eyes and ears to receive that you might fulfill the seven scriptures that say, "He that hath an ear, let him hear what the Spirit saith unto the churches."

REV. JOHNNY B. HIGDON
Church Planter, Pastor
State of Oklahoma District Chairman, ALJC

HOW TO READ THIS BOOK

THIS BOOK IS INTENDED to be a no-nonsense, get-to-the-point, user-friendly guide to understanding difficult Biblical passages. Each chapter begins with a PREMISE, so you *(the reader)* clearly understand what I *(the author)* am presenting.

This book is refreshingly unique because it offers an alternative to the dramatic, fear-mongering interpretations of the Book of Revelation. Rather than creating anxiety and MORE confusion, this book instills hope and clarifies scripture, keeping salvation through Jesus Christ as the central theme.

Each chapter highlights an important key principle. Each key is designed to open your understanding and make your Bible easier to read and navigate.

To get the most out of this book, ask God to open your understanding and start at the beginning. Read one chapter at a time. The material is presented logically and orderly, with easy-to-read pictures and charts. So, take time to read for comprehension. After reading each chapter, stop and ponder what you have just read. Let each chapter sink in before moving to the next.

PREFACE

WELCOME, fellow scholar and adventurer! Climb aboard and sail with us on an amazing treasure hunt of epic proportions! It is not for the fearful or faint of heart, nor for those who prefer to keep their ship in the harbor tethered safely to the dock. Instead, it is for you, oh captain, the thrill-seeking romantic at heart, who inwardly longs to set sail into the unpredictability of the sea for which you and your ship were designed. So, with a hardy bellowing "Aargh!" throw off the dock lines and come along and explore the beauty beyond the horizon!

Fair warning, mate! As you explore unchartered territory, do not grow weary; do not lose heart. You will be challenged. You will be stretched. You may even become consumed in this true-to-life, exhilarating treasure hunt. But, I promise, if you stay at the helm and embrace this journey without prejudice, you will uncover the mysteries of the deep.

You will lay claim to treasures—peculiar treasures that are incorruptible. You will see Jesus Christ from a fresh, intimate, personal perspective that will take your breath away! You will see very clearly the identity of the Bride of Christ, the True Church. You will be relieved and encouraged to know that everything will turn out just fine, that you can trust The Lord, and that He does have a future hope and reward for us.

Allow the Word to unfold before you and prepare for an adventuresome ride. No matter your belief or philosophy, I challenge you to keep an open mind. Ask God for wisdom and understanding. He desires to open His Word to you. John 16:13 declares, "when he, the Spirit of truth, is come, he will guide you into all truth." If something has a ring of truth, consider it, and search it out. If it is false, discard it. You do have that discretion and privilege, you know.

Because prophecy is so profoundly shrouded in symbolism and our ability to comprehend at times seems beyond our grasp, we tend to gravitate to the interpretation we have heard most often. The danger of this natural tendency is that an unchallenged statement repeated often enough will eventually become acceptable and viewed as truth, even if there is no truth in the statement.

The natural prejudice towards the information we have repeatedly heard grows stronger as time progresses. This prejudice is all but impossible to overcome. What we think to be true will always win over what is actually true. Add to the mix our human ego and pride, and, oh boy!

It is healthy to question, analyze, critique and challenge. However, we must also embrace criticism. It is how we grow. Where and what would we be if we were never challenged? We question to find the truth, not excuse it. We question to find a way *in*, not a way *out;* access to truth, not a detour around it.

Scripture will never contradict itself. Scripture application to an individual's life may vary, but a scripture's meaning or principal message will remain constant. If scripture or scripture passages appear to contradict in meaning or principle, we are either not reading it correctly or our interpretation is wrong.

You can understand the Bible. You *can* understand the Bible. *You* can understand the Bible! And yes, we simple ones can read and comprehend it as well, even the seemingly most difficult parts. Has not God chosen the simple things of the world to confound the wise? Therefore, He gets the glory, and we cannot boast. Besides, it is too easy to get puffed up with pride and think *our* understanding is based on *our* intellect. And that, my friend, is the moment we sabotage our journey. Whatever truth we possess, it is because God revealed it to us through His unfathomable grace.

This book was not born out of contention nor formulated as a rebuttal to any of the many interpretations of the Book of Revelation. Instead, it began as a compilation of notes to answer a simple yet profound question: *If Revelation 1:1 begins, The Revelation of Jesus Christ which God gave unto him [John], then just how does the Book of Revelation actually reveal Jesus Christ?*

Here is the main theme and where the journey begins: If the Book of Revelation is the Revelation (the revealing or the unveiling) of Jesus Christ, then:

1. How does it reveal the identity of Jesus Christ and One God?
2. How does it reveal His plan for salvation?
3. How does it reveal the True Church?

I have endeavored to keep my illustrations as simple as possible. I do not intend to lure the reader through emotion brought about by dramatic artistic representations.

Are you ready? Then, let's begin our journey into the *Treasures of Revelation*!

Louis Holub, Jr.

CHAPTER 1

THE SEVEN CHURCHES OF ASIA

Revelation 1 through 3

THE PREMISE:

The Seven Churches of Asia represent a cross-section of the churches of John's generation. They are typical, perhaps, of churches in all generations in various stages of truth, apostasy, and compromise.

SCRIPTURE TEXT:

Revelation 1:4 *John, to the seven churches which are in Asia: Grace be unto you, and peace, from him which is, and which was, and which is to come, and from the seven Spirits which are before his throne.*
Revelation 1:11 *I am the Alpha and Omega, the first and the last: and, what thou seest, write in a book, and send it unto the seven churches which are in Asia; unto Ephesus, and unto Smyrna, and unto Pergamos, and unto Thyatira, and unto Sardis, and unto Philadelphia, and unto Laodicea.*

SEVEN DOMINANT CHURCHES

Three were part good/part bad - Ephesus, Pergamum, and Thyatira
Two were very bad - Sardis and Laodicea
Two were very good - Smyrna and Philadelphia

LOCATION OF THE SEVEN CHURCHES

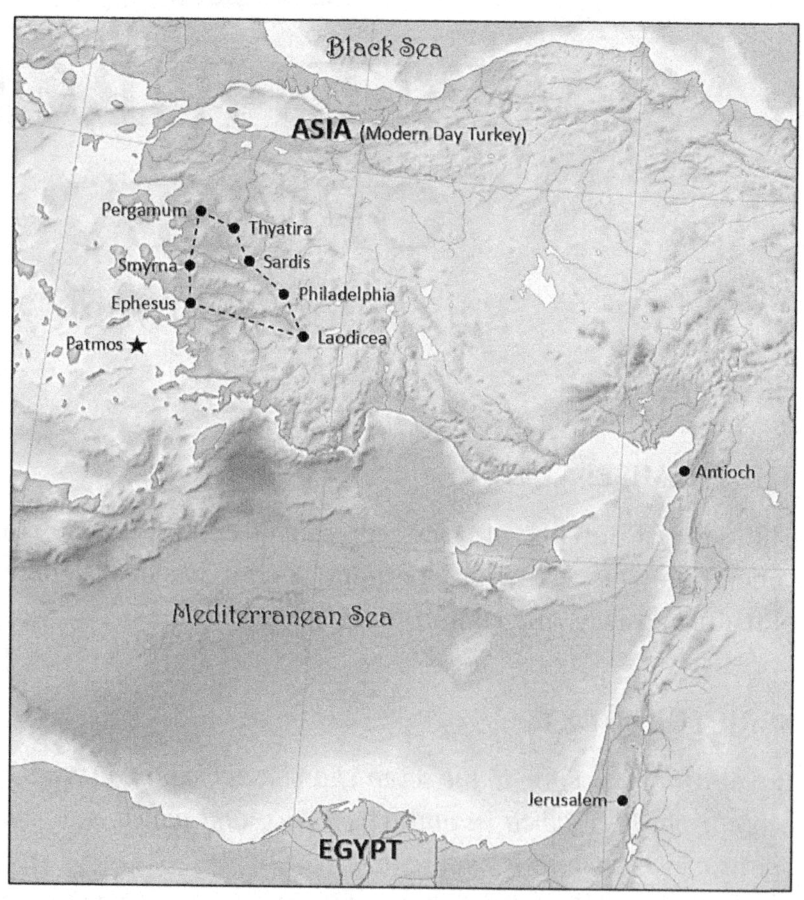

Asia was a Roman Province in the west part of what we know as Asia Minor, and now a part of Turkey. A great triangular highway connected the seven cities. Although there were many churches in Asia, each city contained a main church or a dominant body of believers. These cities are named in their geographical order, beginning with **Ephesus**, then north about 100 miles to **Pergamos** (passing thru **Smyrna** along the way), and then southeast to **Laodicea,** which was about 100 miles east of Ephesus. **Thyatira**, **Sardis,** and **Philadelphia** lay in between Pergamos and Laodicea.

It is important to note that each message from The Lord was addressed "unto the angel of the church." (e.g., Revelation 12:13). The angel (*or messenger*) of each church is the pastor. God's divine order is to speak to the local assembly through the pastor. It is then the pastor's responsibility to deliver the message to the local church body. Although God can and does speak to people individually, God appointed pastors as leaders to promote accountability and unity in the faith within the local church body.

BACKGROUND

It had only been about 50 years since the resurrection of Jesus Christ, and Christianity had been growing by leaps and bounds. However, with the rapid growth and the infant stage of the church, Satan was doing all he could to corrupt and kill it.

SATAN'S TACTICS – HERESY AND COMPROMISE

The heresy was the acceptance of *fornication* and the *eating of things sacrificed to idols* among church members. Sexual vice was a part of heathen worship and accepted as standard practice in heathen festivals. Nearly 50 years earlier, a circular letter was sent from the Apostles at Jerusalem to the Gentile churches, insisting that Christians *must abstain from pollutions of idols, and from fornication, and from things strangled and from blood*. (Acts 15:20)

The allurements of Diana worship had a tremendous appeal to human nature, and it was not easy for those accustomed to such practices to give them up. So, naturally, there were all sorts of attempts to harmonize these practices with Christianity. Many self-professed Christian teachers claimed inspiration from God and advocated the right to participate in these immoral activities. Ephesus excluded such teachers, while Pergamum and Thyatira tolerated them.

God instructed John to write what he saw, including a unique, brief message to each of the seven churches. Each letter ends with, "He that hath an ear, let him hear what the Spirit saith unto the churches." It appears that seven copies of the letters were made and sent to each city. Each church could thus read the Lord's analysis, not only of itself but also regarding the other six.

The Seven Spirits of God represent a seven-fold, or complete operation of the Holy Ghost, the Spirit of Jesus Christ, revealing Himself to each church relevant to each church's particular need. Therefore, no matter the situation or condition, the answer always lies in Jesus Christ. Furthermore, He will reveal Himself to us as He sees fit, whether rebuke, encouragement, healing, etc. And since Jesus Christ is the Word of God made flesh, all our answers lie in the sacred scriptures of the Holy Bible.

THE ORIGIN OF IDOL GODS AND GODDESSES

After the flood, the entire earth's population had been reduced to only eight people: Noah, his wife, his three sons, Shem, Ham, and Japheth, and their wives. From Shem came the Jews, from Ham came the Canaanites (the cursed lineage), and from Japheth came the Gentiles. One of Ham's sons was Cush, the father of Nimrod. Therefore, Nimrod was the great-grandson of Noah and a powerful and ambitious young man known for being a mighty hunter.

Noah and his family settled in the fertile lands of Shinar. This area was where the Euphrates and Tigris Rivers had built up rich soil deposits, making it easy to produce crops in abundance. This wonderful fertile land of Shinar was not only a great place for human habitation but also for animals. And unfortunately, it wasn't long before it was overrun with wild animals threatening the peace and safety of the people.

The threat of wild animals was a new challenge that did not exist before the flood. Before the flood, both man and animals adhered to a plant-based diet. Neither man nor the animals consumed meat. Therefore, because meat was not a part of the diet, fear did not exist between man and animals.

> *And God said, Behold, I have given you every herb bearing seed, which is upon the face of all the earth, and every tree, in the which is the fruit of a tree yielding seed; to you it shall be for meat. And to every beast of the earth, and to every fowl of the air, and to every thing that creepeth upon the earth, wherein there is life, I have given every green herb for meat: and it was so.*
>
> GENESIS 1:29-30

The peaceful cohabitation of man and animals, along with a plant-based diet, made it possible for a harmonious stay in the ark while the floodwaters were upon the earth. However, all this would change after they went forth from the ark.

> *And God blessed Noah and his sons, and said unto them, Be fruitful, and multiply, and replenish the earth. And the fear of you and the dread of you shall be upon every beast of the earth, and upon every fowl of the air, upon all that moveth upon the earth, and upon all the fishes of the sea; into your hand are they delivered. Every moving thing that liveth shall be meat for you; even as the green herb have I given you all things.*
>
> GENESIS 9:1-3

The fear of man was now upon the animal kingdom, and like the green herb, animal flesh was introduced as a part of the diet. No longer did all the animals peacefully cohabitate with man because God put the fear and dread of man upon every beast of the earth.

And not only did man multiply and replenish the earth, but so did the animals, including predatory animals. Unlike before the flood, predatory animals now threatened the peace and safety of the people. Therefore, if a man was a successful hunter, he was highly esteemed and greatly honored because he served as a protector and a provider.

Nimrod, being a great and mighty hunter, seized this opportunity to shine (pun intended, for he later became known as the sun god.) He organized the people into fenced cities for protection, and he became the first to establish kingdoms which accounted for his rapid rise into power. This process happened in two stages. The *first* was in Shinar, including Babel, Erech, Accad, and Calneh. The *second* was in Assyria, referred to as the land of Nimrod in Micah 5: 6.

Nimrod in Hebrew means "rebel." The Jewish historian Flavius Josephus says that it was Nimrod who moved the people to such contempt for God by persuading them to believe their own courage brought about their happiness. Nimrod, also through tyranny, gradually took governmental control seeing no other way of turning men from the fear of God to total dependence on his power.

Traditions and legends give Nimrod credit for building the Tower of Babel. Rather than obeying God by going forth and replenishing the earth, Nimrod influenced the people to rebel, build a kingdom, and make a name for themselves. They began to build a temple to reach heaven, which some historians believe was also made waterproof in the possibility of another flood. Whatever the case, this was a contemptible act and a mockery against God! Therefore, in Genesis 11:9, God confounded the language and scattered the people throughout the earth.

Sin and rebellion will always lead to further demise. If left unrepented, it will affect not only the individual at fault but those around him. As the story of Nimrod continues, his legacy introduced idolatry, immorality, and self-indulgence into every counterfeit religion we have today. According to ancient Babylonian and Egyptian tradition, Nimrod's mother, Semiramis, was also referred to as his "wife" on occasion, leading to the belief that Nimrod married his mother.

As Nimrod rose to power, so did Semiramis. When Nimrod died, Semiramis pronounced him a god (the sun god), naturally making her a goddess (the moon god). One story says that after Nimrod's death, Semiramis claimed that an evergreen tree sprouted out of a dead tree stump, indicating that Nimrod would be reincarnated. From then on, gifts were brought to the tree every year on the anniversary of Nimrod's death (the root of some Christmas traditions).

Semiramis had another problem. Although she claimed to be a virgin, she had become pregnant and gave birth to another son named Tammuz. Claiming to be a virgin was quite ridiculous, seeing she was already the mother of Nimrod. Howbeit, to keep her goddess status, she alleged Tammuz was conceived by a sunbeam, thus making Nimrod the father and Tammuz the reincarnation of Nimrod. Semiramis became known as the *Virgin Mother*, *Holy Mother*, and the *Queen of Heaven* and was symbolized by the moon. Thus began the worship of a mother-goddess and a child-god. As seen in the following image, this religious practice would soon permeate virtually every significant culture in history.

In this early Babylonian time, the worship of Nimrod, Semiramis, and Tammuz established the idea and teaching of a triple or triune deity. For this reason, the pagan-rooted religious institution of the last days is called "Mystery Babylon." From various ancient sources, Semiramis was considered the high priestess of the Babel religion and the founder of all mystery religions. After the Tower of Babel was destroyed and God confounded the language, Nimrod, Semiramis, and Tammuz continued to be worshipped as deities under many different names in many languages. Here are a few examples:

Babylon:	Nimrod (Baal)	Semiramis	Tammuz
Egypt:	Osiris	Isis	Horus
Greece:	Zeus	Athena (Aphrodite)	Apollo (Eros)
Rome:	Jupiter	Venus	Mercury (Cupid)
Phoenicia:	Baal	Astarte (Ashtoreth)	Adonis

This religious custom also influenced the One True God to be viewed in triple form. Therefore, God's first and great commandment is, "*Hear, O Israel: The LORD our God [is] one LORD:*" (Deuteronomy 6:4). The emphasis here is on ***one*** Lord.

According to Wikipedia, the most prominent ancient Triple Goddess was Diana, who was equated with the Greek goddess Hecate (pronounced **heh**·kuh·tee). She and Hecate were each represented in triple form from the early days of their worship. Diana ultimately was viewed as a triunity of three goddesses in one: goddess of the *hunt*, goddess of the *moon*, and goddess of the *underworld*.

Often Hecate is accented with sunrays and holding a torch, a symbol we still see in our culture today. The Columbia Torch Lady, the Statue of Liberty, and the woman atop the Palais Garnier Opera House in Paris, France, all share a striking resemblance to the Greek goddess, Hecate (see images on previous page. In every case, the worship of these various pagan gods and goddesses was associated with sexual immorality and self-indulgence.

When the Roman Catholic Church began the Christianization of the world during the crusades, she was amazed to find the worship of a virgin mother and her child already a part of the religious culture. This allowed the Catholic Church to quickly shift the worship from *Isis* and *Horus* in Egypt, *Aphrodite* and *Eros* in Greece, *Venus* and *Cupid* in Rome, and so on, to the worship of *Mary* and *baby Jesus.*

Columbia Torch Lady

Statue of Liberty

Palais Garnier Opera House, Paris, France

Hecate

And thus, the climate for the mixture of paganism and Christianity was established. So, likewise, the worship of other gods and goddesses was easily changed into saints with corresponding similarities.

The point is that Satan has always had a counterfeit to anything pure and holy and belonging to God. The counterfeit would manifest itself in various ways throughout time to undermine God's True Redemptive Plan for mankind.

Solomon instructed, *"Good understanding giveth favor: but the way of transgressors is hard."* (Proverbs 13:15). Jesus taught, *"My yoke is easy, and my burden is light."* (Matthew 11:30). Paul declared, *"But I fear, lest by any means, as the serpent beguiled Eve through his subtlety, so your minds should be corrupted from the simplicity that is in Christ."* (2 Corinthians 11:3).

Serving the Lord is simple! It is not grievous and complicated, full of rites and rituals. Instead, as alluded to in scripture, it is like a beautiful, joyous, and romantic relationship between a husband and his wife.

EPHESUS: PART GOOD/PART BAD

Unto the angel of the church of Ephesus write: These things saith he that holdeth the seven stars in his right hand, who walketh in the midst of the seven golden candlesticks;

REVELATION 2:1

Once a proud, rich, and busy trading port, Ephesus was now silted up. It was built near the shrine of an old Anatolian fertility goddess and became the seat of an oriental cult. Around the cult clustered much trade. It became a place of pilgrimage for tourist-worshipers and brought about the prosperous guild of silversmiths. These artisans manufactured silver shrines and images of the meteoric stone, said to be Diana's image fallen from heaven. As a result, Ephesus depended increasingly on the trade and commerce which followed the cult.

GOD'S ASSESSMENT: THE PROUD CHURCH

Fallen from their first love—this was their offense. The Church of Ephesus had become prideful in its identity and reputation and complacent in its attitude toward a lost and dying world. Their zeal for doctrinal purity was commendable; however, their love was for *their* doctrine and righteousness and not for God and their fellow man. They no longer loved God as they once did. God admonishes us to love Him with all our heart, soul, and strength and to love our neighbor as He loves us. All scriptural teaching can be summed up in these two simple commandments.

> *By this shall all men know that ye are my disciples, if ye have love one to another.*
>
> JOHN 13:35

To become doctrinally strong, only to look down upon those who are not like us or do not share our beliefs, is not the love of Christ. Consequently, the Church of Ephesus received a stinging rebuke to repent, or their candlestick would be removed. And it has—the site of Ephesus is now deserted.

PROMISE TO THE OVERCOMER

The Tree of Life was promised to those who would *repent*, return to their *first love* and overcome the natural temptations of fleshly indulgences and worldly ease. The promise of the Tree of Life still holds for those individuals in any church who overcome.

PERGAMUM: PART GOOD/PART BAD

> *And to the angel of the church in Pergamos write; These things saith he which hath the sharp sword with two edges;*
>
> REVELATION 2:12

Pergamum developed into a major city in the new province of Asia. The first temple of a Caesar cult was erected there for Rome and Augustus in 29 BC. The worship of Asklepios (the god of medicine) and Zeus was also native to this region. So it was natural that Nicolaitanism should flourish in a place where politics and paganism were so closely allied and where pressure on Christians to compromise must have been heavy. Nicolaitanism was generally associated with eating things offered to idols and fornication (sexual immorality).

GOD'S ASSESSMENT: THE TOLERANT CHURCH

The Church of Pergamum was faithful to the name of Christ (even unto martyrdom) but tolerant of false teachers, probably the same class of false teachers as those in Ephesus. Pastors at Ephesus, as a body, stood solidly against the false teachers. But here in Pergamum, the pastors, though not themselves holding to the false teaching, tolerated within their ranks those who did. The false teaching was the right of Christians to indulge in heathen immoralities. False doctrine was being intermingled with the truth, and The Lord wanted this wickedness removed from the church.

For the word of God is quick, and powerful, and sharper than any two-edged sword, piercing even to the dividing asunder of soul and spirit, and of the joints and marrow, and is a discerner of the thoughts and intents of the heart.

HEBREWS 4:12

Pergamum was a seat of Emperor worship, where people offered incense before the emperor's statue as to God. Quite often, the refusal of Christians to do so meant death. Also, an altar to Jupiter and a temple of Esculapius (another name for *Asklepios*), a healing god in the form of a serpent, were worshipped. This city was also a stronghold of Balaamite and Sicolaitan teachers. Sicolaitan doctrine, the teaching of the Nicolaitans, refers to *dominating* the people compared to the teaching of Balaam, which refers to *seducing* the people. Thus, as a notorious center of heathenism and wickedness, Pergamum was called Satan's Throne.

PROMISE TO THE OVERCOMER

Those who would overcome the temptations of sinful pleasures were promised Hidden Manna and A White Stone with a New Name written on it.

THE HIDDEN MANNA, A WHITE STONE, A NEW NAME

There are different views within commentaries concerning The Hidden Manna and A White Stone with a New Name written in it. God provided manna for Israel in the wilderness after leaving Egypt. Still, the Old Testament is a schoolmaster for the New Testament. What was *veiled* in the Old Testament is *unveiled* in the New Testament.

And had rained down manna upon them to eat and had given them of the corn of heaven. Man did eat angels' food: he sent them meat to the full.

PSALM 78:24-25

Then Jesus said unto them, Verily, verily, I say unto you, Moses gave you not that bread from heaven; but my Father giveth you the true bread from heaven. For the bread of God is he which cometh down from heaven, and giveth life unto the world.
I am that bread of life. Your fathers did eat manna in the wilderness and are dead.
As the living Father hath sent me, and I live by the Father, so he that eateth me, even he shall live by me. This is that bread which came down from heaven; not as your fathers did eat manna and are dead: he that eateth of this bread shall live forever.

JOHN 6:32-33; 48-49; 57-58

And he was clothed with a vesture dipped in blood: and his name is called The Word Of God.

REVELATION 19:13

Jesus was not referring to eating his natural body but to studying and obeying the scriptures and making the Word of God the guiding light of our life. The scriptures above, along with many others, such as Matthew 15:22-27, Mark 7:27, and Luke 4:4, illustrate that when we hear Jesus Christ, the Word of God, taught or preached, we are feasting on angels' food. This is the true manna that comes from God out of Heaven. The Bible calls it "hidden manna."

But if our gospel is hidden, it is hid to them that are lost:

2 CORINTHIANS 4:3

Not everyone finds this Pearl of Great Price. The oddity is that a person will not even know it unless they have received it.

A white stone was generally regarded as a token of favor, prosperity, or success. It could have been in the form of a vote or reward to a victor. The name engraved on the stone would be marked to indicate its origin, the name of the giver, and/or the victor's name as a pledge of friendship, favor, and reward.

In Christianity, the White Stone has a spiritual connotation and denotes the approval and favor of our Redeemer, Jesus Christ. The Christian victor receives such a token of divine favor evidenced by pardoned sin, joy in the Holy Ghost, and the hope of everlasting life. He bears it about as a precious stone and a promise from the Redeemer that heaven awaits. The world does not understand it or attach any value to it. It is considered enthusiasm, fanaticism, or delusion to the world. But, to the Christian, it is joy unspeakable and full of glory (see 1 Peter 1:7-9).

A friend of mine spoke of his pastor years ago, who was of Jewish descent. The Jewish pastor shared some interesting cultural history on the significance of a white stone. He said that in Jewish custom, if a notable deed was performed, such as saving the life of another, it was customary to find a smooth white stone as a witness to a lasting friendship between the two parties. Then, they would break the stone in half, and each would keep his half as a covenant of friendship. When the next generation or two came along, their half of the white stone could then be put up with the half of their family friend's white stone. And, if there was a match, the covenant of friendship would be validated and renewed.

When we come to the house of God and hear the Gospel of Jesus Christ taught or preached, or any scripture for that matter, we are feasting on angels' food—the Word of God. Suppose we follow and obey the Word of God and are born again according to scripture and live an overcoming life. In that case, we, too, are promised to partake of the Hidden Manna and receive a White Stone with a New Name written on it. If we continue to focus on God and stand firm upon the Word of God, allowing the Holy Ghost to lead us, God will divide true doctrine from false doctrine, just as he was doing in the Church of Pergamum.

THYATIRA: PART GOOD/PART BAD

And unto the angel of the church in Thyatira write; These things saith the Son of God, who hath his eyes like unto a flame of fire, and his feet are like fine brass;

REVELATION 2:18

Thyatira had no illustrious history and was barely mentioned by ancient writers. However, the city was a center of commerce. It is interesting to find another Jezebel, nicknamed after King Ahab's wicked wife, leading a party of compromise in the church of Thyatira.

GOD'S ASSESSMENT: THE COMPROMISING CHURCH

The Church of Thyatira was the Church of Compromise. They did have some good qualities: *love, service, faith, and patience.* They were even growing in zeal, *their last works more than their first.* (Revelation 2:19). Thyatira was just the opposite of Ephesus.

WHO WAS JEZEBEL?

Thyatira was most famous for the temple of Artemis (another name for Diana). Jezebel was likely a prominent woman devotee of Diana with an aptitude for leadership who had a following of influential people in the city. Attracted to the growing cause of Christianity, she attached herself to the Church, militantly insisting she was entitled to teach and practice promiscuous indulgence, claiming inspiration for her teaching.

The comparison between this so-called Jezebel and the original Jezebel, who was married to King Ahab, is perhaps due to the powerful influence she had in causing the people of God to commit spiritual harlotry. Just as Jezebel of the Old Testament had introduced the abominations of Astarte worship into Israel (I Kings 16), this New Testament Jezebel was infecting the Christian Church with the same vile practices.

Not all Thyatira pastors accepted her teaching. But they received her as a fellow saint, trying to be liberal, open-minded, politically correct, and relevant, and thinking that she might help reach and win the whole city to Christianity. With that, the Lord was greatly displeased. And, in a stinging rebuke, He presented Himself with eyes like fire and feet like brass.

> *Be ye not unequally yoked together with unbelievers: for what fellowship hath righteousness with unrighteousness? And what communion hath light with darkness?*
> 2 CORINTHIANS 6:14

THE DEEP THINGS OF SATAN

This is the third mention of Satan in the letters to the churches. In Smyrna, the Church was being persecuted by the blasphemy of a group of professed Jews who God referred to as the synagogue of Satan. In Pergamum, Satan's throne, the seat of idolatry, was infecting the Church. And here in Thyatira, Jezebel's infectious spirit of compromise was known as the deep things of Satan.

Compromise, like cancer, takes root in the body and begins to grow, giving place to all types of outlandish beliefs. Left alone, it continues to grow and spread undetected throughout the body. All too often, by the time it is finally manifested, it has attached itself so tightly to vital organs of the body that removal would ultimately cause death to the entire body. Therefore, we must never compromise the truth.

PROMISE TO THE OVERCOMER

Power is promised to those who overcome the spirit of compromise, along with the capability to rise above worldliness and rule with spiritual authority. The overcomer is also promised the *morning star*, the glory of God revealed in Jesus Christ (Revelation 22:16). It is a robe of righteousness and a sure place in God's kingdom, as opposed to the ungodly who are *wandering stars* doomed to the blackness of darkness forever (Jude 1:13).

SARDIS: VERY BAD

And unto the angel of the church in Sardis write; These things saith he that hath the seven Spirits of God, and the seven stars; I know thy works, that thou has a name that thou livest, and art dead.

REVELATION 3:1

Sardis was the chief city of Lydia and was famous for arts and crafts. It was the first center to mint gold and silver coinage, legendary for riches, pride, and arrogance.

GOD'S ASSESSMENT: THE DEAD CHURCH

The Church of Sardis was alive in name only. Only a few had not defiled their garments. Yet, in the 6th century BC, Sardis was one of the world's wealthiest and most influential cities. The Church of Sardis had works, but their works were not found perfect before God. Thus they were admonished to repent, or He would come upon them as a thief in the night.

PROMISE TO THE OVERCOMER

But, to him that overcometh, white raiment and God would not blot out his name out of the book of life. (Revelation 3:5).

LAODICEA: VERY BAD

And unto the angel of the church of the Laodiceans write; These things saith the Amen, the faithful and true witness, the beginning of the creation of God;

REVELATION 3:14

Laodicea was also a wealthy city in Asia Minor and head of the circuit of The Seven Churches of Asia. It was located on a sizeable Asian trade route which caused significant commercial prosperity. Laodicea also contained a major banking center.

With the city's exposed position and easy wealth, growth in the community fostered a spirit of compromise and worldly-mindedness where the cares of this world, the deceitfulness of riches, and the lusts of other things, choked the Word (see Mark 4:19).

GOD'S ASSESSMENT: THE LUKEWARM CHURCH

Laodicea was a banking center, proud of its wealth, beautified with splendid temples and theaters, and noted for being a manufacturer of rich garments of black glossy wool. The Church of Laodicea was rich and increased with goods and needed nothing. Thus, the Lord said, "Buy of me gold tried in the fire, that thou mayest be rich; and white raiment, that thou mayest be clothed." (Revelation 3:18).

I STAND AT THE DOOR AND KNOCK

Here is a strange picture—a Church of Christ, with Christ Himself on the outside, asking to be let in. Yet, in measure, it is indicative of many churches today that exist under the Name of Christ, but with the operation of the Spirit of Christ in little evidence. With wealth and provision also comes an attitude of self-sufficiency. We must never forget our daily dependency upon The Lord and allow Him to have supreme authority in our midst at all times.

God is sovereign, and He alone knows what is best for us. Evidently, the church of Laodicea forgot their reliance on Him, and with a stinging rebuke, the Lord said He would spew them out of His mouth if they didn't repent. And He has done accordingly because Laodicea no longer exists.

PROMISE TO THE OVERCOMER

The overcomer will be granted to sit with The Lord in His throne. Only by being totally dependent upon God can an individual achieve such spiritual heights.

SMYRNA: VERY GOOD

> *And unto the angel of the church in Smyrna write; These things saith the first and the last, which was dead, and is alive;*
>
> REVELATION 2:8

Smyrna had an early checkered history. The Lydians destroyed it in 627 BC, and for three centuries, Smyrna was little more than just a village. Reestablished in the middle of the 4th century before Christ, it rapidly became the chief city of Asia. The city had worshipped Rome as a spiritual power since 195 BC; hence Smyrna's historical pride in her Caesar cult. Polycarp, Smyrna's martyred bishop of AD 155, had been a disciple of John.

GOD'S ASSESSMENT: POOR BUT RICH

Smyrna was known as the "Suffering Church." The Church of Smyrna received no admonishment, only loving comfort. About 50 miles north of Ephesus, Smyrna was a splendid city, of rare beauty, on a fine bay. Its bishop, at the time, was the beloved Polycarp, appointed bishop by John. The Church was composed of poor people, nothing like the prestige of the large congregation of the Church in Ephesus. According to God, they were *poor* but *rich*.

To those facing martyrdom, the One who was dead and is alive reminded them that He had already suffered what they were about to suffer. And they, too, would be alive forever.

PROMISE TO THE OVERCOMER

The Lord promised those who overcome a Crown of Life and that the Second Death shall not hurt them. In another sense, as a city, Smyrna has been given a Crown of Life. It has survived through all the centuries and is now one of the largest cities in Asia Minor. As seen in the photo on the following page, it is a city of splendid beauty known as modern-day Izmir, Turkey.

Modern-Day Izmir, Turkey

PHILADELPHIA: VERY GOOD

> *And to the angel of the church in Philadelphia write; These things saith he that is holy, he that is true, he that hath the key of David, he that openeth, and no man shutteth; and shutteth, and no man openeth;*
>
> REVELATION 3:7

Philadelphia was also a Lydian city. Despite Muslim invasion and pressure, a Christian witness was maintained in Philadelphia through medieval times and into modern times.

GOD'S ASSESSMENT: THE FAITHFUL CHURCH

The Church of Philadelphia was the epitome of humility. Philadelphia was derived from *philadelphos*, which literally means "one who loves his brother" or "city of brotherly love." Content to exemplify the life of Christ amid a pagan and corrupt society, the Philadelphia Church was a lover of God's Word and intent on keeping it. Philadelphia was greatly beloved of the Lord, with no word of reproof.

AN OPEN DOOR THAT NO MAN CAN SHUT

God had warned Ephesus and Sardis against boasting of their influential standing. So here, God encourages the Church of Philadelphia not to be discouraged because it was not affluent or of excellent reputation, for God is not dependent on worldly prestige.

One of the pagan gods worshipped in Asia Minor was Janus, the pagan god of doors and hinges, also referred to as "the god of beginnings" and the "opener and shutter." In our Roman calendar, the beginning month, January, comes from this name. Even today, the man entrusted with all the door keys to a building is called a janitor, another word derived from Janus. Because this counterfeit pagan god was worshipped this way, the chosen words of Jesus to the church in Philadelphia carry a deeper and more personal meaning.

The Philadelphia church was reminded that this god among the pagans was nothing more than a powerless counterfeit and that Jesus was the *true* opener and shutter of doors. In fact, not only is Jesus the opener and shutter of doors, but Jesus *is* the door!

PROMISE TO THE OVERCOMER

To those who overcome, a new name is promised. The overcomer is granted a new identity in Christ. It is very interesting to note that the city of Philadelphia was even given a new identity. It was eventually given the name Alasehir or Ala-Shehir, which means "the city of God." It is still a prosperous town today, with many residents, including a large Christian population.

SUMMARY OF THE SEVEN CHURCHES

Three were partly good and partly bad:

- **Ephesus**
  Orthodox in teaching, but losing their first love
- **Pergamum**
  Tolerant of heresy, but faithful to the Name of Christ
- **Thyatira**
  Compromising, tolerating Jezebel, but growing in zeal

Two were very bad:

- **Sardis and Laodicea**
  Rich, ruling class, nominally Christian but pagan in life

Two were very good:

- **Smyrna and Philadelphia**
  Humble class of people facing persecution

This chapter shows that the seven Spirits of God were not seven individual and distinct spirits. But instead, they were seven different ways in which God needed to reveal Himself to each Church according to the specific situation. This teaching is relevant to us today. The answer to our dilemma is *always* Jesus Christ. How He chooses to manifest Himself is His business. It is only our business to have faith, believe, and act accordingly.

THE EARLY CHURCH AND THE CHURCH TODAY

With the onslaught of idolatry and false teaching infiltrating the early church, one can certainly conclude that the church today faces the same challenges. Satan's strategy then was doing severe damage, and he is, without a doubt, using the very same demonic tactics to derail Christians today. Not only the church but we as individuals cycle through seasons of life encumbered with distractions and challenges.

Therefore, it is extremely vital that we die daily to the carnal desires of our flesh. We must live a repentant life, casting aside the works of the flesh in order to bring forth Spiritual fruit. Repentance and humility are the keys to having the right perspective and a profitable life in Christ. And repentance and humility only come about if we love God with all our heart, mind, and strength and love our neighbor as ourselves.

So, what do we do about false doctrines in and around us? In the Book of Acts, Gamaliel, a Pharisee, and a doctor of the law, had a good philosophy on the matter:

And now I say unto you, Refrain from these men, and let them alone: for if this counsel or this work be of men, it will come to naught: But if it is of God, ye cannot overthrow it; lest haply ye be found even to fight against God.

ACTS 5:38-39

The point is to keep preaching and teaching the truth. If the seed of truth is planted in the heart of an individual, that seed will grow—provided it has fallen on good ground. But unfortunately, until the Second Coming of Jesus Christ, there will continue to be an overwhelming abundance of false teaching, idolatry, and worldly-mindedness. Therefore, it is imperative that we love the Word of God more than anything else and stay ever so close to His Word continually.

CONCLUSION:

The Seven Churches of Asia represented a fair cross-section of the churches of John's generation: typical, perhaps, of churches in *all* generations, in varying stages of truth and apostasy, and humanized with worldly traditions.

CHAPTER 2

AROUND THE THRONE

Revelation 4

THE PREMISE:

The Twenty-Four Elders and the Four Beasts are the Old Testament and the New Testament, which further reveal the identity of Jesus Christ.

INTRODUCTION:

Revelation 1:1 will continue to serve as a reminder that the underlying theme of the Book of Revelation is the revealing and unveiling of the identity of Jesus Christ.

> *The Revelation of Jesus Christ, which God gave unto him, to shew unto his servants things which must shortly come to pass; and he sent and signified it by his angel unto his servant John: Who bare record of the word of God, and of the testimony of Jesus Christ, and of all things that he saw. Blessed is he that readeth, and they that hear the words of this prophecy, and keep those things which are written therein: for the time is at hand.*
>
> REVELATION 1:1-3

We are promised to be blessed if we read and hear the words of this book and keep them in our hearts. They are indeed relevant to our time.

THE BOOK OF REVELATION IS DIVIDED INTO TWO PARTS

Part I, Chapters 1–3: Things that ***are,*** things that pertain to John's day: Seven Letters to the Seven Churches (all, of course, applicable to the Churches of today).
Part II, Chapters 4–22: Things that shall be ***hereafter,*** from John's day until the end of time.

WRITING STYLE OF THE BOOK OF REVELATION

The Book of Revelation is not written in chronological order as we are accustomed to reading in modern literature. Instead, it is written in a cyclical style. It will narrate a subject to give the first glance and then go back to fill in various details at a later juncture.

This type of order can make it challenging to interpret. But it can be made easier by looking at it as a puzzle, or better yet, a treasure map, with clues leading to a beautiful treasure. The treasure being Jesus!

A CALL TO REPENTANCE

The first three chapters of the Book of Revelation send a very clear message to the Christian Church. The underlying message to each individual church body was a call to repentance. Repentance must take precedence in the daily life of the Christian believer. Even the great apostle Paul confessed his need for repentance by dying daily to keep his own body under subjection to the will of God. Repentance is more than deliverance *from* something. It is a turning *to* and a *pressing towards* something greater.

Paul declared in Acts 19:4 that John the Baptist *verily baptized with the baptism of repentance*. Therefore, when Jesus was baptized by John, Jesus was baptized with the baptism of repentance. Although Jesus was sinless and needed no repentance from sin, He still exampled the act of repentance by turning from being a carpenter and son of Joseph and Mary so that He could become the Atoning Sacrifice and Son of God.

For this, the glory of God was revealed, and a voice from heaven declared, "*Thou art my beloved Son; in thee, I am well pleased.*" (Luke 3:22). Of the seven churches, only Smyrna and Philadelphia were not directly admonished to repent. However, in their humble and persecuted state, it was still necessary to remind them of their hope in Christ and to keep their eyes on things eternal. Consequently, repentance is the bridge one must cross to transition from Chapters 1-3 to Chapters 4-22.

THE TRANSITION FROM THINGS THAT ARE TO THINGS THAT SHALL BE

After this I looked, and behold a door was opened in heaven: and the first voice which I heard was as it were of a trumpet talking with me: which said, Come up hither, and I will shew thee things which must be hereafter. And immediately, I was in the spirit: and, behold, a throne was set in heaven, and one sat on the throne. And he that sat was to look upon like jasper and a sardine stone: and there was a rainbow round about the throne, in sight like unto an emerald.

REVELATION 4:1-3

Some theologians believe, at this point, the Rapture of the Church takes place. However, the book does not indicate this, nor does scripture support such teaching. Instead, the scripture only notes that John was called up into a heavenly realm to see visions, just as the man Paul spoke of in II Corinthians 12:1-6 was caught up into the third heaven and saw visions.

John first saw a dramatic vision of God as the veil of the future lifted. Apparently, to assure the Church that no matter how disheartening some of the events still to come might be, GOD IS STILL ON THE THRONE. In fact, the throne of God is mentioned in every chapter of Revelation except 2, 8, and 9. That's 19 out of a total of 22 chapters!

God's form is not described, except that He had the appearance of jasper and sardius in a Rainbow of Emerald. Jasper was the color of a clear diamond. Sardius was red, and emerald was green. Thus, God revealed Himself to John as one enswathed in a halo of clear, dazzling white, shaded with red and green.

And round about the throne were four and twenty seats: and upon the seats I saw ***four and twenty elders*** *sitting, clothed in white raiment; and they had on their heads crowns of gold. And out of the throne proceeded lightnings and thunderings and voices: and there*

> *were seven lamps of fire burning before the throne, which are the seven Spirits of God. And before the throne there was a sea of glass like unto crystal: and in the midst of the throne, and round about the throne, were* ***four beasts*** *full of eyes before and behind. And the first beast was like a* ***lion****, and the second beast like a* ***calf****, and the third beast had a face as a* ***man****, and the fourth beast was like a flying* ***eagle****. And the four beasts had each of them six wings about him; and they were full of eyes within: and they rest not day and night, saying, Holy, holy, holy, LORD God Almighty, which was, and is, and is to come. And when those beasts give glory and honour and thanks to him that sat on the throne, who liveth forever and ever, The* ***four and twenty elders*** *fall down before him that sat on the throne, and worship him that liveth for ever and ever, and cast their crowns before the throne, saying, Thou art worthy, O Lord, to receive glory and honour and power: for thou hast created all things, and for thy pleasure they are and were created.*
>
> REVELATION 4:4-11

DEFINITION OF BEAST IN SCRIPTURE TEXT

In Scripture, the word "beasts" is translated from a different word than *the* "Beast" mentioned in Revelation, Chapter 13—a horrible monster that figures so largely in the latter part of the book. "Living Creatures" is another translation of these Four Beasts in Chapter 4, Verse 6, and is a better description. We will explore the Four Beasts first, which will shed more light on the identity of the Twenty-Four Elders.

THE FOUR LIVING CREATURES AND THE FOUR GOSPELS

Identifying the Four Beasts makes it easier to identify the Twenty-Four Elders correctly. Several years ago, Reverend G. T. Haywood expounded on the Four Beasts, or Four Living Creatures, who worshiped around the throne. He paralleled them to the Four Gospels.

THE FOUR GOSPELS

The Four Gospels are, by far, the most crucial part of the Bible—more important than all the rest of the Bible combined, more important than all the rest of the books in the whole world put together. It would be better to be without the knowledge of everything else than to be without the knowledge of Christ Jesus.

Bible books that precede the Gospels are Anticipatory, and those that follow are Explanatory of the Hero of the Four Gospels. In other words, all the Old Testament books point to and look for the main character of the Gospels and His redemptive power for mankind. The New Testament books from Acts to Revelation explain how to take action and mature in accordance with the redemptive plan of the Gospels.

WHY FOUR?

There were many more than four to start with (Luke 1:1). As Dr. Henry Halley, author of the famed *Halley Bible Handbook*, states, "It was a period of great literary activity. The story of Jesus had spread over the known world and had enlisted countless thousands of devoted followers. Naturally, there arose a great demand for written narratives" of the life of Christ.

We believe God took a hand in preparing and preserving these four as containing what He wanted us to know about Christ. Of course, in the Old Testament, there are some double narratives. But only here are four of the Bible books about the same person. It must mean that the main character is of colossal importance.

OLD TESTAMENT REFERENCES TO THE FOUR BEASTS

Ezekiel also saw the Four Beasts (Living Creatures) of Revelation 4 but in a different setting. The likeness of their faces is described in Ezekiel 1:10. (See also Isaiah 40:3-4 concerning a *straight* path for *straight* feet).

And I looked, and, behold, a whirlwind came out of the north, a great cloud, and a fire infolding itself, and a brightness was about it, and out of the midst thereof as the colour of amber, out of the midst of the first. Also out of the midst thereof came the likeness of ***four living creatures****. And this was their appearance; they had the likeness of a man. And every one had four faces, and every one had four wings. And their feet were straight feet; and the sole of their feet was like the sole of a calf's foot: and they sparkled like the color of burnished brass. As for the likeness of their faces, they four had the face of a* ***man****,* *and the face of a* **lion**, *on the right side: and they four had the face of an* **ox** *on the left side; they four also had the face of an* **eagle**. *And they went every one straight forward: whither the spirit was to go, they went; and they turned not when they went. As for the likeness of the living creatures, their appearance was like burning coals of fire, and like the appearance of lamps: it went up and down among the living creatures; and the fire was bright, and out of the fire went forth lightning. And above the firmament that was over their heads was the likeness of a throne, as the appearance of a sapphire stone: and upon the likeness of the throne was the likeness as the appearance of a man above upon it. And I saw as the colour of amber, as the appearance of fire round about within it, from the appearance of his loins even upward, and from the appearance of his loins even downward, I saw as it were the appearance of fire, and it had brightness round about. As the appearance of the bow that is in the cloud in the day of rain, so was the appearance of the brightness round about. This was the appearance of the likeness of the glory of the* L*ORD*. *And when I saw it, I fell upon my face, and I heard a voice of one that spake.*

EZEKIEL 1:4-7; 10, 12-13, 22, 26-28

- Deuteronomy 4:24a — *For the Lord thy God is a consuming fire…*
- Deuteronomy 9:3a — *… the Lord thy God is he which goeth over before; as a consuming fire …*
- I Kings 18:38a — *Then the fire of the Lord fell, and consumed the burnt sacrifice …*
- II Kings 1:12b — *… And the fire of God came down from heaven, and consumed …*
- Luke 3:17 — *Whose fan is in his hand, and he will thoroughly purge the floor, and gather the wheat into his garner; but the chaff he will burn with fire unquenchable.*

This description parallels how the Lord presented Himself to the Church of Thyatira, the Son of God, who had eyes like a flame of fire, and his feet were like fine brass. Interestingly, both John and Ezekiel saw essentially the same grand vision!

ALL FOUR "LIVING CREATURES" ARE REPRESENTATIVE OF JESUS CHRIST

The **Lion** is supreme among beasts, the noblest, the powerful and compelling work of Jesus, His leadership and royal power, the Lion of the Tribe of Judah.

The **Ox** is supreme among cattle—the strongest, the priestly side of his work, our sacrificial atonement, and also the bearer of our burdens.

Man is supreme among all creatures, the wisest, His incarnation, His humanity, a man of like passion, tempted as we are yet without sin.

The **Eagle** is supreme among birds, the most majestic, His spiritual nature, His deity, He is high and lifted up.

LION: Matthew is written to the **Jews** emphasizing the declaration that Jesus is the Messiah as foretold by the Old Testament prophets. He is the Lion of the tribe of Judah. Matthew quotes from the Old Testament repeatedly. (Matthew 1:1-17). *What Jesus said.*

CALF or OX: Mark is written to **Rome** emphasizing the superhuman power of Jesus, demonstrating His deity through His miracles. Jesus Christ was the ultimate sacrifice that took on the sins of the world. Only Jesus has the strength to bear our burdens. Mark omits most of the discourses of Jesus and narrates things Jesus did rather than things He said. (Mark 1:1-4,8). *What Jesus did.*

MAN: Luke is written to the **Greeks** (i.e., the Gentiles) with emphasis on the humanity of Jesus, representing Jesus as the Son of God by virgin birth. Luke speaks of the kindness of Jesus toward the weak, the suffering, and the outcast. (Luke 1:31). *What Jesus felt.*

EAGLE: John is written to the **religious culture** worshiping every god but the One True God. John takes the reader back to creation and declares the Word made everything of God and that the **Word was God** and the **Word became flesh**. Emphasis is placed on the deity of Jesus and consists chiefly of his discourses. Here Jesus openly presents himself as the Son of God. John narrates the conversations of Jesus to reveal who he was (i.e., the Word made flesh, the bread of life, the light of the world, the good shepherd, the door, the life, the resurrection, the way, etc.) The Gospel of John, out of all the gospels, reaches the highest heights of thought. (John 1:1-14). *Who Jesus was.*

These are spoken of as "Living Creatures" because Christ is yet alive forever. They are full of eyes before and behind. They can look back and see the fulfillment of scripture (The Old Testament) concerning the Messiah and look forward with the understanding of grace (The New Testament), Christ in us, *the hope of glory* (Colossians 1:27).

THE TWENTY-FOUR ELDERS SYMBOLIZE THE OLD TESTAMENT

The Hebrew Old Testament contains the same books as our English Old Testament but in a different arrangement. It was divided into three categories:

- Law = 5 books — Genesis, Exodus, Leviticus, Numbers, Deuteronomy
- Prophets = 8 books
  - 4 Earlier: Joshua, Judges, Samuel, Kings
  - 4 Later: Isaiah, Jeremiah, Ezekiel, & the 12 Minor Prophets
- Writings = 11 books
  - 3 Poetical: Psalms, Proverbs, Job
  - 5 Rolls: Song of Solomon, Ruth, Lamentations, Ecclesiastes, Esther
  - 3 Books: Daniel, Ezra-Nehemiah, Chronicles

This comes to a total of **Twenty-Four** books. These were elder to Jesus. They were before Christ but gave their attention, credence, and obeisance to the Coming of Christ.

IT TAKES TWO TO ESTABLISH CREDIBILITY

The credibility of any word must have at least two witnesses.

> *In the mouth of two or three witnesses shall every word be established.*
>
> II CORINTHIANS 13:1B

> *Search the scriptures; for in them ye think ye have eternal life; and they are they which testify of me. For had ye believed Moses, ye would have believed me: for he wrote of me.*
>
> JOHN 5:39, 46

THE NEW TESTAMENT BEARS WITNESS AND TESTIFIES OF JESUS CHRIST

The New Testament – The Gospels testify of Jesus Christ the Messiah, His gracious works, and all the Father had sent Him to accomplish.

> *But I have greater witness than that of John [the Baptist]: for the works which the Father hath given me to finish, the same works that I do, bear witness of me, that the Father hath sent me.*
>
> JOHN 5:36

God cannot be separated from His Word. They are one and the same. *Hear, Oh Israel: the Lord our God is One Lord.* (Deuteronomy 6:4).

THE OLD TESTAMENT BEARS WITNESS AND TESTIFIES OF JESUS CHRIST

The Old Testament – The Law & The Prophets testify of the Messiah who was to come and all that God will accomplish in Jesus Christ.

But now the righteousness of God without the law is manifested, being witnessed by the law and the prophets; Even the righteousness of God which is by faith of Jesus Christ unto all and upon all them that believe: for there is no difference.

ROMANS 3:21-22

To him [Jesus Christ] give all the prophets witness, that through his name whosoever believeth in him shall receive remission of sins.

ACTS 10:43

THE OLD AND NEW TESTAMENTS ESTABLISH JESUS AS THE MESSIAH

It takes both the New Testament and the Old Testament together to bear witness and establish the validity that Jesus Christ is God manifest (revealed) in the flesh.

For unto us a child is born, unto us a son is given: and the government shall be upon his shoulder: and his name shall be called Wonderful Counsellor, The mighty God, The everlasting Father, The Prince of Peace.

ISAIAH 9:6

And without controversy great is the mystery of godliness: God was manifest in the flesh, justified in the Spirit, seen of angels, preached unto the Gentiles, believed on in the world, received up in glory.

I TIMOTHY 3:16

For in him [Jesus] dwelleth all the fullness of the Godhead bodily.

COLOSSIANS 2:9

And he was clothed with a vesture dipped in blood; and his name is called The Word of God.

REVELATION 19:13

CONCLUSION:

The Twenty-Four Elders represent the Old Testament, and the Four Beasts represent the New Testament's Four Gospels. Together, they are the Word of God, which was with God in the beginning, which *is* God, made flesh, which *is* JESUS

CHAPTER 3

THE TWO WITNESSES – PART I

Revelation 11

THE PREMISE:

The Two Witnesses are the Old Testament and the New Testament, which testify to the validity of Jesus Christ. All scriptural truths ultimately flow to the Golden Candlestick of One God and bear witness to Jesus Christ as the Messiah.

SCRIPTURE TEXT:

Revelation 11:3-4 *And I will give power unto my two witnesses, and they shall prophesy a thousand two hundred and threescore days, clothed in sackcloth. These are the two olive trees and the two candlesticks standing before the God of the earth.*

THE BELIEF IN ONE GOD

The belief in One God is the most fundamental foundation of Biblical teaching. That being true, everything must and will ultimately lead back to, support, and further reveal the existence of only One God. The incarnation of One God in Jesus Christ is the *Revelation of Jesus Christ*.

Hear, O Israel: The Lord our God is one Lord: And thou shalt love the Lord thy God with all thine heart, and with all thy soul, and with all thy might.

DEUTERONOMY 6:4-5

In Matthew, the declaration *The Lord our God is One Lord* is the unwritten but understood prelude to the First and Greatest Commandment.

Master, which is the great commandment in the law? Jesus said unto him, Thou shalt love the Lord thy God with all thy heart, and with all thy soul, and with all thy mind. This is the first and great commandment.

MATTHEW 22:36-38

The response of Jesus to the question, *Which is the great commandment in the law?*, was essentially: "There exists only One God, eternal, indivisible, all-powerful, and all-knowing. He is the Creator of everything visible and invisible. That goes without saying because you are Israelites and already acknowledge this great truth. With that settled in your hearts, you are to love, worship, and serve Him with everything within you! And that, my friend, is the great commandment!"

In Mark, we find a direct quote from Deuteronomy 6:4:

And Jesus answered him, 'The first of all the commandments is, Hear, O Israel; the Lord our God is one Lord;

MARK 12:29

Before we try to figure out the 1260 days, which will be explained later, let us explore some scripture that will give more understanding about the Two Witnesses.

The Two Witnesses are given the power to prophesy and, interestingly enough, are called Olive Trees and Candlesticks—not men or angels. Now it is only natural to imagine them as human beings because our mind automatically rejects the notion of two trees or candlesticks walking around, prophesying, and doing exploits.

OLD TESTAMENT REFERENCE TO OLIVE TREES AND CANDLESTICKS

The olive tree, an object of symbolism throughout the Bible, was an integral part of building the temple of the Old Testament. The two cherubims that stood in the temple's oracle (the Holy of Holies), where the ark of the covenant sat, were made of an olive tree.

> *And the oracle he prepared in the house within, to set there the ark of the covenant of the Lord. And within the oracle he made two cherubims of olive tree, each ten cubits high. And he set the cherubims within the inner house: and they stretched forth the wings of the cherubims, so that the wing of the one touched the one wall, and the wing of the other cherub touched the other wall; and their wings touched one another in the midst of the house.*
>
> I KINGS 6:19, 23, 27

Zechariah 4, however, gives us the clearest revelation of the Two Witnesses.

ZECHARIAH'S VISION

Here is what Zechariah saw in his vision.

> *And said unto me, What seest thou? And I said, I have looked, and behold a candlestick all of gold, with a bowl upon the top of it, and his seven lamps thereon, and seven pipes to the seven lamps, which are upon the top thereof:*
>
> ZECHARIAH 4:2

THE BACKGROUND TO ZECHARIAH'S VISION

Zerubbabel was in the process of rebuilding both the wall of Jerusalem and the temple in very troublous times (see Ezra 3, 4). He had already laid the foundation. In this very trying time, Zechariah, the prophet of God, had a vision to assure him and everyone else that God was in control and that Zerubbabel would indeed finish the rebuilding of Jerusalem. Zerubbabel was the governor of Jerusalem who was given money by Cyrus, King of Persia, to rebuild Jerusalem.

The prophet Zechariah asks the angel of the Lord for the understanding of the vision. The angel reveals that it is *not by might, nor by power, but by my SPIRIT, saith the Lord* (Zechariah 4:6), and that Zerubbabel will be victorious *with those seven;* (the seven lamps) *they are the eyes of the Lord, which run to and fro through the whole earth* (Zechariah 4:10). The seven lamps are the seven eyes of the Lord, which are the seven Spirits of God as referred to in Revelation 5:6.

THE SEVEN SPIRITS OF GOD

Here is one example of how scripture will ultimately lead to and support the doctrine of One God. As we read Revelation chapters 1 through 3 concerning the Letters to the seven Churches, it is apparent that One God reveals himself in seven different ways to seven different churches according to seven different situations, whether through rebuke, encouragement, or admonishment.

God is NOT a conglomerate of seven separate and distinct spirits, entities, or streams of consciousness. He is simply One God revealing Himself differently according to the situation at hand. Therefore, no matter the situation, Jesus Christ is the answer. In fact, according to Rev. Johnny Higdon, in a lesson entitled *The Name of God*, the actual Greek transliteration of the full name "Jesus Christ" is "Through anointed contact, God becomes our Salvation to furnish what is needed."

THE PROPHECY TO ZERUBBABEL

In Zechariah 4:7, the angel also made known that from Zerubbabel would come forth the headstone. Twelve generations later, the stone prophesied in Psalms 118:22 would *become the headstone of the corner,* that is, of course, Jesus Christ.

THE ANGEL ANSWERS ZECHARIAH'S QUESTION, "WHAT ARE THESE?"

Zechariah inquires in verse 11 of Chapter 4, "*What are these* ***two olive trees*** *upon the right side of the candlestick and upon the left side thereof? What be these* ***two olive branches*** *which through the* ***two golden pipes*** *empty the golden oil out of themselves?*"

The angel answers Zechariah's question in verse 14, "*These are the* ***two anointed ones*** *that stand by the Lord of the whole earth.*"

The two anointed ones that stand beside The Lord are ***Two Olive Trees***. However, please remember this is figurative language. It is representative imagery.

On the "Mount of Transfiguration" (Matthew 17:1-3), Jesus was transformed before Peter, James, and John and was seen talking with Moses and Elijah. This event was a manifestation of the Old Testament, the Law, and the Prophets, represented by Moses and Elijah, and the New Testament, the Gospels, represented by Jesus. The purpose of the vision was to validate Jesus as the incarnation of God, bearing witness that Jesus Christ is the embodiment of the Word of God and *all the fullness of the Godhead dwelleth in Him* (Colossians 2:9).

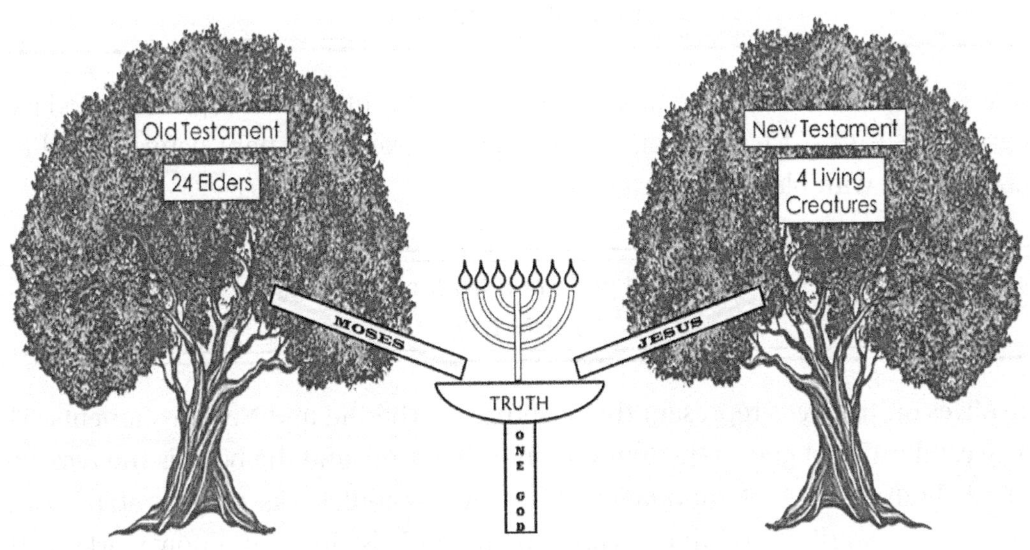

THE INTERPRETATION OF ZECHARIAH'S VISION

The two olive trees, the two anointed ones, represent the Old Testament and the New Testament (the 1st Covenant and the 2nd Covenant).

Whereupon neither the first testament was dedicated without blood. For when Moses had spoken every precept to all the people according to the law, he took the blood of calves and of goats, with water, and scarlet wool, and hyssop, and sprinkled both the book, and all the people, saying, This is the blood of the testament which God hath enjoined unto you. Moreover he sprinkled with blood both the tabernacle, and all the vessels of the ministry.

HEBREWS 9:18-21

Moses was the pipe, or conduit, for the 1st Covenant. For through him, God gave the Law. Moses was the one who sealed the covenant between God and Israel with blood.

For the law having a shadow of good things to come. Then said he, Lo, I come to do thy will, O God. He taketh away the first, that he may establish the second. By the which will we are sanctified through the offering of the body of Jesus Christ once and for all.

HEBREWS 10:1A; 9-10

Likewise, Jesus Christ was the pipe for the 2nd Covenant. For through Him, God gave us grace. Jesus Christ was the one who sealed the New Covenant between God and ALL mankind with blood, His *own* blood!

For the law was given by Moses, but grace and truth came by Jesus Christ.

JOHN 1:17

The olives on the trees represent the scriptures of the Old and New Testaments. The single candlestick of gold is the foundation of One God, and the bowl is the reservoir of faith built upon that foundation. The seven candlesticks on top of the bowl represent the Spirit of God that became the man Christ Jesus and now works in the church today as the Holy Ghost (Rev. 1:13). Jesus is referred to often as the Branch.

- Isaiah 4:2 — *In that day shall the branch of the Lord*
- Jeremiah 23:5 — *I will raise unto…a righteous Branch*
- Jeremiah 33:15 — *will I cause the Branch of righteousness*
- Zechariah 3:8 — *I will bring forth my servant the Branch*
- Zechariah 6:12 — *Behold…whose name [is] The Branch*

THE PARALLEL BETWEEN MOSES AND JESUS

Just as the law foreshadowed an inner spiritual, moral law, Moses was a foreshadowing of Jesus Christ.

- Moses was the deliverer of Israel out of Egyptian bondage.
  Jesus Christ is the deliverer of all humanity out of spiritual bondage.
- Moses was the mediator between God and Israel.
  Jesus Christ is the mediator between God and all mankind. (Hebrews 12:24).
- Israel was baptized unto Moses.
  We are baptized unto Jesus Christ.

Moreover, brethren, I would not that ye should be ignorant, how that all our fathers were under the cloud, and all passed through the sea; And were all ***baptized unto Moses in the cloud and in the sea****; And did all eat the same spiritual meat; And did all drink the same spiritual drink: for they drank of that spiritual Rock that followed them: and that Rock was Christ.*

I CORINTHIANS 10:1-4

The sea and cloud mentioned in this passage symbolize water and spirit baptism unto salvation in the New Testament.

Jesus answered, "Verily, verily, I say unto thee, Except a man be born of water and of the Spirit, he cannot enter into the kingdom of God."

JOHN 3:5

> *Therefore we are buried with him [Jesus Christ] by baptism into death: that like as Christ was raised up from the dead by the glory of the Father, even so we also should walk in newness of life.*
>
> ROMANS 6:4

- Israel taught and preached *Moses.*
- Today, we teach and preach *Jesus Christ.*

> *For Moses of old time hath in every city them that preach him [Moses], being read in the synagogues every sabbath day.*
>
> ACTS 15:21

They read and preached Moses (the Law—the first five books of the Bible: Genesis, Exodus, Leviticus, Numbers, and Deuteronomy).

> *But even unto this day, when Moses is read, the vail is upon their heart.*
>
> II CORINTHIANS 3:15

> *And daily in the temple, and in every house, they ceased not to teach and preach Jesus Christ.*
>
> ACTS 5:42

To teach and preach Jesus Christ is to teach and preach the Gospel: Matthew, Mark, Luke, and John. The Gospel is the Death, Burial, and Resurrection of Jesus Christ. In response to the Gospel, *our* actions should align with those in the book of Acts. The book of Acts is a book of *action*. It is where the sinner can find examples of how people, whether Jew, Samaritan, or Gentile, were "Born Again." God's desired response to the message of the Gospel is found throughout the book of Acts. Acts is the book describing where individuals were first born again. Acts is where individuals repented (died), were buried (born of water), and were filled with the Holy Ghost (born of spirit). It is where the church began.

Notice Christ is preached just like Moses was preached. The Gospel is preached just like the Law was preached. Matthew, Mark, Luke, and John are being taught and preached just like Genesis, Exodus, Leviticus, Numbers, and Deuteronomy were being taught and preached.

MOSES AND JESUS: SERVANTS IN THE HOUSE

Wherefore, holy brethren, partakers of the heavenly calling, consider the Apostle and High Priest of our profession, Christ Jesus; Who was faithful to him that appointed him, as also Moses was faithful in all his house. For this man [Jesus] was counted worthy of more glory than Moses, inasmuch as he who hath builded the house hath more honour than the house. For every house is builded by some man; but he that built all things is God. And Moses verily was faithful in all his house, as a servant, for a testimony of those things which were to be spoken after; But Christ as a son over his own house; whose house are we, if we hold fast the confidence and the rejoicing of the hope firm unto the end.

HEBREWS 3:1-6

Here we observe that both Moses and Jesus were servants in the house. The difference is that Jesus OWNED the house because he BUILT the house; *whose house are we* (the church). Moses and Jesus were the servants (or conduits) in the house of God. Moses brought us the Law (the Old Testament), and Jesus brought us Grace (the New Testament).

SUMMARY OF ZECHARIAH'S VISION

Thus, the two branches, *which through the two golden pipes empty the golden oil* into the bowl, are Moses and Jesus. The one candlestick of gold upon which the bowl and the lamps stand is the fundamental axiom of One God. *Hear, O Israel: The Lord our God is one Lord:* Deuteronomy 6:4 (also known as The Great Commandment).

Whenever one squeezes the olives (the Holy Scriptures) from either tree, the oil flows through Moses and Jesus (the branch) into the bowl (the reservoir of truth built upon the Golden Candlestick of One God), providing the power to keep the lamps burning in and amongst His people. Is it any wonder the Psalmist declared, *"Thy word is a lamp unto my feet and a light unto my path?"* (Psalm 119:105).

AT LEAST TWO WITNESSES MUST ESTABLISH THE WORD OF TRUTH

> *...that in the mouth of two or three witnesses every word may be established.*
>
> MATTHEW 18:16B

> *...in the mouth of two or three witnesses shall every word be established.*
>
> II CORINTHIANS 13:1B

> *Search the scriptures; for in them ye think ye have eternal life: and they are they which **testify** of me.*
>
> JOHN 5:39

The Old and New Testaments together testify that Jesus Christ is the manifestation of God Almighty in the flesh and that we find our salvation in Him. Only God, by the authority of His Word, can validate the holiness of Jesus Christ to be the propitiation (atonement) for the sins of all mankind. (Romans 3:25, I John 2:2, 4:10).

THE WORD OF GOD IS GOD

> *In the beginning was the Word, and the Word was with God, and the Word was God. The same was in the beginning with God. All things were made by him; and without him was not any thing made that was made.*
>
> JOHN 1:1-3

"Word" is simply an expression of thought. Therefore, God and the Word of God are synonymous, and one cannot be separated from the other.

Since the Word of God is the expression of the mind of God and comprises both the Old and New Testament (The Two Witnesses), God could establish all things alone without going against His Word and becoming self-contradictory. Therefore, God could *swear by himself* without creating a paradox.

> *For when God made promise to Abraham because he could swear by no greater,* ***he sware by himself****.*
>
> HEBREWS 6:13

THE WORD BECOMES JESUS CHRIST

> *And the Word was made flesh, and dwelt among us, (and we beheld his glory, the glory as of the only begotten of the Father,) full of grace and truth.*
>
> JOHN 1:14

> *And he was clothed with a vesture dipped in blood: and his name is called the Word of God.*
>
> REVELATION 19:13

> *And I fell at his feet to worship him. And he said unto me, See thou do it not: I am thy fellowservant, and of thy brethren that have the testimony of Jesus: worship God: for the testimony of Jesus is the spirit of prophecy.*
>
> REVELATION 19:10

The testimony of Jesus Christ is the Spirit of prophecy. The *marturia* (witness of Jesus Christ) is the *pneuma* (the wind or breath) of *propheteia* (public exposition).

JESUS IS THE LIGHT OF THE WORLD

And I turned to see the voice that spake with me. And being turned, I saw seven golden candlesticks; And in the midst of the seven candlesticks one like unto the Son of man, clothed with a garment down to the foot, and girt about the paps with a golden girdle.

REVELATION 1:12-13

To understand prophecy is to understand the testimony (or witness) of Jesus Christ. The Bible's highly figurative passages that seem so profoundly shrouded in imagery are given to help us further understand the mystery that in Jesus *dwells all the fullness of the Godhead bodily* (Colossians 2:9). The Doctrine of One God is the foundation upon which all Biblical truths are built (Deuteronomy 6:4).

CONCLUSION:

The Two Witnesses of Revelation 11 are the Old and New Testament, the Word of God, Jesus Christ. Therefore, nothing can testify to the validity of Jesus Christ except for the Word (Himself). And thus, all scriptural truths ultimately flow to the Golden Candlestick of One God and bear witness to Jesus Christ as the Messiah.

CHAPTER 4

THE 144,000

Revelation 7, 14

THE PREMISE:

The 144,000 of Revelation chapters 7 and 14 represent the first Jewish converts to obey the gospel unto salvation.

INTRODUCTION:

The 144,000 are mentioned on two occasions, Revelation, Chapter 7, and Chapter 14. Naturally, there are many opinions and speculations about whom, when, and where concerning the 144,000. The Bible, however, very plainly reveals their identity.

SCRIPTURE TEXT:

Revelation 7:4, 9 *And I heard the number of them which were sealed: and there were sealed* ***a hundred and forty and four thousand*** *of all the tribes of the children of Israel. After this I beheld, and lo, a great multitude, which no man could number, of all nations, and kindreds, and people, and tongues, stood, before the Lamb, clothed with white robes, and palms in their hands;*

Revelation 14:1, 3-4 *And I looked, and, lo, a Lamb stood on the mount Sion, and with him* ***a hundred forty and four thousand****, having his Father's name written in their foreheads...and no man could learn that song but the hundred and forty and four thousand which were redeemed from the earth. These are they which were not defiled with women; for they are virgins. These are they which follow the Lamb whithersoever he goeth. These were redeemed from among men, being the* ***firstfruits*** *unto God and to the Lamb.*

THREE NOTABLE CLUES IN THE SCRIPTURE TEXT

1. The 1st Group, the 144,000, are Israelites or Jews.
2. The 2nd Group, the "great multitude," are Gentiles. "Nations" is the same Greek word interpreted elsewhere as Gentiles.
3. The 1st Group, the 144,000, are called "Firstfruits."

THE 144,000 VS. THE "GREAT MULTITUDE"

John was able to identify and number the 144,000 (Jews) in comparison to the "great multitude" (Gentiles) that "no man could number." John clearly recognized and counted the Jewish Group but not the Gentile Group because the multitude was so large.

THE ROLE OF NUMBERS IN THE BIBLE

Numbers have always played an essential role in the Word of God. For instance, the book of Revelation is built upon the number 7. Seven letters, seven spirits of God, seven churches, seven seals, seven trumpets, seven vials, seven thunders, and even seven beatitudes are all mentioned in the book of Revelation.

The Old Testament is also full of sevens. The Sabbath is the seventh day. The Levitical system centers around the number 7. Jericho fell after seven priests with seven trumpets led a march for seven days and seven times on the seventh day around the walled city.

It is generally accepted that the number 12 is representative of the Children of Israel (e.g., the 12 tribes). The number 12 is also used to reference the apostles and their Foundational Teachings (Apostolic Doctrine).

Neither pray I for these alone, but for them also which shall believe on me through ***their*** *word;*

JOHN 17:20

And they continued steadfastly in the ***apostles' doctrine*** *and fellowship, and in breaking of bread, and in prayers.*

ACTS 2:42

Now therefore ye are no more strangers and foreigners, but fellowcitizens with the saints, and of the household of God; And are built upon the ***foundation of the apostles*** *and prophets, Jesus Christ himself being the chief corner stone;*

EPHESIANS 2:19-20

The cornerstone is Jesus Christ. Upon that is the Foundation of the Apostles' Doctrine. The number 1000 is a bit more ill-defined. According to Midrash (an old Jewish hermeneutical interpretation of Rabbinical scripture text), the number 1000 was a mystical number used throughout the Rabbinical writings and even the Bible itself.

The term *thousand,* in this instance, is comparative to modern-day sayings such as, "I must have traveled that road a thousand times" or "You have a million-dollar smile." These sayings are only descriptive and do not refer to an exact amount.

EXAMPLE OF THE SYMBOLIC USE OF THE WORD "THOUSAND" IN OTHER SCRIPTURE TEXT

...Saul hath slain his thousands, and David his ten thousands. And Saul was very wroth, and the saying displeased him; and he said, They have ascribed unto David ten thousands, and to me they have ascribed but thousands...

I SAMUEL 18:7-8A

The focal point of this scripture is not about an exact number. Instead, David was given higher regard than Saul. It shows that David was more significant and beloved than Saul in the people's minds.

THE REPRESENTATION OF THE NUMBER 144,000

The Children of Israel (12) times the Apostles' Doctrine (also represented by 12) equals 144—a perfect union denoted by a perfect numerical square. Thus, Israel multiplied by Apostolic Doctrine equals a perfect people, in both a natural and spiritual genealogical sense. These are Jews (natural heirs) who believed in Jesus Christ unto salvation and have now also become spiritual heirs. Natural heir times Spiritual heir equals a Perfect People.

Multiplying 144 by that mystical number 1000 gives us 144,000 representing redeemed Jewish Born Again Christians. It does not suggest that salvation for the Jews is only limited to precisely 144,000 individuals. Instead, it simply means that there are both Jewish and Gentile converts, and Jewish converts are smaller in number in comparison to the great multitudes of Gentile converts.

In Revelation 14:1, the Lamb stands on Mount Zion with the 144,000. Scripture states that these were *redeemed from among men* and were the ***firstfruits** unto God and to the Lamb*. The 144,000 were the **firstfruits** or the **first converts** to the Lamb. According to mainstream teaching, the 144,000 are the "last ones" to be saved. This idea contradicts scripture because the Bible clearly says they are the **firstfruits** or the **first** ones to receive salvation, not the **last fruits** or the **last** ones to be saved.

In his book *His Truth is Marching On, Advanced Studies on Prophecy in the Light of History*, Christian author and historian Ralph Woodrow wrote this: In the Old

Testament, the term "firstfruits' designated the FIRST gatherings of a crop which were presented to the Lord (Exodus 23:19, Leviticus 2:14, Nehemiah 10:35). John D. Keyser discussed this in his writing, "The Mystery of the Wave Sheaf Offering." Keyser says that in the New Testament, Christ, who was "the FIRST that should rise from the dead" to immortality (Acts 26:23), is called "the FIRSTFRUITS of them that slept" (I Corinthians 15:20). The FIRST converts that Paul made in Achaia were called "the FIRSTFRUITS of Achaia" (I Corinthians 16:15). Likewise, the 144,000, the firstfruits unto the Lamb, are the first converts to Christ!

In Paul's writings to the Romans and the Corinthians, he spoke of Epaenetus and the house of Stephanas as being the FIRSTFRUITS of the town of Achaia. Paul was not saying they were among the last ones to be converted in Achaia. He was explicitly declaring they were among the FIRST. Even our tithe is to be the firstfruits, the FIRST tenth of our increase, not the last.

JAMES IDENTIFIES THE "FIRSTFRUITS"

James, an apostle, a Jew, and a pastor of Jerusalem, wrote, "*to the **twelve tribes** which are scattered abroad.*" (James 1:1). Note that he addresses his letter to the Israelites (Jews). Now pay close attention to verse 18.

*Of his own will begat he us [Jews] with the word of truth, that we [Jews] should be a kind of **firstfruits** of his creatures.*

JAMES 1:18

Again, comparing the first ingathering of crops as the firstfruits, we can surmise that the 144,000 must represent those Jews who FIRST received the Gospel in the Book of Acts. In fact, the very first example of Baptism of Water and Spirit is found in Acts, Chapter 2, and ALL the people that experienced this New Birth were either Jewish or converts to Judaism.

The Gospel was *to the Jew FIRST, then to the Greek.* So the Jews in Acts, Chapter 2, were the **"Firstfruits of the Lamb."**

JEWS, BY BIRTHRIGHT, HAVE THE FIRST RIGHT TO SALVATION

Matthew 15:21-28 tells the story of the healing of the Syrophoenician woman's daughter. When the woman made her request known to Jesus, his first response was, "*I am not sent but unto the lost sheep of the house of Israel.*" The same story is told in Mark 7:25-30. Here Jesus is recorded saying, "*Let the children (Israelites) first be filled.*"

Jesus not only ministered to the Jews first but instructed his disciples to do the same. He commanded them to go FIRST to the JEWS with the gospel.

> *These twelve Jesus sent forth, and commanded them, saying, Go* ***not*** *into the way of the Gentiles, and into any city of the Samaritans, enter ye* ***not****: But go rather to the lost sheep of the house of Israel.*
>
> MATTHEW 10:5-6

> *And that repentance and remission of sins should be preached in his name among all nations, beginning at Jerusalem.*
>
> LUKE 24:47

Notice the sequential order in Acts, Chapter 1:

> *Ye shall be witnesses unto me both in Jerusalem, and in Judea, and in Samaria, and unto the uttermost part of the earth.*
>
> ACTS 1:8

Therefore, the Gospel must be preached:

First: To Jerusalem and Judea (Jews)
Second: To Samaria
Third: To the uttermost (those everywhere else., i.e., Gentiles)

Was this done? Absolutely! Three thousand souls were added to the Church when the Holy Ghost was first poured out in Acts, Chapter 2. Pay close attention to Peter's address in the following verses:

> *Ye men of Israel, hear these words . . . Now when they heard this, they were pricked in their heart, and said unto Peter and to the rest of the apostles, Men, and brethren, what shall we do? Then Peter said unto them, Repent, and be baptized every one of you in the name of Jesus Christ for the remission of sins, and ye shall receive the gift of the Holy Ghost . . . Then they that gladly received his word were baptized: and the same day there were added unto them about three thousand souls.*
>
> ACTS 2:22, 37-38, 41

These first three thousand converts were all Israelites! They were all Jews and Jewish converts. Peter further declared in Acts:

> *Ye are the children of the prophets, and of the covenant which God made with our fathers, saying unto Abraham, And in thy seed shall all the kindreds of the earth be blessed.*
> *Unto you* ***first*** *God, having raised up his Son Jesus, sent him to bless you, in turning away every one of you from his iniquities.*
>
> ACTS 3:25-26

In Acts Chapter 13, Verse 46, Paul and Barnabas said, "*it was necessary that the Word of God should* ***first*** *have been spoken to you,*" referring to the Jews of a synagogue at Antioch.

Paul declares at the beginning of his letter to the Romans, "*For I am not ashamed of the gospel of Christ: for it is the power of God unto salvation to everyone that believeth; to the Jew first, and also to the Greek.*" God's promises were to the Jews first.

THE THREE PILGRIMAGE FESTIVALS OF JUDAISM

Three significant holidays are mentioned in the Torah: Passover, Shavuot, and Sukkot. These Pilgrimage Festivals of Judaism occur annually and are a time when Jews and Jewish converts embark on a pilgrimage back to Jerusalem to celebrate three important holy days, as instructed by Moses.

Passover	Feast of Unleavened Bread, The Exodus
Shavuot (Pentecost)	Feast of FirstFruits, Beginning of Wheat Harvest
Sukkot (Tabernacles)	Feast of Tabernacles, End of Wheat Harvest

It is no coincidence that when the Baptism of the Holy Ghost was first poured out, it occurred on the Day of Pentecost, the beginning of Wheat Harvest, a holy day when Jews had made their pilgrimage back to Jerusalem to celebrate the Feast of Firstfruits.

THE JEWS RECEIVE THE NEW COVENANT PROMISE

As prophesied by the prophet Joel, the outpouring of the Holy Ghost occurred during the Jewish **Feast of Firstfruits**. The timing of this was historically perfect! God ordained the day the promise of the Comforter, the Holy Ghost, would come, and the message of salvation would be preached to the Jews.

And when the day of Pentecost was fully come … And they were all filled with the Holy Ghost, and began to speak with other tongues, as the Spirit gave them utterance. And they were all amazed, and were in doubt, saying one to another, What meaneth this? Others mocking said, These men are full of new wine. But Peter, standing up with the eleven, lifted up his voice, and said unto them, ***Ye men of Judea****, and* ***all ye that dwell at Jerusalem****, be this known unto you, and hearken to my words: For these are not drunken, as ye suppose, seeing it is but the third hour of the day. But this is that which was spoken by the prophet Joel; And it shall come to pass in the last days, saith God, I will pour out of my Spirit upon all flesh.*

ACTS 2:1, 4, 12-17

The Jewish Feast of Firstfruits is celebrated on the fiftieth day after Passover. Peter preached the message of salvation first to the Jews who had come from far and wide to celebrate the Feast of Firstfruits. Little did they know, *they* would become firstfruits. They would be redeemed from among men, being the **firstfruits** unto God and to the Lamb. They would become the first to receive salvation under the New Covenant.

On a side note: In Exodus, three thousand souls died when the Law was given. In Acts, three thousand souls gained New Life when Grace was given! Both events occurred fifty days after Passover. This was an incredible demonstration of God's Law vs. His Grace!

THE SAMARITANS RECEIVE THE NEW COVENANT PROMISE

Four years after Pentecost, the first Non-Israelites experienced this wonderful New Birth by being baptized in water and Spirit, just as the Jews did in Acts, Chapter 2! These Samaritans were also born again when they were baptized in the name of Jesus Christ and filled with the Holy Ghost. The prophecy in Acts 1:8 was being fulfilled.

Then Phillip went down to the city of ***Samaria****, and preached Christ unto them. Now when the apostles which were at Jerusalem heard that Samaria had received the word of God, they sent unto them Peter and John.*
... that they might receive the Holy Ghost. (For as yet he [the Holy Ghost] was fallen upon none of them; only they were baptized in the name of the Lord Jesus.) Then laid they their hands on them, and they received the Holy Ghost.

ACTS 8:5, 14, 15A, 16-17

THE GENTILES RECEIVE THE NEW COVENANT PROMISE

Then, in keeping with the natural order God had ordained, a few years later, in Acts, Chapter 10, Cornelius, who was a Gentile, received the Gospel. Cornelius had prayed for years, yet he and his house did not receive the Gospel of Jesus Christ until some ten years after Pentecost.

The Bible states that Cornelius's prayers and alms were a memorial to God. But why didn't the Lord send the Gospel to him sooner? The answer is Acts 1:8, which reads, "*to the Jew first, then to Samaria, and then to the uttermost* [Gentiles]."

I speculate that while Cornelius was born again of water and Spirit, the Feast of Tabernacles was happening back in Jerusalem. However, these are only my thoughts for which I have no historical proof.

In Romans 11:13-16, Paul explains to the Gentiles their position as the ones who were grafted into the olive tree. He speaks of the Israelites as the ***"firstfruits"*** on that olive tree and as a foundation for us.

> *For I speak to you Gentiles...For if the* ***firstfruits*** *be holy, the lump is also holy: and if the root be holy, so are the branches.*
>
> ROMANS 11:13A, 16

What a great feeling to know that we are also "holy" if we receive the Gospel the same way the Israelites did at the beginning. This is described by Peter in Acts 2:38, where he says, "*repent and be baptized every one of you in the name of Jesus Christ for the remission of sins, and ye shall receive the gift of the Holy Ghost.*"

THE NATURAL BRANCHES AND WILD BRANCHES OF ROMANS 11

> *And if some of the branches [the natural heirs, the Jews] be broken off, and thou [the unnatural, a foreigner], being a wild olive tree [a Gentile], wert grafted in among them [Jews], and with them partakest of the root and fatness of the olive tree; Boast not against the branches. But if thou boast, thou bearest not the root, but the root thee. Thou wilt say then, The branches [Jews] were broken off, that I [Gentile] might be graffed in. Well; because of unbelief they [Jews] were broken off, and thou [Gentile] standest by faith. Be not highminded, but fear: For if God spared not the natural branches [Jews], take heed lest he also spare not thee [Gentile]...if they [Jews] abide not still in unbelief, shall be graffed in: for God is able to graff them [Jews] in again. ...how much more shall these [Jews], which be the natural branches, be graffed into their own olive tree?*
>
> ROMANS 11:17-21; 23, 24B

Many Jews received salvation, but the majority were blinded (hardened). Therefore, the natural branches were broken off because of unbelief. But the root, which was spiritually Israel (*the city of the Lord* as referred to in Isaiah 60:14), remained.

Now the lump or the wild branches (Gentile nations) were given the good fortune of being grafted in. The natural are more easily grafted in if they simply believe that Jesus *was* and *is* the Messiah. If they can accept by faith that Jesus is the Messiah, they will have no issue with obeying the scripture that calls us to repent and be baptized of water and Spirit.

NO MORE OUTWARD DISTINCTION BETWEEN JEWS AND GENTILES

Romans 11:32 declares that God has *concluded* (or shut all up together) both the natural and the unnatural branches into one unbelieving pile, that He may have mercy upon all. After the Gospel was preached to the entire world (the Jews, the Samaritans, and then the Gentiles), the world would no longer be divided as **bound** or **free** according to the flesh.

An individual is now considered either **bound** or **free** according to the spirit. All mankind, whether Jew or Gentile, is considered in bondage to sin until that individual is *born again*. Once an individual has been *born of water and Spirit*, that individual is made **free**.

There is neither Jew nor Gentile anymore in the eyes of God when it comes to salvation. We are all sinners until we are born again of water and Spirit and become joint-heirs with Christ. There is One Lord, One Faith, One Baptism (Ephesians 4:5). Seeking or preaching in any other way is equated to being a thief and a robber. (John 10:1) Paul constantly reminded the early church that there was neither Jew nor Greek, circumcision or uncircumcision.

For he is not a Jew, which is one outwardly; neither is that circumcision, which is outward in the flesh: But he is a Jew, which is one inwardly; and circumcision is that of the heart, in the spirit, and not in the letter; whose praise is not of men, but of God.

ROMANS 2:28-29

According to Scripture, we are no longer regarded as Gentiles but as heirs of God through Christ (Galatians 4:7). And when we are baptized, we take on the Blood of Jesus. We are known by, and *only* by, the Blood. The Blood is our identity. It was the identifying mark of the Passover, and today it is the identifying mark of the authentic Christian.

The Hastings Encyclopedia of Religion describes the events of Acts 2:38 in this way: a **name** was an ancient synonym for a person. The payment was always made in the **name** of some person, referring to ownership. Therefore, someone baptized in the **name** of Jesus Christ becomes the personal property of Jesus Christ—*Ye are Christ's.*

Even today, many religious teachers still attempt to put a separation between Jews and Gentiles concerning salvation. Such teaching lends itself to an alternate plan or another way to salvation for the Jews. This wayward teaching even goes so far as to suggest a "Third coming of the Lord" for Jews. And it states that Jews will have special access to places in Heaven where Gentiles will not.

It is all quite absurd when given any critical thought. It was necessary for Paul then, and it is still required today, to teach and preach that there is only *one* way to salvation and there is no difference between Jew and Greek in God's eyes. God is no respecter of persons. Period.

SUMMARY:

...Thou seest, brother, how many thousands of Jews there are which believe...

ACTS 21:20B

Although there were thousands, the Jews were a small number compared to all the Gentiles who received the same salvation. The door to the New Birth experience was made available first to the Jews (Acts 2:37-38). Next, the door was opened to the Samaritans (Acts 8:14-17) because they were part Jew and part Gentile. And finally, the door of salvation swung wide open so that salvation was made available to the Gentiles, all nations under heaven, and people with no Jewish blood or heritage (Acts 10:44-48). There is ***no*** other salvation message!

CONCLUSION:

The 144,000 spoken of in Revelation, Chapters 7 and 14 represent the first Jewish converts to obey the Gospel unto salvation.

CHAPTER 5

ORDER OF WORLD KINGDOMS

Daniel 2, 4, 7 & Revelation 13

THE PREMISE:

God gave Nebuchadnezzar, Daniel, and John visions of the world's kingdoms and the order in which they would appear.

INTRODUCTION:

The visions are what God made known unto Nebuchadnezzar, Daniel, and John concerning the Kingdoms of the World. This chapter identifies what the three visions have in common and how they correspond.

SCRIPTURE TEXT:

Daniel 2:28-29, 31-33 and 38-44 *But there is a God in heaven that revealeth secrets, and maketh known to the king Nebuchadnezzar what shall be in the latter days. Thy dream, and the visions of thy head upon thy bed, are these; As for thee, O king, thy thoughts came into thy mind upon thy bed, what should come to pass hereafter: and he that revealeth secrets maketh known to thee what shall come to pass. Thou, O king, sawest, and behold a great image. This great image, whose brightness was excellent, stood before thee; and* *the form thereof was terrible. This image's head was of fine gold, his breast and his arms of silver, his belly and his thighs of brass, His legs of iron, his feet part of iron and part of clay …Thou [Nebuchadnezzar] art this head of gold. And after thee shall arise another kingdom inferior to thee, and another third kingdom of brass, which shall bear rule over all the earth. And the fourth kingdom shall be strong as iron: forasmuch as iron breaketh in pieces and subdueth all things: and as iron that breaketh all these, shall it break in pieces and bruise. And whereas thou sawest the feet and toes, part of potter's clay, and part of iron, the kingdom shall be divided; but there shall be in it of the strength of the iron, forasmuch as thou sawest the iron mixed with miry clay. And as the toes of the feet were part of iron, and part of clay, so the kingdom shall be partly strong, and partly broken. And whereas thou sawest iron mixed with miry clay, they shall mingle themselves with the seed of men: but they shall not cleave one to another, even as iron is not mixed with clay. And in the days of these kings shall the God of heaven set up a kingdom, which shall never be destroyed: and the kingdom shall not be left to other people, but it shall break in pieces and consume all these kingdoms, and it shall stand forever.*

NEBUCHADNEZZAR'S DREAM OF THE GREAT IMAGE - BACKGROUND

Nebuchadnezzar was in the second year of his reign over Babylon when he had a disturbing dream. So much so that he would have his own wise men and magicians killed if they did not reveal his dream and the meaning of it, even though he had already forgotten the details. So finally, God made the dream known and the interpretation unto him through Daniel.

THE PURPOSE OF THE DREAM

God desired to make known to Nebuchadnezzar the kingdoms that were to follow Babylon to the end. Each kingdom would be significant but less illustrious than the one before. Each kingdom would rule over the whole world but, eventually, fall. God purposefully mapped out His plan to show that He Alone is Omnipotent (All-powerful), Omniscient (All-knowing), and Omnipresent (Ever-present, not bound by time).

THE KINGDOMS REPRESENTED

Babylon, represented by gold, was the greatest. The Medio-Persian Empire came next and was represented by silver, then the Grecian Empire, represented by brass. Next was Rome, represented by iron, and finally, the ten toes, represented by iron and clay.

Five world powers, five world governments, and *only* five are mentioned. Four of these were single, and one was divided.

Daniel, Chapter 2, Verse 43 declares that the ten toes *shall not cleave one to another.* There is no mention of another singular one-world government because the scripture clearly states that these ten nations *shall not cleave one to another.*

The Ten Toes are the Ten Germanic Gothic Tribes that resulted from the Fall of Rome. They are the following:

- Heruli
- Suevi
- Burgundians
- Huns
- Ostrogoths
- Visigoths
- Vandals
- Lombards
- Franks
- Anglo-Saxons

Since the time of Nebuchadnezzar, the world has been under the political control of four single powers (one-world governments): **Babylon,** the **Medo-Persian Empire, Greece**, and **Rome**, along with one divided-world government: the **Ten Germanic Gothic Tribes**.

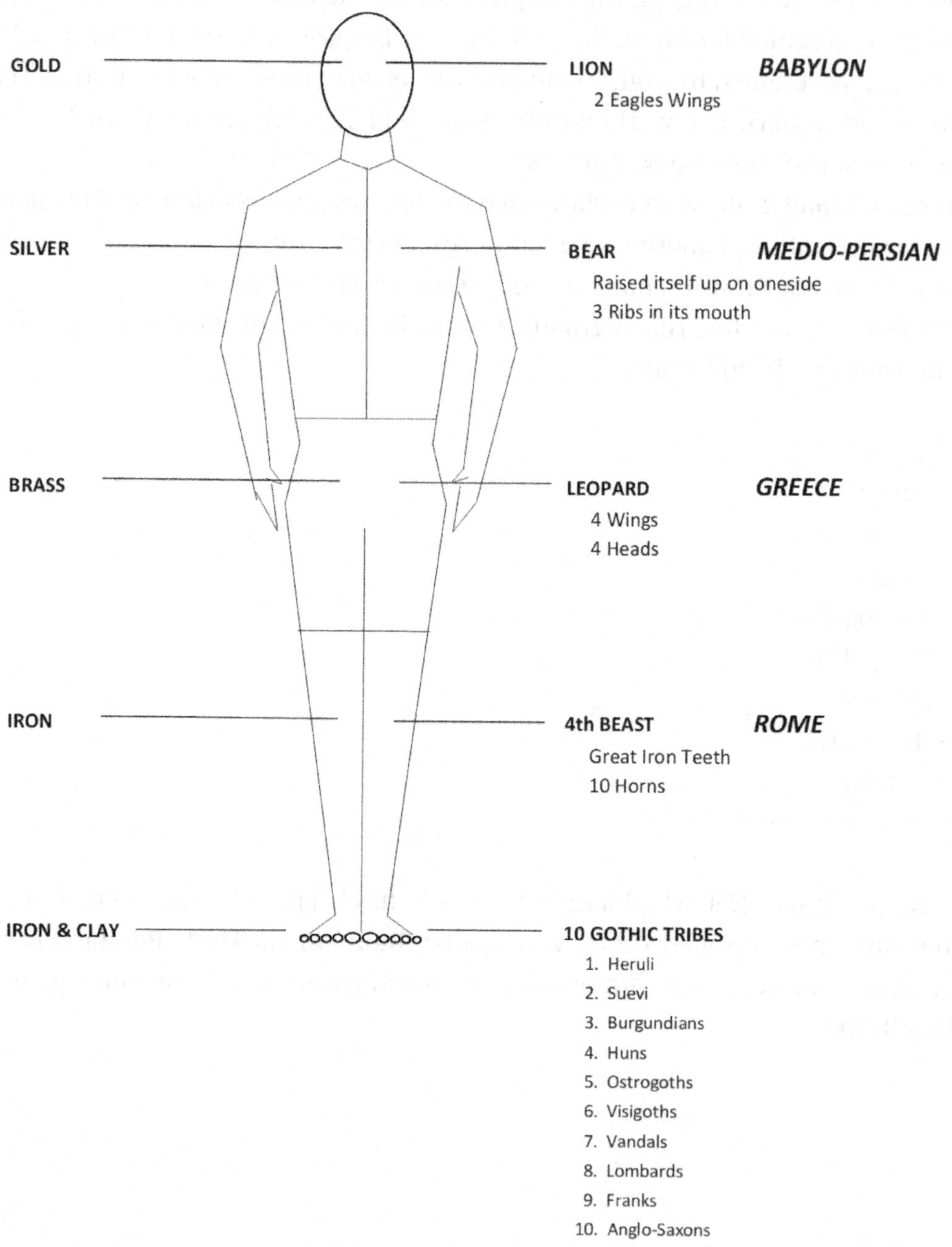
Nebuchadnezzar's Dream
GOLD
LION
BABYLON
2 Eagles Wings
SILVER
BEAR
MEDIO-PERSIAN
Raised itself up on oneside
3 Ribs in its mouth
BRASS
LEOPARD
GREECE
4 Wings
4 Heads
IRON
4th BEAST
ROME
Great Iron Teeth
10 Horns
IRON & CLAY
10 GOTHIC TRIBES
1. Heruli
2. Suevi
3. Burgundians
4. Huns
5. Ostrogoths
6. Visigoths
7. Vandals
8. Lombards
9. Franks
10. Anglo-Saxons

DANIEL'S VISION OF THE SEA BEAST

Daniel spake and said, I saw in my vision by night, and, behold, the four winds of the heaven strove upon the great sea. And four great beasts came up from the sea, diverse one from another. The first was like a lion, and had eagle's wings: I beheld till the wings thereof were plucked, and it was lifted up from the earth, and made stand upon the feet as a man, and a man's heart was given to it. And behold another beast, a second, like to a bear, and it raised up itself on one side, and it had three ribs in the mouth of it between the teeth of it: and they said thus unto it, Arise, devour much flesh. After this I beheld, and lo another, like a leopard, which had upon the back of it four wings of a fowl; the beast had also four heads; and dominion was given to it. After this I saw in the night visions, and behold a fourth beast, dreadful and terrible, and strong exceedingly; and it had great iron teeth: it devoured and brake in pieces, and stamped the residue with the feet of it: and it was diverse from all the beasts that were before it; and it had ten horns. I considered the horns, and, behold, there came up among them another little horn, before whom there were three of the first horns plucked up by the roots: and, behold, in this horn were eyes like the eyes of man, and a mouth speaking great things.

DANIEL 7:2-8

THE PURPOSE OF THE DREAM

God desired to make known to Daniel the kingdoms that were to follow Babylon to the end and give another perspective and greater detail to Nebuchadnezzar's dream.

THE KINGDOMS REPRESENTED

Daniel also saw the Five kingdoms represented. Four single kingdoms and one divided kingdom.

- **1st Kingdom – "Lion" – Babylon**

The lion represents Babylon. The two wings on the lion represent Nebuchadnezzar and Belshazzar, the two kings who ruled (carried about) Babylon. The eagle reference, the plucking of the wings, the standing upright, and the giving of a man's heart are prophecies directed to King Nebuchadnezzar, as stated in Daniel, Chapter 4.

This same passage also tells the story of another dreadful dream of King Nebuchadnezzar. King Nebuchadnezzar is warned of the day that he will become a beast and live like a wild animal and eat grass for seven years.

Let his heart be changed from man's, and let a beast's heart be given unto him: and let seven times pass over him. All this came upon the king Nebuchadnezzar. At the end of twelve months he walked in the palace of the kingdom of Babylon. The king spake, and said, Is not this great Babylon, that I have built for the house of the kingdom by the might of my power, and for the honour of my majesty? While the word was in the king's mouth, there fell a voice from heaven, saying, O king Nebuchadnezzar, to thee it is spoken; The kingdom is departed from thee. And they shall drive thee from men, and thy dwelling shall be with the beasts of the field: they shall make thee to eat grass as oxen, and seven times shall pass over thee, until thou know that the most High ruleth in the kingdom of men, and giveth it to whomsoever he will. The same hour was the thing fulfilled upon Nebuchadnezzar: and he was driven from men, and did eat grass as oxen, and his body was wet with the dew of heaven, till his hairs were grown like eagle's feathers, and his nails like birds' claws. And at the end of the days I Nebuchadnezzar lifted up mine eyes unto heaven, and mine understanding returned unto me, and I blessed the most High, and I praised and honoured him that liveth forever.

DANIEL 4:16; 28-34A

Notice how Nebuchadnezzar's fate was ultimately fulfilled, as stated, down to every detail. First, Nebuchadnezzar went insane for declaring Babylon was built by his own power and for not giving the glory to God. Then, Nebuchadnezzar's hair and nails grew for seven years, and he dwelt in the field like a wild animal until God restored his sanity. Finally, God made it very clear that He alone is God, and He is in control!

- 2nd Kingdom – "Bear" - Medo-Persian

The "Bear" raised itself on one side because Cyrus, King of Persia, conquered Babylon and gave his uncle Darius the Mede half of the kingdom. Cyrus gained his victory by overthrowing Babylon, Lydia, and Egypt. Babylon, Lydia, and Egypt are the three ribs in the Bear's mouth.

- **3rd Kingdom – "Leopard" - Greece**

The Medio-Persian Empire fell to Alexander the Great. The **four wings** were the **four generals** who ruled over the four provinces of Greece. The **four heads** were the **four provinces**.

1. Cassander over Greece
2. Ptolemy over Egypt
3. Lysimachus over Asia Minor
4. Seleucus over Syria and Babylon

- **4th Kingdom – "Iron" – Rome**

The Iron reference signifies this empire was Roman. The two legs were the Eastern and Western Roman Empires.

- **5th Kingdom – "part Iron and part Clay" – The Ten Gothic Tribes**

As the Roman Empire declined, it decayed into a divided kingdom, the Ten Gothic Tribes. They are described here as horns because they grew out of the Roman Empire. The Ten Toes of Nebuchadnezzar's dream and the Ten Horns of Daniel's dream are the same. They are the Ten Gothic Tribes that resulted from the Fall of Rome. They were the following:

1. Heruli
2. Suevi
3. Burgundians
4. Huns
5. Ostrogoths
6. Visigoths
7. Vandals
8. Lombards
9. Franks
10. Anglo-Saxons

After this, a Little Horn arises from this Iron Beast plucking up three of the prior horns by their roots. It is also referred to as a "horn" because it, too, grows out of the Roman Empire. During the Crusades, the Heruli 493 A.D., the Vandals 534 A.D., and the Ostrogoths 553 A.D. were conquered or plucked up. The one that commissioned the Crusades is that Little Horn, which will be explained further, coming up later in this book.

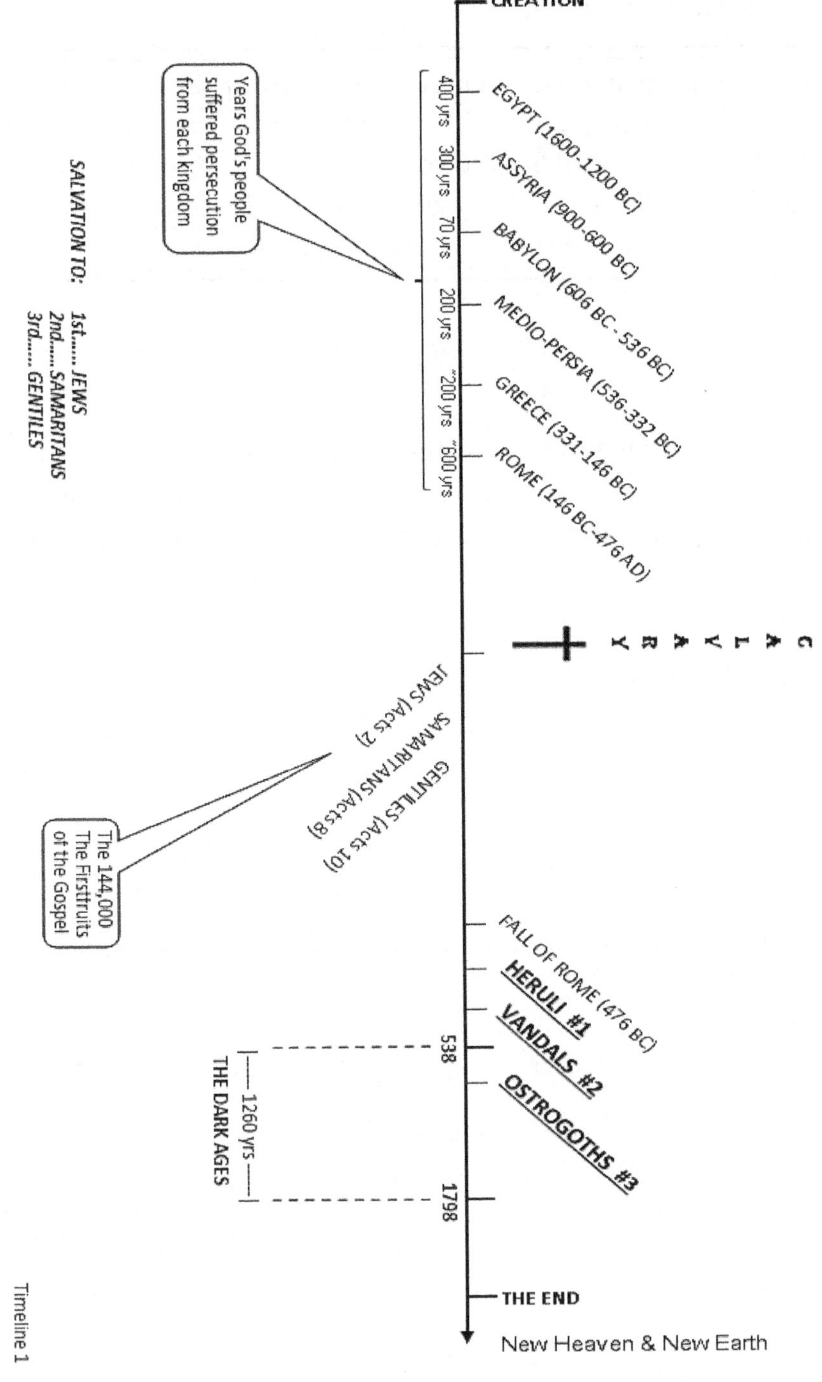
CREATION
EGYPT (1600-1200 BC)
ASSYRIA (900-600 BC)
BABYLON (606 BC - 536 BC)
MEDIO-PERSIA (536-332 BC)
GREECE (331-146 BC)
ROME (146 BC-476 AD)
400 yrs
300 yrs
70 yrs
200 yrs
200 yrs
600 yrs
Years God's people suffered persecution from each kingdom
SALVATION TO:
1st..... JEWS
2nd..... SAMARITANS
3rd..... GENTILES
CALVARY
JEWS (Acts 2)
SAMARITANS (Acts 8)
GENTILES (Acts 10)
The 144,000 The Firstfruits of the Gospel
FALL OF ROME (476 BC)
HERULI #1
VANDALS #2
OSTROGOTHS #3
538
1798
1260 yrs
THE DARK AGES
THE END
New Heaven & New Earth

Timeline 1

JOHN'S VISION OF THE SEA BEAST

And I stood upon the sand of the sea, and saw a beast rise up out of the sea, having seven heads and ten horns, and upon his heads the name of blasphemy. And the beast which I saw was like unto a leopard, and his feet were as the feet of a bear, and his mouth as the mouth of a lion: and the dragon gave him his power, and his seat, and great authority.
REVELATION 13:1-2

THE PURPOSE OF THE VISION

God desired to make known unto John the kingdoms of the world from Babylon to the end but in **reverse** order. So while Nebuchadnezzar and Daniel view the world's kingdoms from the past looking forward, John is in the future looking towards the past.

THE KINGDOMS REPRESENTED

John sees a *composite* of all Daniel sees but in reverse order. This small but important detail about the order has great significance. Daniel is looking forward in time. John is looking backward in time.

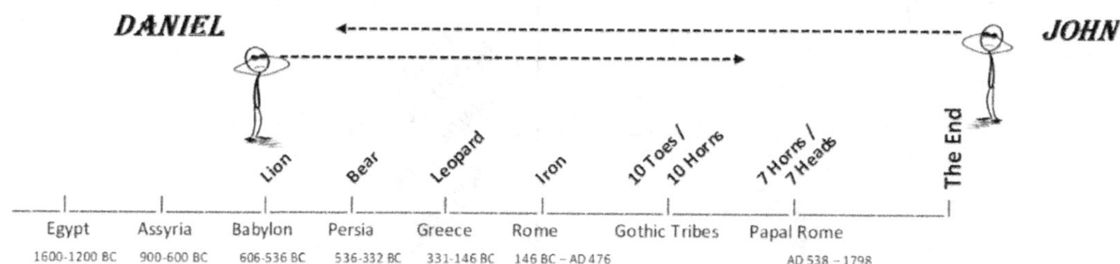

COMPARING THE ORDER

Daniel	**John**
Lion	7 Heads
Bear	10 Horns
Leopard	Leopard
Iron	Bear
10 Horns	Lion
10 – 3 = 7 Horns Left	

The order's significance is that Daniel and John are seeing the same thing but from different positions in time. Daniel is looking from the beginning of Babylon to the end of Time. John is standing at the end of Time, looking back toward Babylon. This explains how each sees his view of the world's kingdoms and how they unfold.

John sees a consolidation of the images from the visions of Nebuchadnezzar and Daniel morphed into one dreadful beast. This composite beast comprised of all worldly kingdoms also reveals how Satan, the prince of this world, continues to exist and operate.

Although each kingdom eventually dies, giving rise to another, the same evil spirit of our adversary, the devil continues to reappear in whatever form to persecute and oppress God's people. But God declares His Kingdom ***shall stand forever!***

DOMINATE KINGDOMS THROUGHOUT HISTORY

Before the Modern Era in which we live, eight world powers towered above and largely dominated the course of history. These Powers seem to represent the spirit of one evil power manifesting itself in various forms and to various degrees in various ages. Each of these afflicted and persecuted God's people.

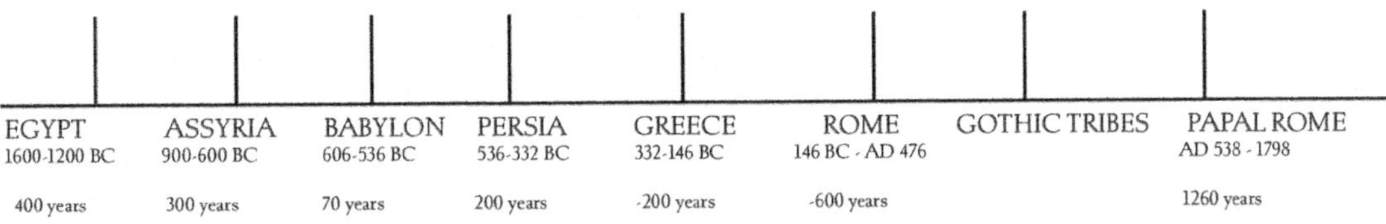

CONCLUSION:

God gave Nebuchadnezzar, Daniel, and John visions of the Kingdoms of the World and the order in which they would appear.

CHAPTER 6

THE SEVENTY WEEKS OF DANIEL

Daniel 9

THE PREMISE:

The pronoun "he" in Daniel 9:27 refers to Jesus Christ, not an antichrist

SCRIPTURE TEXT:

Daniel 9:24-27 *Seventy weeks are determined upon thy people and thy holy city, to finish the transgression, and to make an end of sins, and to make reconciliation for iniquity, and to bring in everlasting righteousness, and to seal up the vision and prophecy, and to anoint the most Holy. Know therefore and understand, that from the going forth of the commandment to restore and to build Jerusalem unto the Messiah the Prince shall be seven weeks, and threescore and two weeks: the street shall be built again, and the wall, even in troublous times. And after threescore and two weeks shall Messiah be cut off, but not for himself: and the people of the prince that shall come shall destroy the city and the sanctuary; and the end thereof shall be with a flood, and unto the end of the war desolations are determined. And he shall confirm the covenant with many for one week: and in the midst of the week he shall cause the sacrifice and the oblation to cease, and for* *the overspreading of abominations he shall make it desolate, even until the consummation, and that determined shall be poured out upon the desolate.*

THE BACKGROUND FOR DANIEL, CHAPTER 9

Chapter 9 of the book of Daniel foretells the coming Messiah. Daniel, a praying man who sought the Lord with fasting, interceded fervently on behalf of his people, the children of Israel. As a result, God sent the angel Gabriel to Daniel to make him skillful in understanding, not only with visions, as mentioned in Chapter 8, but also with the knowledge of Scripture.

THE BIG QUESTION - WHO IS "HE?"

The main subject in verses 24 through 26 is the Messiah or, as he was referred to in verse 25, "Messiah the Prince," revealed in the New Testament as Jesus Christ. However, much debate has resulted from the attempt to identify "he" in verse 27.

One interpretation suggests the embodiment of the Holy Spirit (Jesus Christ), while another suggests the embodiment of a Satanic spirit (the Antichrist). With such polar opposite interpretations of the little personal pronoun "he," the many intense and spirited discussions on this topic are no wonder.

FOUR REASONS TO SUPPORT THAT "HE" IS JESUS IN DANIEL 9:27

1. Sentence structure
2. Context
3. Fulfillment of scripture
4. Parables

"HE" IS JESUS ACCORDING TO SENTENCE STRUCTURE

Let's begin at the most elementary level and try to identify "he" in Daniel 9:27 according to sentence structure.

- The primary individual in verse 24 is "the most Holy" (JESUS).

- The primary individual in verse 25 is "Messiah the Prince" (JESUS).
- The primary individual in verse 26 is "Messiah" (JESUS).

The personal pronoun "he," whether capitalized or not, refers to the main subject matter of the passage. The personal pronoun "himself" refers to Messiah in verse 26, although the "h" in himself is not capitalized. Therefore, the reference to "he" in verse 27 can only be the Messiah (JESUS).

"He" cannot refer to "prince" in verse 26 simply because "prince" is the object of a prepositional phrase, and "of the prince" is an adjectival prepositional phrase describing "the people." An adjectival prepositional phrase is added to a sentence for the sole purpose of describing the preceding noun. And "he" cannot refer to "people" because "he" is singular, and "people" is plural.

It is important to remember that similar logic is used to understand baptism.

> *Go ye therefore, and teach all nations, baptizing them in the name of the Father, and of the Son, and of the Holy Ghost:*
>
> MATTHEW 28:19

Each adjectival prepositional phrase describes the preceding noun "name." Therefore, "of the Father," "of the Son," and "of the Holy Ghost" could be dropped without changing the structure or meaning of the sentence. We know the name is Jesus. These three adjectival prepositional phrases are added to describe the one name in the sentence. More prepositional phrases could be added, such as "of the Messiah," "of the Holy One," "of the Anointed One," "of the seed of David," "of the Comforter," "of the Second Adam," or "of the Savior," and so on. The only purpose is to describe that same name in the sentence further. The name is still Jesus.

"HE" IS JESUS ACCORDING TO CONTEXT

Seventy weeks are determined implies a single continuous timespan without interruption. There simply is no implication of any gaps in the passage.

Gaps are added to support a predetermined philosophy. One example of this arises in the various interpretations of the days of creation. Many creationists suggest a gap somewhere in the six days of creation in Genesis simply to satisfy the influence of evolution in their education. Such comments are spouted such as, "One day with the Lord is as a thousand years, so no one knows how long creation actually took" or "God created all the plants and animals, and they had to multiply and evolve, and the dinosaurs had to die off before Adam was created."

These statements are absurd once Truth is revealed in scripture. In his Creation Seminars, Steve Grohman has taught exceptionally well the Biblical truths of creation, dinosaurs, giants, the flood, and even global warming. His excellent Bible-based teaching explaining how the earth was created in precisely six consecutive 24-hour days without the aid or insertion of a gap period made creation clear and straightforward to understand. However, oddly enough, it remains unpopular and controversial even in Christianity.

Interestingly, a gap theory was formulated in the arrival of the 1st Adam, and a gap theory is again used in the appearance of the 2nd Adam (Jesus). Verse 24 of Daniel implies that seventy weeks is a continuous, uninterrupted period. Nothing remotely alludes to a portion of this timespan occurring in the past and the other part some 2,000 years in the future. There simply is *no* gap.

Verse 25 takes the first 69 weeks and divides it into two parts, seven weeks and 62 weeks. It does not mention or even imply a gap between the first seven weeks and the following 62 weeks here, either. The reason for the division serves only to point out that in the first 7-week period, a special event occurs, and then there are 62 weeks before the final week, the 70th week, in which another special event also occurs. In verse 26, the scripture reads, *And after 62 weeks Messiah shall be cut off.* Again, the scripture does not say or imply any gap. It merely states that after 69 weeks, the Messiah, or Jesus Christ, would be cut off.

So, what week would logically follow week sixty-nine? Week seventy, of course! And it does. Week 1 is followed immediately by weeks 2, 3, and so on until week 69, which is immediately followed by week 70. This is so elementary; however, confusion begins when a gap or a suspension in time is inserted to imply that the 70th week does not immediately follow the 69th. It may be redundant and perhaps overemphasizing the point here, but this is vital to comprehending the Book of Revelation.

Now, it follows that if immediately after the 69th week comes the 70th week, and the final week is singled out to denote the occurrence of a special event, *and* also after 69 weeks the Messiah is cut off, then the Messiah is cut off in the 70th week. So the "cutting off" of the Messiah is that special event occurring in the final week and the reason the one week is singled out. *See Timeline Pic 2.*

For he was cut off out of the living: for the transgression of my people was he stricken.

ISAIAH 53:8B

And he shall confirm the covenant with many for one week:

DANIEL 9:27A

Therefore, the confirmation of the covenant (the Covenant God made to mankind through the patriarchs) in the final week is the "cutting off" of the Messiah. The Messiah confirms the covenant by allowing himself to be cut off.

The phrase **"cut off"** (as defined in Strong's Concordance H3772) comes from the Hebrew word "karath" כָּרַת **kârath,** pronounced kaw-rath' which means to covenant (i.e., make an alliance or bargain, originally by cutting flesh and passing between the pieces).

In Genesis 15, the Lord promised Abraham that in his seed, all the nations of the earth would be blessed. To seal the covenant, the Lord instructed Abraham to bring five animals and divide the pieces of their carcass, one against the other, before the Lord. The Lord then passed through the pieces, and He alone established His Covenant with Abraham.

And it came to pass, that, when the sun went down, and it was dark, behold a smoking furnace, and a burning lamp that ***passed between those pieces****. In the same day the LORD made a covenant with Abram, saying, Unto thy seed have I given this land.*

GENESIS 15:17-18A

This same Hebrew word, **karath,** is interpreted elsewhere as **covenanted.**

Then will I establish the throne of thy kingdom, according as I have ***covenanted*** *with David thy father, saying, There shall not fail thee a man to be ruler in Israel.*

II CHRONICLES 7:18

According to the word that I ***covenanted*** *with you when ye came out of Egypt, so my spirit remaineth among you: fear ye not.*

HAGAI 2:5

The cutting off of Jesus by the sacrifice of himself upon the cross was the act that put the New Testament into motion. By his death, we have the right to the inheritance promised to Abraham! Through the New Birth experience, we are made partakers of ALL the blessings of God!

Now I say that Jesus Christ was a minister of the circumcision for the truth of God, to ***confirm*** *the* ***promises*** *made unto the fathers:*

ROMANS 15:8

Even as the ***testimony of Christ*** *was* ***confirmed*** *in you: So that ye come behind in no gift; waiting for the coming of our Lord Jesus Christ: Who shall also* ***confirm*** *you unto the end, that ye may be blameless in the day of our Lord Jesus Christ.*

I CORINTHIANS 1:6-8

Jesus Christ is the only one who can confirm or establish His covenant with us, which is only accomplished when we obey the gospel unto salvation. Strong's Concordance 01396 states that the word "confirm" comes from the Greek word "gabar." Gabar [gaw-bar'] means to be strong; by implication, to prevail, act insolently: -exceed, confirm, be great, be mighty, prevail, put to more (strength), strengthen, be stronger, be valiant.

The word confirm is further defined as: Con-FIRM /ken'ferm- *a verb;* to establish or strengthen as with new evidence or facts; strengthen or make more firm; support a person for a position; administer the rite of confirmation to; to make firm or firmer; to add strength to; to establish, to strengthen in judgment or purpose; to give new assurance of the truth of; to render certain; to verify; to corroborate; to render valid for formal assent; to complete by a necessary sanction; to ratify; as to confirm the appointment of an official; to administer the rite of confirmation.

SYNONYM DISCUSSION OF *CONFIRM*

None of the definitions or synonyms relate to "terminate, diminish, end, or make null and void." The notion that an antichrist, the embodiment of some satanic spirit, breaks a covenant does not even remotely fit the definition!

Daniel 9:27 is expressly speaking that "he" (Jesus Christ) is validating, making effective as in probating a will, authenticating, certifying, endorsing, guaranteeing, undergirding a covenant or contract that has already been in place but until this point not in effect. This is precisely what Jesus did when he died on the cross. The death of the testator confirms the testament or covenant. The New Testament or New Covenant does not have any power until the testator dies.

A will does not benefit the heirs until the will's maker dies. The will becomes validated once the maker of the will dies. And authority is now given to the heirs to partake of the promises of that will. God's covenant with Abraham was validated when Jesus died; not only the Jews but Samaritans (half-Jews) and Gentiles became heirs to the promise of washing away of sin, regeneration, and eternal life.

Please note that God is the maker of the Covenant. The maker of the Covenant must die to make the covenant effective, and herein lies the paradox. God cannot die because God is eternal! But, as I Timothy 3:16 states, *Great is the mystery of godliness: God was manifest in the flesh.*

Therefore, God created a body in the womb of Mary and placed His Spirit in that little baby. The baby grew into the man Christ Jesus, but God Almighty was the Spirit inside that man's body. Thus, *God was in Christ, reconciling the world unto himself.* (II Corinthians 5:19). God took on the form of man not only to redeem us from sin but to make us heirs to all He possesses!

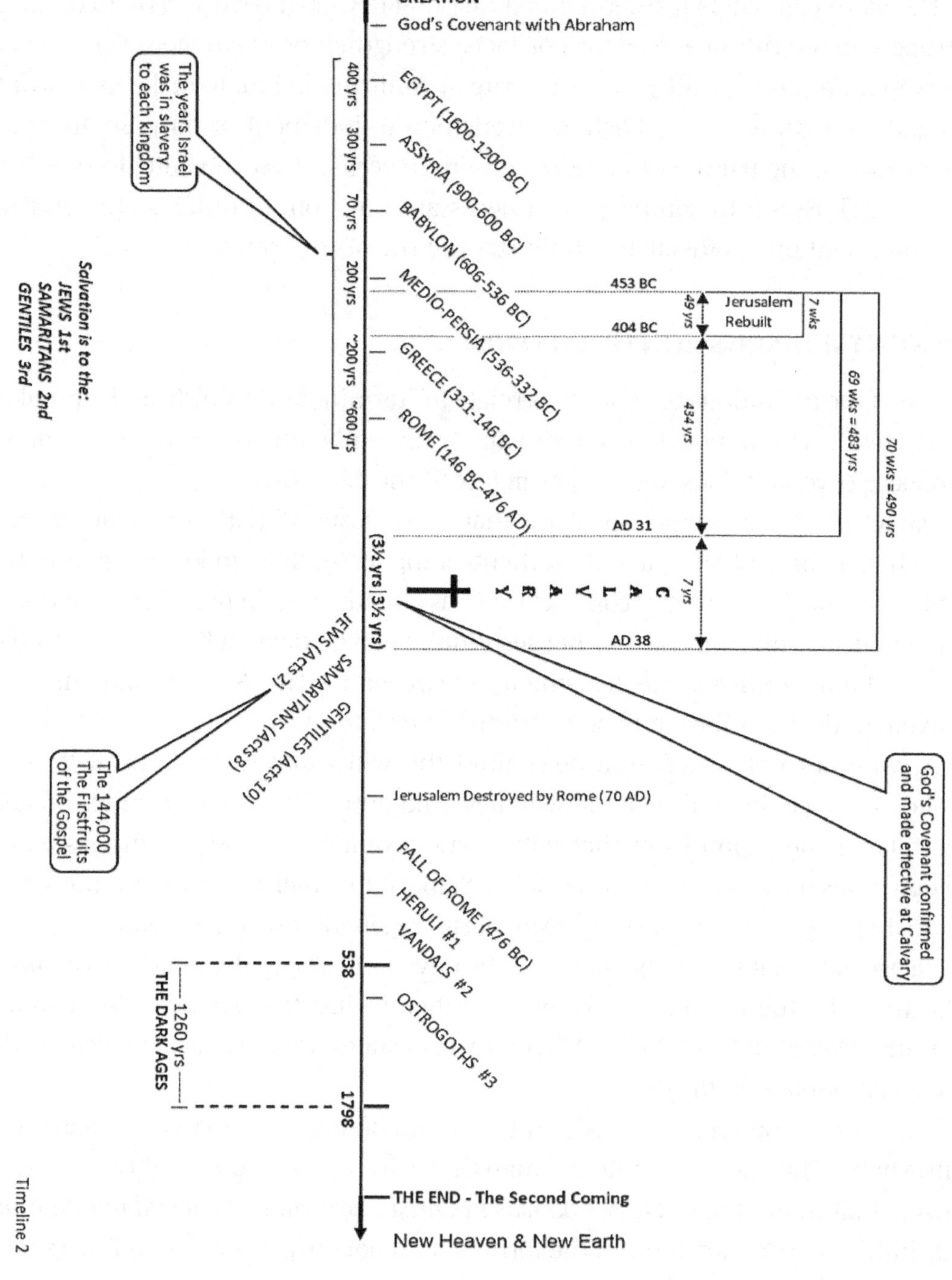
CREATION
God's Covenant with Abraham
EGYPT (1600-1200 BC)
ASSYRIA (900-600 BC)
BABYLON (606-536 BC)
MEDIO-PERSIA (536-332 BC)
GREECE (331-146 BC)
ROME (146 BC-476 AD)
400 yrs
300 yrs
70 yrs
200 yrs
~200 yrs
~600 yrs
The years Israel was in slavery to each kingdom
Salvation is to the:
JEWS 1st
SAMARITANS 2nd
GENTILES 3rd
453 BC
404 BC
49 yrs
Jerusalem Rebuilt
7 wks
434 yrs
69 wks = 483 yrs
70 wks = 490 yrs
AD 31
7 yrs
CALVARY
AD 38
(3½ yrs | 3½ yrs)
JEWS (Acts 2)
SAMARITANS (Acts 8)
GENTILES (Acts 10)
The 144,000 The Firstfruits of the Gospel
God's Covenant confirmed and made effective at Calvary
Jerusalem Destroyed by Rome (70 AD)
FALL OF ROME (476 BC)
HERULI #1
VANDALS #2
OSTROGOTHS #3
538
1798
1260 yrs
THE DARK AGES
THE END - The Second Coming
New Heaven & New Earth

Timeline 2

"HE" IS JESUS ACCORDING TO BIBLICAL REFERENCES AND THE FULFILLMENT OF SCRIPTURE

An excerpt from Haley's Bible Handbook has this to say: *The Captivity, which was then drawing to a close, had lasted 70 years. The angel here tells Daniel that it would yet be "70 weeks" till the coming of the Messiah.*

The "70 weeks" is generally understood as 70 weeks of years, that is, 70 sevens of years, seven times 70 years, or 490 years. It is as if the angel says, "The Captivity has been 70 years; the period between the Captivity and the Coming of the Messiah will be seven times that long."

Seven, and cycles of seven, sometimes have symbolic meanings; yet the facts of this prophecy are most remarkable, as follows:

The date from which the 70 weeks were to be counted was the decree to rebuild Jerusalem. Persian kings issued three decrees for this purpose (536 B.C., 457 B.C., 444 B.C., see under Ezra). The principal one of these was 457 B.C.

The 70 weeks are subdivided into seven weeks, 62 weeks, and one week. It is difficult to see the application of the "7 weeks." Still, the 69 weeks (including the 7) equal 483 days, that is, on the year-day theory (Ezekiel 4:6), which is the commonly accepted interpretation, 483 years.

This 483 years is the period between the decree to rebuild Jerusalem and the coming of the "Anointed One." The mandate to rebuild Jerusalem, as noted above, was in 457 B.C. Adding 483 years to 457 B.C. brings us to A.D. 26, the exact year that Jesus was baptized and then began his public ministry. What an exciting fulfillment of Daniel's prophecy—even to the year!

Further, within 3 ½ years, Jesus was crucified, that is, "in the midst of the one week," "the Anointed One" was "cut off" and "purged away sin and brought in everlasting righteousness."

Thus, Daniel foretold the time when the Messiah would appear, how long his public ministry would last, and the need for his death to atone for human sin.

Haley's Bible Handbook (4th Edition) also points out that some believe God's chronology was suspended at the death of Christ to remain so while Israel is scattered and that the last half of the "one week" belongs to the time of the End.

NOTE: I agree with Haley's summary, but I do not support the idea that God's chronology was suspended at Calvary and the final 3 ½ years are future. Now, because it was 483 years from the date of the *going forth of the commandment* of Daniel 9:25 to the day that Jesus began his ministry at age 30 (Luke 3:23), which would be AD 31 (there is no year "0"), I place the decree of King Cyrus to rebuild Jerusalem in the year 453 BC. And the 1st seven weeks were singled out to represent the time it took to rebuild Jerusalem and the Temple, a decree set forth and put in writing by Cyrus, king of Persia.

Now in the first year of Cyrus king of Persia, that the word of the Lord by the mouth of Jeremiah might be fulfilled, the Lord stirred up the spirit of Cyrus king of Persia, that he made a proclamation throughout all his kingdom, and put it also in writing, saying, Thus saith Cyrus king of Persia, The Lord God of heaven hath given me all the kingdoms of the earth; and he hath charged me to build him a house at Jerusalem, which is in Judah. Who is there among you of all his people? His God be with him, and let him go up to Jerusalem, which is in Judah, and build the house of the Lord God of Israel, (he is the God,) which is in Jerusalem.

EZRA 1:1-3

ANOTHER NOTE: The 1st seven weeks are equivalent to 49 years.
(7 weeks = 49 days. Using the "day for a year" formula found in Numbers 14:34 and Ezekiel 4:6, the 1st seven weeks represent the 1st 49 years.)
Looking again at Daniel 9:24:

Seventy weeks are determined upon thy people and upon thy holy city, to finish the transgression, to make an end of sins, to make reconciliation for iniquity, and to bring in everlasting righteousness, and to seal up the vision and prophecy, and to anoint the most Holy.

DANIEL 9:24

Seventy weeks are to *thy people and upon thy holy city*. It is to Israel, the Jews. Seventy prophetic weeks until the Promise of a New Covenant of salvation would be fulfilled and established with the people of Israel. The Promise was to the Jew first. Only after the New Covenant was established with Israel could the same New Covenant of salvation be extended to the Samaritans and then to the Gentiles.

EVERY PROPHECY OF DANIEL 9:24 IS FULFILLED

1. **—to finish the transgression**

Isaiah 53:5	he was wounded for our transgressions
Hebrews 9:15	for the redemption of the transgressions that were under the first testament
John 19:30	he said, "It is finished," and he bowed his head and gave up the ghost

2. **—to make an end of sins**

Matthew 1:21	and thou shalt call his name JESUS: for he shall save his people from their sins.
Hebrews 9:6	to put away sin by the sacrifice of himself
I John 3:5	he was manifested to take away our sins
I Peter 2:24	by whose stripes ye were healed.
I Peter 3:18	For Christ also hath once suffered for sins
I Corinthians 15:3	Christ died for our sins

3. **—and to make reconciliation for iniquity**

Isaiah 53:6	and the Lord hath laid on him the iniquity of us all.
Isaiah 53:11	by his knowledge shall my righteous servant justify many; for He shall bear their iniquities.
Titus 2:14	that he might redeem us from all iniquity
Hebrews 2:17	to make reconciliation for the sins of the people.
Colossians 1:20-22	to reconcile all things unto himself…now hath he reconciled
Ephesians 2:16	that he might reconcile both unto God
II Corinthians 5:19	God was in Christ, reconciling the world unto himself

4. **—and to bring in everlasting righteousness**

Romans 5:17-21	the gift of righteousness shall reign in life by one, Jesus Christ.
I Corinthians 1:30	God is made unto us wisdom, righteousness, sanctification, and redemption.
I Peter 2:24	that we, being dead to sins, should live unto righteousness
Romans 3:21-26	But now the righteousness of God without the law is manifested
II Corinthians 5:21	that we might be made the righteousness of God in him.

5. **—and to seal up the vision and prophecy**

Matthew 11:13	For all the prophets and the law prophesied until John.
Acts 3:18	But those things, which God before had showed by the mouth of all his prophets, that Christ should suffer, he hath so fulfilled.

6. **—and to anoint the most Holy**

Luke 4:18-21	The Spirit of the Lord is upon me because he hath anointed me to preach the gospel This day is this scripture fulfilled in your ears.

After Jesus was baptized by John in the river Jordan and returned after being tempted for forty days in the wilderness, he came to Nazareth, went into the synagogue on the Sabbath, and stood up and read from the prophet Esaias. (Isaiah 61:1)

The Spirit of the Lord is upon me, because he hath anointed me to preach the gospel to the poor; he hath sent me to heal the brokenhearted, to preach deliverance to the captives, and recovering of sight to the blind, to set at liberty them that are bruised, To preach the acceptable year of the Lord.

LUKE 4:18-19

Then in Luke 4:21, Jesus says, "*This day is this scripture fulfilled in your ears.*" At this point, the 69-week period ends, and the final 70th week begins. The confirmation of God's covenant with Abraham would take one week, that is, seven years. In the middle of the seven-year period, Jesus was crucified, and within the 3 ½ years after the crucifixion, Peter preached on the day of Pentecost to the Jews the good news of salvation of being *Born Again* under a New Covenant. Not until God's promise to Israel from hundreds of years earlier to "the children" was fulfilled could an open door to the Gentile nations be revealed.

"HE" IS JESUS ACCORDING TO PARABLES

Parables are profitable because they're designed to help us understand heavenly things by paralleling them with everyday examples and lessons in life.

All scripture is given by inspiration of God, and is profitable for doctrine, for reproof, for correction, for instruction in righteousness.

II TIMOTHY 3:16

Hear another parable: There was a certain householder, which planted a vineyard, and hedged it round about, and digged a winepress in it, and built a tower, and let it out to husbandmen, and went into a far country; And when the time of the fruit drew near, he sent his servants to the husbandmen, that they might receive the fruits of it. And the husbandmen took his servants, and beat one, and killed another, and stoned another. Again, he sent other servants more than the first: and they did unto them likewise. But last of all he sent unto them his son, saying, They will reverence my son. But when the husbandmen saw the son, they said among themselves, This is the heir; come, let us kill him, and let us seize on his inheritance. And they caught him, and cast him out of the vineyard, and slew him. When the lord therefore of the vineyard cometh, what will he do unto those husbandmen? They say unto him, He will miserably destroy those wicked men, and will let out his vineyard unto other husbandmen, which shall render him the fruits in their seasons. Jesus saith unto them, Did ye never read in the scriptures, The stone which the builders rejected, the same is become the head of the corner: this is the Lord's doing, and it is marvelous in your eyes? Therefore say I unto you, The kingdom of God shall be taken from you, and given to a nation bringing forth the fruits thereof.

MATTHEW 21:33-43

In this parable, Jesus refers to the Old Testament prophets (his servants) sent by God (the householder) to Israel (the husbandmen). But Israel (the husbandmen) rejected the prophets (God's servants) and ultimately persecuted and killed the householder's son (Jesus Christ), hoping to seize on the inheritance. Israel wanted total control of the vineyard. Because Israel as a nation in general (the natural branches and natural heirs to the promise) rejected Jesus as the Messiah, God cut them off so that the Gentiles (other husbandmen, the wild branches) might be grafted in. God's judgment for rejecting Jesus as the Messiah caused Jerusalem to be destroyed by the Roman armies. Salvation is a Free Gift to All! The Promises of God are for whosoever will!

And Jesus answered and spake unto them again by parables, and said, The kingdom of heaven is like unto a certain king, which made a marriage for his son, And sent forth his servants to call them that were bidden to the wedding: and they would not come. Again, he sent forth other servants, saying, Tell them which are bidden, Behold, I have prepared my dinner: my oxen and my fatlings are killed, and all things are ready: come unto the marriage. But they made light of it, and went their ways, one to his farm, another to his merchandise: And the remnant took his servants, and entreated them spitefully, and slew them. But when the king heard thereof, he was wroth: and he sent forth his armies, and destroyed those murderers, and burned up their city. Then saith he to his servants, The wedding is ready, but they which were bidden were not worthy. Go ye therefore into the highways, and as many as ye shall find, bid to the marriage.

MATTHEW 22:1-9

Again, we see the same scenario. The king (God) sent forth his servants (the prophets) to prepare the wedding for his son (Jesus Christ). When the servants (the prophets) went to call those that were bidden (Israel), they made light of the event and excuses not to come and then went so far as to slay the servants (the prophets).

When the nation of Israel rejected Jesus as the Messiah, God turned to the Gentiles, laid waste to Jerusalem, and destroyed the temple at the hand of the Roman army.

And, lo there was a great earthquake; and the sun became black as sackcloth of hair, and the moon became as blood; and the stars of heaven fell unto the earth, even as a fig tree casteth her untimely figs, when she is shaken of a mighty wind.

REVELATION 6:12a-13

The metaphors used in this passage refer to Joseph's dream in Genesis 37:9-11, where the sun, moon, and stars bowed to him; the sun referred to his father, Israel, the moon to his mother, and the stars to his eleven brothers. The sun, moon, and stars in Revelation 6 now represent Israel as the entire Hebrew nation with all of her pomp and pride in her beautiful Temple.

And he dreamed yet another dream, and told it his brethren, and said, Behold, I have dreamed a dream more; and, behold, the sun and the moon and the eleven stars made obeisance to me. And he told it to his father, and to his brethren: and his father rebuked him, and said unto him, What is this dream that thou hast dreamed? Shall I and thy mother and thy brethren indeed come to bow down ourselves to thee to the earth? And his brethren envied him; but his father observed the saying

GENESIS 37:9-11

The light of the nation of Israel went out, never to shine as in her former glory when the Lord used his armies to besiege Jerusalem and destroy it and her temple. The Roman armies are called "his armies" because they were used to carry out His will—not because they were holy. Nebuchadnezzar was even referred to as the servant of God, but only because he was under God's direction, not because he was a follower and worshiper of Him.

Does this mean that Jews are without any hope of salvation? Of course not! They must be *born again,* just as those Jews were in Acts, Chapter 2. The first step for a Jew or anyone is to believe that Jesus Christ is the Messiah. A person must first believe that Jesus is the way to salvation. Belief in Him leads to repentance and a new birth experience.

Herein, four explanations support that "he" is the Messiah, Jesus Christ, in Daniel 9:27, through sentence structure, context, fulfillment of scripture, and parallels in parables. To say that "he" refers to "The Antichrist" is to take a notable reference to the cross of Calvary, the most integral part of the Bible, the crux of both the Old and New Testament, and attribute it to a covenant of Satan. Now that is atrocious!

CONCLUSION:

The pronoun "he" in Daniel 9:27 refers to Jesus Christ, not an antichrist.

CHAPTER 7

COUNTDOWN TO THE NEW BIRTH

Daniel 8, 9 & 12

THE PREMISE:

The time periods of Daniel 8, 9, and 12 (2300 days, 490 days, 1290 days, and 1335 days) reveal the establishment of God's Covenant and its fulfillment in Jesus Christ through the New Birth experience as exampled in the Book of Acts. Furthermore, the formula one day = one year is the correct interpretation for *all* the time periods of Daniel's dreams and visions.

THE ESTABLISHMENT AND FULFILLMENT OF GOD'S COVENANT

God's Covenant was:

1.	Established with Noah	Genesis 6:18
2.	Established with Abraham	Genesis 15:18, Galatians 3:18
3.	Established with Isaac	Genesis 17:21
4.	Established with Jacob (Israel)	Genesis 32:28, Exodus 2:24
5.	Established with Moses	Exodus 24:7-8, 34:27-28, Hebrews 9:18-20
6.	Established with David	Isaiah 9:7, Psalm 51:5-6
7.	**Confirmed by Jesus**	Romans 15:8
8.	Partaken of by us	Colossians 1:12

God's Covenant was and still is a promise, a pledge, a divine ordinance between God and man. It is a **testament** authored by God Himself. By definition, a **will** or **testament** is a legal document by which a person, known as the **testator**, states their desires as to how their property is to be distributed at death and names one or more persons, the **executor(s)**, to manage the **estate** until its final distribution.

The creator of a testament is called the testator. The testament is just a promise until the testator dies. Please note that **God is the testator**, and since God cannot die, God needed to indwell the man Christ Jesus so that flesh could die. Therefore, the Spirit that was in Christ was God Almighty!

*To wit, that **God was in Christ**, reconciling the world unto himself…*

II CORINTHIANS 5:19A

*And without controversy great is the mystery of godliness: **God was manifest in the flesh…***

I TIMOTHY 3:16A

GOD'S COVENANT WITH MAN WAS:

1st Established with Noah through the washing of water
Sign: Rainbow in the cloud. (Genesis 9:13)
Foreshadowing: Baptism washes away our sins.

2nd Established with Abraham through the dividing of the pieces
The Spirit of the Lord passed through the pieces. (Genesis 15:17-18)
Sign: Abraham's seed would be a stranger in Egypt. (Genesis 15:13)
Foreshadowing: God separates us from the world unto Him.

3rd Established with Isaac through the cutting-off of the flesh
Sign: Circumcision. (Genesis 17:11, 21)
Foreshadowing: Our former unclean nature is cut off.

4th Established with Jacob through a change in identity.
Sign: A new name. (Genesis 32:28).
Foreshadowing: We are identified as belonging to Jesus Christ.

5th Established with Moses by obedience to God's Written Word.
Sign: Application of blood. (Exodus 24:7-8).
Foreshadowing: We are given a protective covering.

6th Established with the throne of David with judgment and justice. (Isaiah 9:7).
David understood that God desired truth in the inward part of the heart. (Psalm 51:6).
Sign: David desired in his heart to build a house of rest for the ark of the covenant of the LORD and made ready for the building. (I Chronicles 28:2).
Foreshadowing: We now have a new inner direction and desire to consecrate.

7th Confirmed by Jesus through his Death, Burial & Resurrection.
God's covenant is validated. Power and authority are made available.
Jesus was a minister of the circumcision and confirmed the promises made unto our spiritual fathers of the Old Testament. (Romans 15:8).
Sign: The Resurrection. (Romans 1:4, I Peter 1:3, 3:21).
Foreshadowing: Spirit Baptism. (Acts 2, Acts 8, Acts 10).

8th Partaken of by believers who are made heirs through the New Birth
This is The Rest, the Times of Refreshing! (Isaiah 28:12, Acts 3:19).
Sign: Outpouring of Holy Ghost & Fire! (Acts 2:1-4).
Fulfillment: Born Again Believers inherit spiritual power and spiritual authority.

All born-again Believers are partakers of God's Covenant and inherit ALL rights of spiritual freedom, spiritual power, and spiritual authority in this life through the Name of Jesus Christ, along with the promise of eternal life after death.

Just as the Lord created all things in six days and rested on the seventh, in six significant instances, God established His Covenant with mankind and rested on the seventh by laying down his life for us. All mankind now has the opportunity to obey the gospel (the death, burial, and resurrection of Jesus Christ) and find, as the prophet

Isaiah declared, *the rest wherewith ye may cause the weary to rest* and become heirs of the Promise with all rights and authority exercised therein!

2,300 DAYS OF DANIEL 8

SCRIPTURE TEXT:

Daniel 8:13-14 *Then I heard one saint speaking, and another saint said unto that certain saint which spake, How long shall be the vision concerning the daily sacrifice, and the transgression of desolation, to give both the sanctuary and the host to be trodden under foot? And he said unto me, Unto* ***two thousand and three hundred days; then shall the sanctuary be cleansed.***

The first period mentioned in Daniel is 2,300 days, interpreted as 2,300 years. This period of 2,300 years is the grand overview of God's cleansing of the sanctuary.

THE FORMULA: 1 DAY = 1 YEAR

The formula, one day = one year, comes from Numbers 14:34 and Ezekiel 4:6.

> *After the number of the days in which ye searched the land, even forty days,* ***each day for a year,*** *shall ye bear your iniquities, even forty years, and ye shall know my breach of promise.*
>
> NUMBERS 14:34

> *And when thou hast accomplished them, lie again on thy right side, and thou shalt bear the iniquity of the house of Judah forty days: I have appointed thee* ***each day for a year.***
>
> EZEKIEL 4:6

Whenever scripture foretells future events, veiled language is used to describe them in symbolic form. The reason is to keep these events hidden until the appropriate time. For example, just as the scriptures prophesied the circumstances surrounding the birth of Jesus and how he would die, illumination would not come until the appointed time. Therefore, God needed to keep certain events hidden, not only from mankind but from Satan.

Which none of the princes of this world knew: for had they known it, they would not have crucified the Lord of glory.

I CORINTHIANS 2:8

Mankind can now partake of God's Covenant while looking back over history to understand how His plan unfolded and how all humanity has an equal opportunity to salvation through the New Birth Experience.

Of which salvation the prophets have enquired and searched diligently, who prophesied of the grace that should come unto you: Searching what, or what manner of time the Spirit of Christ which was in them did signify, when it testified beforehand the sufferings of Christ, and the glory that should follow. Unto whom it was revealed, that not unto themselves, but unto us they did minister the things, which are now reported unto you by them that have preached the gospel unto you with the Holy Ghost sent down from heaven; which things the angels desire to look into.

I PETER 1:10-12

The same Spirit that indwelt the man Christ Jesus previously moved upon prophets of old to prophesy (foretell) of this glorious gospel. Although they did not fully understand the meaning and magnitude of what they were prophesying, the revelation of it all would not come until the Holy Ghost was poured out, as recorded in the Book of the Acts of the Apostles.

THE SANCTUARY

The Hebrew word for **sanctuary** is **qôdesh** (Strong's Concordance 06944). It refers to something set apart, consecrated, and holy unto the Lord. It is further defined as:

> **qôdesh,** ko'-desh: a sacred place or thing; rarely abstract, sanctity:—consecrated (thing), dedicated (thing), hallowed (thing), holiness, (most) holy (day, portion, thing), saint, sanctuary.

In the original creation plan, mankind was set apart by God from all other living creatures. God's desire was a holy communion with man based on a voluntary relationship. A mere thirteen hundred years after the disobedience of one man, Adam, wickedness had spread to epidemic proportions.

> *God saw that the wickedness of man was great on the earth and that every imagination of the thoughts of his heart was only evil continually.*
>
> GENESIS 6:5

Being grieved, the Lord proceeded to destroy man from the face of the earth. The Lord is holy, and the one part of creation that the Lord set apart to be holy had become so corrupted that he saw no other solution but to cleanse the earth of all mankind.

However, Noah found grace in the eyes of the Lord. Therefore, the Lord made a promise to establish his covenant with Noah. This Covenant is still in effect today. It is a promise, legally bound by the Word of God, of ALL the benefits, blessings, and spiritual authority available from God to us in exchange for our voluntary choice to have that relationship with Him: a relationship that is holy, sacred, pure, set apart, and consecrated unto Him.

God desires from us a relationship that begins in the heart. Truth and righteousness must begin in the inward man to be effective. What is on the inside will ultimately manifest itself on the outside. If the Holy Ghost is in us and influencing us, we will look, talk, and act more like Jesus and less like the world. If the world is in us and influencing us, we will look, talk, act, and follow the things of the world, soon compromising and conforming to the world's standards (or lack thereof). When we truly have Jesus in us, our righteousness will exceed the Pharisees.

It is not enough that we refrain from murder. We are not allowed even to hate our fellow man. It is not enough to refrain from the act of adultery. We are not allowed to even look upon someone with lustful thoughts. It is not enough to refrain from stealing. We are not allowed even to covet. We are not allowed to live any way we choose, for we are not our own. We have been bought with the price of blood, His Blood! We were once a slave to sin, but Jesus paid our ransom to make us free. We now belong to him. Therefore, Paul admonished us that we *present* our *bodies as a living sacrifice, holy, acceptable unto God, which is* our *reasonable service* [Romans 12:1].

> *What? Know ye not that your body is the temple of the Holy Ghost which is in you, which ye have of God, and ye are not your own?*
>
> I CORINTHIANS 6:19

> *But ye are not in the flesh, but in the Spirit,* ***if*** *so be that the Spirit of God dwells in you. Now, if any man has not the Spirit of Christ, he is none of his.*
>
> ROMANS 8:9

This is a conditional statement! If we do not have the Spirit of God, then we do not belong to Him!

WATER & FIRE: GOD'S METHOD OF CLEANSING

> *For this they willingly are ignorant of, that by the word of God the heavens were of old, and the earth standing out of the water and in the water: Whereby the world that then was,* ***being overflowed with water, perished: But the heavens and the earth, which are now, by the same word are kept in store, reserved unto fire against the day of judgment*** *and perdition of ungodly men.*
>
> II PETER 3:5-7

THE CLEANSING BEGINS

In approximately 2255 BC, Noah was five hundred years old. Because Noah was a just man and walked with God, God had mercy upon him and his family and made a way to escape the coming wrath. Noah then commenced building an ark according to

God's detailed instructions. One hundred years later, Noah entered the ark, and the earth was washed with water.

It is interesting to note that God's judgment was not immediate. God allowed man adequate time to repent, one hundred years! However, when the time came, God, not Noah, shut the door to the ark. The impending doom of the wicked was fulfilled, and only Noah and his family were saved, only eight souls. In the New Testament, the Lord likens the coming end of the world to the days of Noah.

Through the New Birth Experience, every man and woman today has the choice to partake in God's Covenant and escape the wrath to come. By being Born Again, according to scripture, man voluntarily enters a covenant relationship with the Lord to enjoy ALL the benefits associated with a holy, sacred, set apart, consecrated life. The Church, the Bride of Christ, is the sanctuary the Lord God Almighty has meticulously cared for throughout the centuries. Not only can we enjoy his benefits every day, but we have a future hope of eternity with him, the likes of which have never entered the mind of man.

The "cleansing of the sanctuary" began approximately 2255 BC with God's promise to Noah and ended when Peter preached the New Birth message to the Gentiles in Acts 10, about 45 AD. It took 2300 years, but salvation is now an equal opportunity for all mankind, whether Jew, Samaritan, or Gentile. Refer to Acts 2 for Jews, Acts 8 for Samaritans, and Acts 10 for Gentiles. In addition, Acts 19 will show that believing does not constitute a New Birth experience since the believers in Acts 19 were commanded to be rebaptized in water and to receive the baptism of the Holy Ghost.

BOTH MAN AND THE EARTH ARE CLEANSED BY WATER AND FIRE

Jesus answered, Verily, verily, I say unto thee, except a man be born of ***water and*** *of the* ***Spirit****, he cannot enter into the kingdom of God.*

JOHN 3:5

I [John] indeed baptize you with ***water*** *unto repentance: but he that cometh after me is mightier than I, whose shoes I am not worthy to bear: he shall* ***baptize*** *you with the* ***Holy Ghost, and*** *with* ***fire****:*

MATTHEW 3:11

Our spirit man is cleansed by water (baptism in water) and fire (baptism in the Holy Ghost). So likewise, once cleansed by water (the flood), the earth will ultimately be cleansed by fire at the Second Coming of the Lord. In both instances, both events must take place for a complete and total cleansing.

Seeing then that all these things shall be dissolved, what manner of persons ought ye to be in all holy conversation and godliness, looking for and hasting unto the ***coming of the day of God, wherein the heavens being on fire shall be dissolved, and the elements shall melt with fervent heat****? Nevertheless* ***we, according to his promise, look for new heavens and a new earth****, wherein dwelleth righteousness.*

II PETER 3:11-13

But as it is written, Eye hath not seen, nor ear heard, neither have entered into the heart of man, the things which God hath prepared for them that love him.

I CORINTHIANS 2:9

When an individual receives the Baptism of the Holy Ghost, they are simultaneously baptized with fire. Although a person may experience a very enthusiastic elation of emotion, the scripture context is not referring to a fire of enthusiasm or zeal but rather a fire to purge us.

...he shall baptize you with the Holy Ghost and with fire: whose fan is in his hand, and he will throughly purge his floor...

LUKE 3:16b-17A

And he shall sit as a refiner and purifier of silver: and he shall purify the sons of Levi, and purge them as gold and silver, that they may offer unto the Lord an offering in righteousness.

MALACHI 3:3

CONVERSION VS. CONSECRATION

The Holy Ghost is given for **conversion**. The Fire is given for **consecration**. **Conversion** is an **Event** (being born again). **Consecration** is a **Process** (a purification). When we receive the Baptism of the Holy Ghost, we are converted, NOT consecrated. Lest this statement is misconstrued, a newborn in Christ IS holy and perfect at this stage of development, although they are not yet fully developed into a "mature" Christian.

It is the trying of our faith by fire, according to I Peter 1:7, that leads to consecration. If we endure trials and temptations and remain faithful, we shall emerge victorious and purified of carnal things that weigh us down. The Holy Ghost working in us leads us and guides us to be more like Jesus.

This is the reason preaching is vital to salvation. I Corinthians 1:21 states that *it pleased God by the foolishness of preaching to save them that believe.* The preaching and teaching of the Word of God are not only *for doctrine* but *for reproof, correction, and instruction in righteousness* (II Timothy 3:16). It is necessary for salvation!

The Baptism of Water and the Baptism of the Holy Ghost and Fire are both required for the total cleansing of our spirit man; therefore, an individual cannot be considered scripturally born again unless both events have occurred.

490 DAYS OF DANIEL 9

SCRIPTURE TEXT:

Daniel 9:24 ***Seventy weeks are determined upon thy people and*** *upon thy holy city, to finish the transgression, and to make an end of sins, and to make reconciliation for* *iniquity, and to bring in everlasting righteousness, and to seal up the vision and prophecy, and to anoint the most Holy.*

The second time period of Daniel is 490 days, which is interpreted as 490 years. This is a prophecy predicting the timing of Calvary and of Jesus's ministry to the nation of Israel, the Jews.

> *He came unto* **his own**, *and* **his own received him not**. *But as many as received him, to them gave he power to become the sons of God, even to them that believe on his name: Which were born, not of blood, nor of the will of the flesh, nor of the will of man, but of God.*
>
> JOHN 1:11-13

His own people, the Jews, for the most part, did not receive him. However, the Jews that did believe in the name of Jesus received salvation when they were born again, not by flesh, but by water and spirit, according to Acts 2:38.

The Gospel was preached:

First	to Jerusalem and Judea (Jews)
Second	to Samaria
Third	to the uttermost (everywhere else: Gentiles)

> *And that repentance and remission of sins should be preached in his name among all nations, beginning at Jerusalem.*
>
> LUKE 24:47

> *…ye shall be witnesses unto me both in Jerusalem, and in Judea, and in Samaria, and unto the uttermost part of the earth.*
>
> ACTS 1:8B

ONE PLAN FOR ALL MANKIND

Once Jesus died and rose again, he alone became the atonement for the sins of **all** mankind. Everyone is born in sin and must be "born again." The New Birth is not limited to Israel but to "whosoever will."

For he is not a Jew, which is one outwardly; neither is that circumcision, which is outward in the flesh: But he is a Jew, which is one inwardly; and circumcision is that of the heart, in the spirit, and not in the letter, whose praise is not of men, but of God.

ROMANS 2:28-29

For ***the promise****, that he should be the heir of the world, was not to Abraham, or to his seed, through the law, but through the righteousness of faith.*

ROMANS 4:13

Neither heritage nor outward customs can cause anyone to be among God's chosen people. It happens only *through the righteousness of faith* and obedience to the Word of God.

Salvation is still for the Jews but only through faith in Jesus Christ. Once a Jew has faith to believe Jesus is the Messiah, he must be born again. Refer to Chapter Six for a more detailed explanation.

And they [Jews] also, ***if*** *they abide* ***not*** *still in unbelief, shall be graffed in: for God is able to graff them in again.*

ROMANS 11:23

1,290 DAYS AND 1,335 DAYS OF DANIEL 12

SCRIPTURE TEXT:

Daniel 12:11-12 *And from the time that the daily sacrifice shall be taken away, and the abomination that maketh desolate set up, there shall be* ***a thousand two hundred and***

ninety days. *Blessed is he that waiteth, and cometh to* ***the thousand three hundred and five and thirty days.***

The last two time periods of Daniel 12 are 1,290 days and 1,335 days, which is interpreted as 1,290 years and 1,335 years. The period of 1,290 years is the time allotted from the giving of the Law by God to Moses until the birth of Jesus Christ as the sacrificial lamb. The period of 1,335 years is the time allotted from the giving of the Law by God to Moses until the day the Holy Ghost was poured out upon the Gentiles in Acts 10. At this point in history, the door of salvation was open to **all** nations, and God's Everlasting Covenant was in full force!

Jesus was the only sacrifice that could ultimately forgive sin and end all animal sacrifice. But, blessed is whosoever comes to the 1,335th day! God's Covenant of salvation was made available to every man and woman on the face of the earth, regardless of race, through the New Birth experience found in the book of Acts. In the book of Acts, one finds examples of individuals being "Born Again" according to scripture. It is in Acts where people (Jew, Samaritan, and Gentile alike) repent of their sins, are baptized in the name of Jesus Christ, and glorify God in an unknown tongue as they are filled with the baptism of the Holy Ghost.

THE NEW BIRTH

Jesus answered, Verily, verily, I say unto thee, Except a man be born of water and of the Spirit, he cannot enter into the kingdom of God.

JOHN 3:5

THE SALVATION MESSAGE WAS FIRST PREACHED TO THE JEWS

And there were dwelling at Jerusalem ***Jews****, devout men, out of every nation under heaven. Then Peter said unto them, Repent, and be baptized every one of you in the name of Jesus Christ for the remission of sins, and ye shall receive the gift of the Holy Ghost.*

ACTS 2:5, 38

NEXT, THE SALVATION MESSAGE PREACHED TO THE SAMARITANS

Now when the apostles which were at Jerusalem heard that ***Samaria*** *had received the word of God, they sent unto them Peter and John: Who, when they were come down, prayed for them, that they might receive the Holy Ghost. (For as yet he was fallen upon none of them: only they were baptized in the name of the Lord Jesus.) Then laid they their hands on them, and they received the Holy Ghost.*

ACTS 8:14-17

FINALLY, THE SALVATION MESSAGE PREACHED TO THE GENTILES

While Peter yet spake these words, the Holy Ghost fell on all them which heard the word. And they of the circumcision which believed were astonished, as many as came with Peter, because that on the ***Gentiles*** *also was poured out the gift of the Holy Ghost. For they heard them speak with tongues, and magnify God. Then answered Peter, Can any forbid water, that these should not be baptized, which have received the Holy Ghost as well as we? And he commanded them to be baptized in the name of the Lord. Then prayed they him to tarry certain days.*

ACTS 10:44-48

Perhaps now, the following timeline will illustrate the importance and focus the Bible places on God's Covenant and his plan for our salvation through Jesus Christ! God's Covenant was:

1. Established with Noah — Genesis 6:18
2. Established with Abraham — Genesis 15:18, Galatians 3:18
3. Established with Isaac — Genesis 17:21
4. Established with Jacob (Israel) — Genesis 32:28, Exodus 2:24
5. Established with Moses — Exodus 24:7-8, 34:27-28, Hebrews 9:18-20
6. Established with David — Isaiah 9:7, Psalm 51:5-6
7. **Confirmed by Jesus** — Romans 15:8
8. Partaken of by us — Colossians 1:12

CONCLUSION:

The time periods of Daniel 8, 9, and 12 (2300 days, 490 days, 1290 days, and 1335 days) reveal the establishment of God's Covenant and its fulfillment in Jesus Christ through the New Birth experience as exampled in the Book of Acts. The formula, one day = one year, is the correct interpretation for all the time periods of Daniel's dreams and visions.

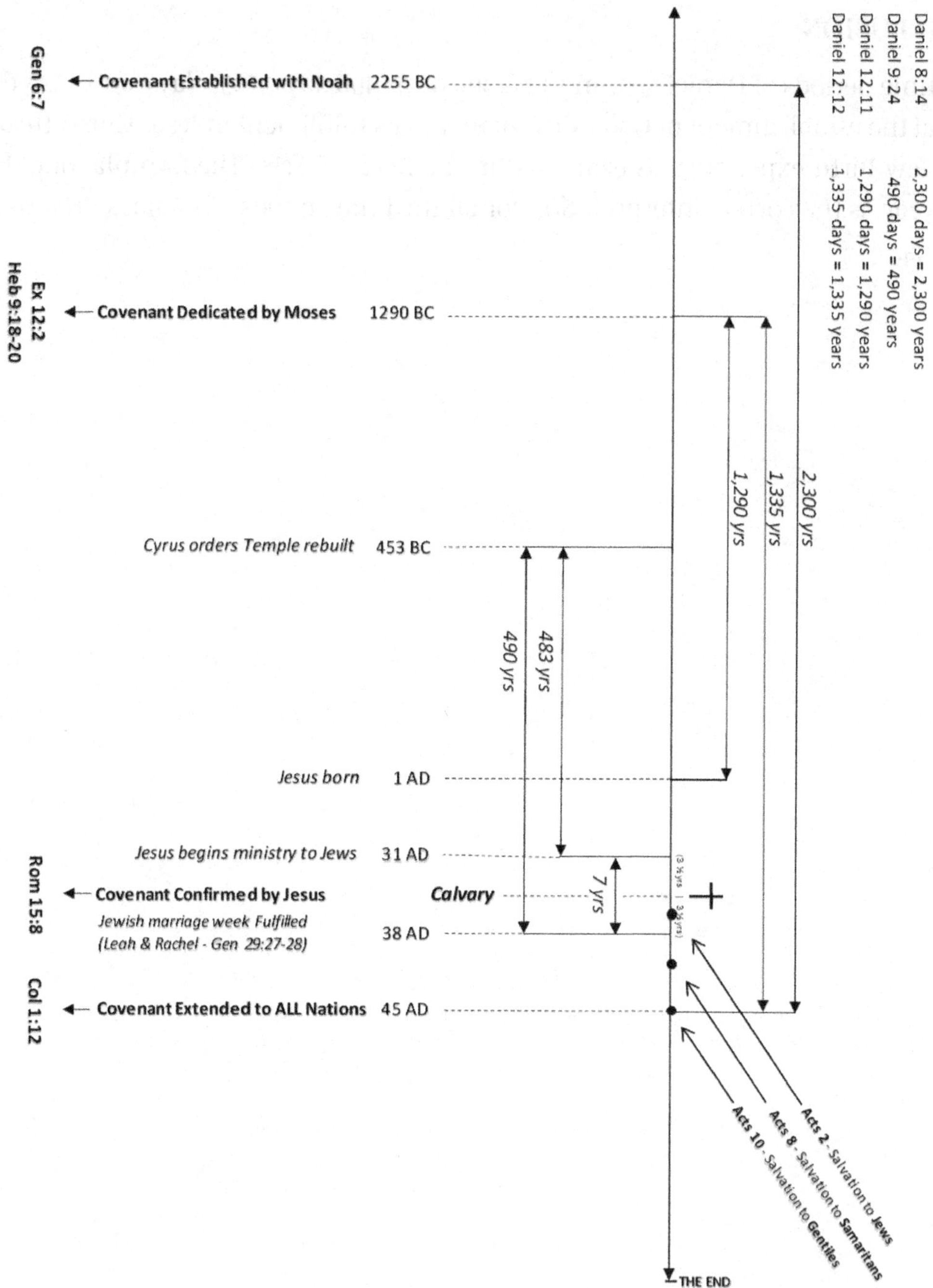

Daniel 8:14 2,300 days = 2,300 years
Daniel 9:24 490 days = 490 years
Daniel 12:11 1,290 days = 1,290 years
Daniel 12:12 1,335 days = 1,335 years
Gen 6:7
Covenant Established with Noah 2255 BC
Ex 12:2
Heb 9:18-20
Covenant Dedicated by Moses 1290 BC
2,300 yrs
1,335 yrs
1,290 yrs
Cyrus orders Temple rebuilt 453 BC
483 yrs
490 yrs
Jesus born 1 AD
Jesus begins ministry to Jews 31 AD
Rom 15:8
Covenant Confirmed by Jesus
Calvary
Jewish marriage week Fulfilled
(Leah & Rachel - Gen 29:27-28)
7 yrs
38 AD
Col 1:12
Covenant Extended to ALL Nations 45 AD
Acts 2 - Salvation to Jews
Acts 8 - Salvation to Samaritans
Acts 10 - Salvation to Gentiles
THE END

CHAPTER 8

THE SEVEN SEALS

Revelation 5, 6, 8

THE PREMISE:

The Seven Seals are God's curse and judgment upon the nation of Israel for failing to turn from idolatry and sin, resulting in the casting down of the light of Israel, its pomp, pride, and power.

QUICK REVIEW

Before diving off into the Seven Seals, the Seven Trumpets, the Seven Vials, and so on, let's celebrate the beautiful gems of truth we have uncovered thus far in this amazing treasure hunt. First, we have found that the Book of Revelation truly is the revelation and unveiling of Jesus Christ. An elementary statement, perhaps, but profound in its implication. We have discovered various perspectives to support that there is only one God according to Deuteronomy 6:4 and the importance and the necessity of the New Birth.

We have seen grand and glorious visions of the throne of God. In fact, the throne of God is mentioned in just about every chapter of the Book of Revelation. We have learned how the seven golden candlesticks are the 7 Churches of Asia and represent a cross-section of The Church even today in various stages as viewed through the eyes of God. We have also identified the 24 Elders, the 4 Beasts, the Two Witnesses, the

144,000, and the Great Multitude. We then recognized how God gave Daniel a vision looking forward in time and gave John a similar vision but looking backward in time. And if that were not enough, we finally cracked the code to the 490, 1290, 1335, and 2300 days of Daniel, all of which point to the "Born Again" Experience! Wow!

INTRODUCTION:

In Deuteronomy 30, God spoke to Israel through Moses and set before them a blessing and a curse: a blessing if they chose to obey and a curse if they did not. Israel chose NOT to obey. In Revelation, Chapters 5 and 6, God holds a book (roll or scroll) in his right hand, sealed with seven seals. Only Jesus Christ was found worthy to loose (remove) the seals and to open the book.

The Sealed Book is a book of curses upon a nation and people who had rejected God, served idols, defiled the sanctuary with all types of abominations and detestable practices, rejected Jesus as the Messiah and crucified him, and then persecuted the bride of Christ, The Church. Therefore, only Jesus Christ was found worthy and given the authority to loose (remove) the seals.

SCRIPTURE TEXT:

And I saw in the right hand of him that sat on the throne a book written within and on the backside, sealed with ***seven seals****. And I saw a strong angel proclaiming with a loud voice, who is worthy to open the book, and to loose the seals thereof? And I beheld, and, lo, in the midst of the throne and of the four beasts, and in the midst of the elders, stood a Lamb as it had been slain, having seven horns and seven eyes, which are the seven Spirits of God sent forth into all the earth. And he came and took the book out of the right hand of him that sat upon the throne.*

REVELATION 5:1-2; 6-7

And I saw when the Lamb opened ***one of the seals****, and I heard, as it were the noise of thunder, one of the four beasts saying, Come and see. And I saw, and behold a white horse: and he that sat on him had a bow, and a crown was given unto him: and he went forth conquering, and to conquer. And when he had opened the* ***second seal****, I heard the second* *beast say, Come and see. And there went out another horse that was red: and power was given to him that sat thereon to take peace from the earth, and that they should kill one another: and there was given him a great sword. And when he had opened the* ***third seal****, I heard the third beast say, Come and see. And I beheld, and lo a black horse; and he that sat on him had a pair of balances in his hand. And I heard a voice in the midst of the four beasts say, A measure of wheat for a penny, and three measures of barley for a penny; and see thou hurt not the oil and the wine. And when he had opened the* ***fourth seal****, I heard the voice of the fourth beast say, Come and see. And I looked, and behold a pale horse: and his name that sat on him was Death, and Hell followed with him. And Power was given unto them over the fourth part of the earth, to kill with sword, and with hunger, and with death, and with the beasts of the earth. And when he had opened the* ***fifth seal****, I saw under the altar the souls of them that were slain for the word of God, and for the testimony which they held: And they cried with a loud voice, saying, How long, O Lord, holy and true, dost thou not judge and avenge our blood on them that dwell on the earth? And white robes were given unto every one of them; and it was said unto them, that they should rest yet for a little season, until their fellowservants also and their brethren, that should be killed as they were, should be fulfilled. And I beheld when he had opened the* ***sixth seal****, and, lo, there was a great earthquake; and the sun became black as sackcloth of hair, and the moon became as blood; And the stars of heaven fell unto the earth, even as a fig tree casteth her untimely figs, when she is shaken of a mighty wind. And the heaven departed as a scroll when it is rolled together; and every mountain and island were moved out of their places. And the kings of the earth, and the great men, and the rich men, and the chief captains, and the mighty men, and every bondman, and every free man, hid themselves in the dens and in the rocks of the mountains; And said to the mountains and rocks, Fall on us, and hide us from the face of him that sitteth on the throne, and from the wrath of the Lamb: For the great day of his wrath is come; and who shall be able to stand?*

REVELATION 6:1-17

And when he had opened the ***seventh seal****, there was* ***silence in heaven*** *about the space of half an hour.*

REVELATION 8:1

THE SEVEN SEALS AT A GLANCE

1st Seal	White Horse: Rider has a bow and a crown and goes forth to conquer
2nd Seal	Red Horse: Rider has the power to remove peace
3rd Seal	Black Horse: Rider has a pair of balances
4th Seal	Pale Horse: Rider's name is Death, and he can kill
5th Seal	Souls of martyrs seen and heard longing to be avenged
6th Seal	Great earthquake, the sun darkens, the moon turns to blood, stars fall, men try to hide from God
7th Seal	Silence in heaven

ISRAEL REJECTS CHRIST AND PERSECUTES THE SAINTS

At the opening of the seventh seal, all heaven is silent. Except for the Jews that believed in Jesus Christ unto salvation, the nation of Israel, God's chosen people, rejected Him as their Messiah because of their unbelief, holding fast to their traditions. For years and years, the temple, Israel's pomp and glory had been overrun with all sorts of abominable practices.

And now, in addition to their rejection of Christ, these same Jews were persecuting the followers of Christ. These Christians included but were not limited to the Jewish converts found in Acts 2, the Samaritan converts of Acts 8, and the Gentile converts of Acts 10. Consequently, God unleashed His fury and curse, bringing destruction upon the nation of Israel. There was a moment of silence as the Lord of Lords turned out the light of Israel's pride and glory forever.

When the Lord sent his armies in 70 A.D., Jerusalem was overthrown, and the temple was destroyed. In this instance, the Lord used the Roman army to carry out his will. Therefore, the Roman army was "His" army as spoken of in the parable in Matthew 21:1-7 and Daniel 9:26-27. It was at that moment that:

> *There was a great earthquake; and the sun became black as sackcloth of hair, and the moon became as blood; And the stars of heaven fell unto the earth*
>
> REVELATION 6:12b-13A

ISRAEL, THE CURSE OF THE FIG TREE

Revelation 6:13 describes the stars falling as figs falling off a fig tree when blown by a mighty wind. In Mark 11:12-21, Just before he entered Jerusalem, Jesus cursed a fig tree for not having any fruit, and the very next morning, it was dried up from the roots. The parable of the cursed fig tree in Mark 11:13 was a foreshadowing of what God would soon do to Israel.

THE PARABLE OF THE VINEYARD AND THE FIG TREE

In Luke 13:6-9, Jesus tells a parable about a fig tree planted in a vineyard.

> *He spake also this parable; A certain man had a fig tree planted in his vineyard; and he came and sought fruit thereon, and found none. Then said he unto the dresser of his vineyard; Behold, these three years I come seeking fruit on this fig tree, and find none: cut it down; why cumbereth it the ground? And he answering said unto him, Lord, let it alone this year also, till I shall dig about it, and dung it: And if it bear fruit well: and if not, then after that thou shalt cut it down.*
>
> LUKE 13:6-9

> *For the vineyard of the Lord of hosts is the house of Israel, and the men of Judah his pleasant plant:*
>
> ISAIAH 5:7

The vineyard is the nation of Israel. The owner of the vineyard is The Lord. The Spirit of The Lord that indwelt Jesus Christ came seeking the fruit of the fig tree and found none. Jesus Christ is the dresser of the vineyard, as the mediator who interceded on behalf of the fig tree.

Just as the owner of the vineyard had already sought fruit for three years but requested just one more, Jesus was halfway into the fourth year of his ministry before his vineyard (the nation of Israel) produced any fruit. Jesus ministered for 3½ years on earth before going to Calvary, and it was only fifty days after his resurrection at the Feast of Pentecost (the Feast of Firstfruits) that God reaped fruit from his vineyard for the first time.

After his resurrection, Jesus appeared to his disciples, instructing them to tarry in Jerusalem for the promise of the Father. (Luke 24:49). Those Jews who were not sealed by receiving the promise of the Father were soon to fall under His chastening rod. For more study on the Lord's Vineyard, refer to Isaiah, Chapter 5.

ZECHARIAH'S VISION OF A *FLYING ROLL* [BOOK] OF CURSES

Then I turned, and lifted up mine eyes, and looked, and behold a ***flying roll****. And he said unto me, What seest thou? And I answered, I see a* ***flying roll****; Then said he unto me,* ***This is the curse that goeth forth over the face of the whole earth:***

ZECHARIAH 5:1-3A

ZECHARIAH'S VISION OF THE FOUR HORSEMEN COMING FROM GOD

I saw by night, and behold a man riding upon a red horse, and he stood among the myrtle trees that [were] in the bottom; and behind him [were there] red horses, speckled, and white. Then said I, O my lord, what [are] these? And the angel that talked with me said unto me, I will shew thee what these [be]. And the man that stood among the myrtle trees answered and said, "These [are they] whom the Lord hath sent to walk to and fro through the earth." And they answered the angel of the Lord that stood among the myrtle trees, and said, "We have walked to and fro through the earth, and, behold, all the earth sitteth still, and is at rest."

ZECHARIAH 1:8-11

And I turned, and lifted up mine eyes, and looked, and, behold, there came four chariots out from between two mountains; and the mountains were mountains of brass: In the ***first chariot were red horses****; and in the* ***second chariot black horses****; And in the* ***third chariot white horses****; and in the* ***fourth chariot grisled and bay horses****; Then I answered and said unto the angel that talked with me. What are these, my lord? And the*

angel answered and said unto me, ***these are the four spirits (winds) of the heavens****,*
which go forth from standing before the Lord of all the earth.

ZECHARIAH 6:1-5

The similarity of imagery in Zechariah 6:1, Ezekiel 1:7, and Revelation 1:15 supports the notion the Four Horsemen come from God. However, the Four Horsemen could do nothing but observe and wait until Christ died on the Cross and returned as the Comforter in the form of the Holy Ghost as recorded in the Book of Acts, and the Promise to Abraham was fulfilled in that ALL nations would be blessed. Now that the New Covenant of Grace was in full swing, the Old Covenant of the Law was ready to be abolished. I Corinthians 13:10 plainly states, "when that which is perfect is come, then that which is in part shall be done away."

SAINTS SEALED BEFORE GOD'S MIGHTY WIND BLOWS

And after these things I saw ***four angels standing on the four corners of the earth, holding the four winds of the earth****, that the wind should not blow on the earth, or on the sea, nor on any tree. And I saw another angel ascending from the east, having the seal of the living God: and he cried with a loud voice to the four angels, to whom it was given to hurt the earth and the sea, Saying,* ***Hurt not the earth, neither the sea, nor the trees, till we have sealed the servants of our God in their foreheads****.*

REVELATION 7:1-3

The Four Horsemen, the Four Spirits of the Heavens, and the Four Angels that hold the four winds are the same. These four are restrained from unleashing the mighty wind of God's fury until the servants of God are sealed in their foreheads. The sealing of God's servants takes place when they are *Born Again*.

THE CHOICE OF BLESSING OR CURSING

In Deuteronomy 28, when Moses led Israel's children out of Egypt, God promised a great blessing to Israel if they would obey His voice and a curse if they did not.

And it shall come to pass, if thou shalt hearken diligently unto the voice of the Lord thy God, to observe and to do all his commandments which I command thee this day, that the Lord thy god will set thee on high above all nations of the earth: And all these blessings shall come on thee, and overtake thee, if thou shalt hearken unto the voice of the Lord the God. But it shall come to pass, if thou wilt not hearken unto the voice of the Lord thy God, to observe to do all his commandments and his statutes which I command thee this day; that all these curses shall come upon thee, and overtake thee: Cursed shalt thou be...
The Lord shall send upon thee cursing, vexation, and rebuke, in all that thou settest thine hand unto for to do, until thou be destroyed, and until thou perish quickly; because of the wickedness of their doings, whereby thou hast forsaken me. The Lord shall make the pestilence cleave unto thee, until he has consumed thee...
And ye shall be left few in number, whereas ye were as the stars of heaven for multitude; because thou wouldest not obey the voice of the Lord thy God.

DEUTERONOMY 28:1-2; 15-16,20-21,62

God *really* meant what He said. Yet we find throughout scripture, repeatedly, Israel rebelling against God and not obeying His commandments. As a result, Israelites were continually falling into all sorts of despair because they lived under a curse. And ultimately, because of their unbelief, God cut Israel off.

The silver lining to the story is that although God cut off Israel as a nation, these *natural branches* can be grafted back into their original place of destiny but *only* by the New Birth. It is important to note that there is only one salvation for all mankind, regardless of race.

SALVATION TO JEWS VS. SALVATION TO GENTILES

Gentiles, wild olive branches, can be grafted. Howbeit, God said to Israel:

Well; because of unbelief they [Jews] were broken off, and thou [Gentiles] standest by faith, Be not highminded, but fear: For if God spared not the natural branches [Jews], take heed lest he also spare not thee [Gentiles]. And they [Jews] also, if they abide not still in unbelief, shall be graffed in: for God is able to graff them in again.

For if thou [Gentiles] wert cut out of the olive tree which is wild by nature, and graffed contrary to nature into a good olive tree: how much more shall these [Jews], which be the natural branches, be graffed into their own olive tree?

ROMANS 11:20-21; 23-24

JOEL WARNS ISRAEL TO REPENT

Blow ye the trumpet in Zion, and sound an alarm in my holy mountain: let all the inhabitants of the land tremble: ***for the day of the Lord cometh****, for it is nigh at hand; A day of darkness and of gloominess, a day of clouds and of thick darkness, as the morning spread upon the mountains:* ***a great people and a strong****: there hath not been ever the like, neither shall be any more after it, even to the years of many generations. A fire devoureth before them; and behind them a flame burneth: the land is as the garden of Eden before them, and behind them a desolate wilderness; yea, and nothing shall escape them.* ***The appearance of them is as the appearance of horses; and as horsemen, so shall they run.*** *Like the noise of chariots on the tops of mountains shall they leap, like the noise of a flame of fire that devoureth the stubble, as a strong people set in battle array.*

Neither shall one thrust another; they shall walk every one in his path: and when they fall upon the sword, they shall not be wounded.

JOEL 2:1-5; 8

Whosoever shall fall upon that stone shall be broken; but on whomsoever, it shall fall, it will grind him to powder.

LUKE 20:18

The earth shall quake before them; the heavens shall tremble: the sun and the moon shall be dark, and the stars shall withdraw their shining: And the Lord shall utter his voice before his army: for his camp is very great: for he is strong that executeth his word: ***for the day of the Lord is great and very terrible****; and who can abide it?* ***Therefore also now, saith the Lord, Turn ye even to me with all your heart****, and* *with fasting, and with weeping, and with mourning: And rend your heart, and not your garments, and turn unto the Lord your God:*

JOEL 2:10-13A

This was a call to repentance by God through the prophet Joel. We see the same images in Jeremiah 4 as God again exhorts Jerusalem to repent.

JEREMIAH WARNS ISRAEL TO REPENT

Behold, he shall come up as clouds, and his chariots shall be as a whirlwind: his horses are swifter than eagles. Woe unto us! For we are spoiled. ***O Jerusalem, wash thine heart from wickedness, that thou mayest be saved.*** *How long shall vain thoughts lodge within thee?*

JEREMIAH 4:13-14

EZEKIEL WARNS ISRAEL TO REPENT

Therefore thus saith the Lord God; Because ye multiplied more than the nations that are round about you, and have not walked in my statutes, neither have kept my judgments, neither have done according to the judgments of the nations that are round about you; Therefore ***thus saith the Lord God; Behold, I, even I, am against thee, and will execute judgments in the midst of thee in the sight of the nations.*** *And I will do in thee that which I have not done, and whereunto I will not do any more the like, because of all thine abominations. Therefore the fathers shall eat the sons in the midst of thee, and the sons shall eat their fathers; and I will execute judgments in thee, and the whole remnant of thee will I scatter into all the winds. Wherefore, as I live, saith the Lord God; surely, because thou hast defiled my sanctuary with all thy detestable things, and with all thine abominations, therefore will I also diminish thee; neither shall mine eye spare, neither will I have any pity.* ***A third part of thee shall die with pestilence, and with famine*** *shall they be consumed in the midst of thee:* ***and a third part shall fall by the sword*** *round about thee; and* ***I will scatter a third part into all the winds, and I will draw out a sword after them.*** *Thus shall mine anger be accomplished, and I will cause my fury to rest upon them, and I will be comforted: and they shall know that I the Lord have* *spoken it in my zeal, when I have accomplished my fury in them. Moreover I will make thee waste, and a reproach among the nations that are round about thee, in the sight of all that pass by. So it shall be a reproach and a taunt, an instruction and an astonishment unto the nations that are round about thee, when I shall execute judgments in thee in anger and in fury and in furious rebukes, I the Lord have spoken it. When I shall send upon them the evil arrows of famine, which shall be for their destruction, and which I will send to destroy you: and I will increase the famine upon you, and will break your staff of bread:* ***So will I send upon you famine and evil beasts, and they shall bereave thee; and pestilence and blood shall pass through thee; and I will bring the sword upon thee. I the Lord have spoken it.***

EZEKIEL 5:7-17

Therefore say unto the house of Israel, ***Thus saith the Lord God; Repent****, and turn yourselves from your idols; and turn away your faces from all your abominations. For every one of the house of Israel, or of the stranger that sojourneth in Israel, which separateth himself from me, and setteth up his idols in his heart, and putteth the stumbling block of his iniquity before his face, and cometh to a prophet to enquire of him concerning me; I the Lord will answer him by myself. And I will set my face against that man, and will make him a sign and a proverb, and I will cut him off from the midst of my people; and ye shall know that I am the Lord. Son of man, when the land sinneth against me by trespassing grievously, then will I stretch out mine hand upon it, and will break the staff of the bread thereof, and will send famine upon it, and will cut off man and beast from it: If I cause noisome beasts to pass through the land, and they spoil it, so that it be desolate, that no man may pass through because of the beasts. Or if I bring a sword upon that land, and say, Sword, go through the land; so that I cut off man and beast from it: Or if I send a pestilence into that land, and pour out my fury upon it in blood, to cut off from it man and beast: For thus saith the Lord God;* ***How much more when I send my four sore judgments upon Jerusalem, the sword, and the famine, and the noisome beast, and the pestilence,*** *to cut off from it man and beast? Yet, behold, therein shall be left a remnant that shall be brought forth, both sons and daughters:*

EZEKIEL 14:6-8; 13; 15; 17; 19; 21-22A

The house of Israel had set up idols in their hearts, bringing about God's punishment. Furthermore, as Jesus said in Luke 11:51, from the murder of Abel to the murder of Zacharias, who was killed between the temple and the altar, blood would be required *of this generation*. The overspreading of such abominations caused the ultimate desolation and destruction of Jerusalem by the hand of God.

GOD IS JUST, AND GOD IS FAITHFUL

God is no respecter of persons. He did not tolerate Israel's disobedience, and we can be sure He will not tolerate our disobedience. But if we do fall, the Bible says:

> *If we confess our sins, He is faithful and just to forgive us our sins, and to cleanse us from all unrighteousness.*
>
> I JOHN 1:9

THE FALL OF JERUSALEM

> *Say thou thus unto them, Thus saith the Lord God: As I live, surely they that are in the wastes* ***shall fall by the sword****, and him that is in the open field will* ***I give to the beasts to be devoured****, and they that be in the forts and in the caves* ***shall die of the pestilence****. For* ***I will lay the land most desolate****, and the* ***pomp of her strength*** *shall cease; and the mountains of Israel shall be desolate, that none shall pass through.* ***Then shall they know that I am the Lord when I have laid the land most desolate because of all their abominations which they have committed.***
>
> EZEKIEL 33:27-29

The pomp of Jerusalem's strength was the temple. Jerusalem was to fall in three parts, as prophesied in Ezekiel.

A third part of thee shall die with pestilence, and with famine shall they be consumed in the midst of thee: and a third part shall fall by the sword round about thee; and I will scatter a third part into all the winds, and I will draw out a sword after them.

EZEKIEL 5:12

Then the Lord said unto me, Out of the north an evil shall break forth upon all the inhabitants of the land.

JEREMIAH 1:14

The Roman Empire came and destroyed Jerusalem and her temple in 70 AD. Jerusalem fell under the 7 Seals, the sun and moon ceased to give light, and the stars fell. The light of Jerusalem was forever put out. Jerusalem, the natural physical city, is referred to in Revelation 11:8 not as the Lamb's wife but as Sodom and Egypt.

Later the Roman Empire would fall in three parts, and then Mystery Babylon would likewise fall in three parts.

THE ABOMINATION OF DESOLATION

When ye therefore shall see the abomination of desolation, spoken of by Daniel the prophet, stand in the holy place, (whoso readeth, let him understand:) Then let them which be in Judaea flee into the mountains:

MATTHEW 24:15-16

When ye shall see the abomination of desolation, spoken of by Daniel the prophet, standing where it ought not, (let him that readeth understand,) then let them that be in Judaea flee to the mountains.

MARK 13:14

And when ye shall see Jerusalem compassed with armies, then know that the desolation thereof is nigh. Then let them which are in Judaea flee to the mountains……and Jerusalem shall be trodden down of the Gentiles…

LUKE 21:20-21,24

The events surrounding the destruction of Jerusalem are pretty amazing. History confirms that Jerusalem was destroyed in 70 AD. But, before this event, EVERY Christian took the opportunity to flee, thereby escaping God's wrath upon that city and country.

In 65 A.D., Judea fell to the control of Florus, one of Nero Caesar's most notorious officers. Florus provoked the Jews into a violent rebellion that was too strong for him to handle. Cestius Gallus then took over; with his army, he subdued Palestine and other towns as he advanced toward Jerusalem. After three days of camping outside the city, his assault began.

The disciples were warned that when they saw Jerusalem compassed with Gentile armies, Jerusalem's desolation was imminent. They were instructed to flee to the mountains. There was a serious problem, though. With this massive army outside the walls of Jerusalem, there was no apparent way of escape. Moreover, Gallus was becoming increasingly successful, and the Jews were just about to open the gate and surrender, which would have saved the city and the temple.

As fate would have it, and as Josephus says, "Without any reason in the world," Gallus withdrew his armies and departed! The Jews, now filled with courage, pursued Gallus and his armies, thus resulting in horrible defeat and the destruction of Jerusalem and the temple, the pomp of Israel's pride. During the brief interval of the retreat of Gallus, the Christians seized their opportunity to flee.

Thomas Newton stated: "We learn from ecclesiastical histories that at this juncture all who believed in Christ departed Jerusalem and removed to Pella and other places beyond the Jordan; so that they all marvelously escaped the general shipwreck of their countrymen; and we do not read anywhere that so much as one of them perished in the destruction of Jerusalem."

British Methodist Theologian Adam Clarke wrote: "It is very remarkable that not a single Christian perished in the destruction of Jerusalem though there were many there when Cestius Gallus invested the city."

With the Christians having fled Jerusalem, the desolation was nigh. Because Cestius Gallus and his armies had retreated, Nero Caesar then ordered Vespasian to take charge, who in turn ordered his son Titus to go to Alexandria and bring more troops from Egypt to subdue Judea. Vespasian, however, had to return to Rome to handle a crisis leaving the capture of Jerusalem totally in the hands of Titus and his armies.

Although Matthew and Mark use somewhat veiled language about the *abomination of desolation*, Luke clearly states it was to be the Gentile armies surrounding the holy place that would bring about the desolation of Jerusalem. This explains why the words, *let him that readeth understand*, are included in Matthew and Mark but not in Luke. This interpretation is complimentary, not contradictory to scripture and history. Furthermore, it glorifies God for making a way of escape for His children in such perilous times.

Oh, what a mighty God we serve!

SUMMARY:

The 1st Seal: A Conquering King

The first Horse, the White Horse, seems to represent Christ setting out to conquer and avenge His bride, the Church. If so, then it is this same White Horse in Revelation 19:11 that finishes what the Rider had set out to accomplish.

The 2nd Seal – 5th Seal: War, Famine, Pestilence, Death

These Four Horsemen were the Four Sore Judgments (Ezekiel 14:21) sent by God upon Jerusalem for their continuous abominations, persecution of the righteous, and for ultimately rejecting Jesus Christ.

The 6th Seal: A Great Earthquake

The Sun darkened, the Moon turned to blood, and the Stars of heaven fell (Joel 2:10). If the Four Horsemen were God's judgments upon Jerusalem, then this would represent the Fall of Jerusalem and the end of its era with her light being forever put out.

The 7th Seal: Silence in heaven

In awe, perhaps, of what God had just executed, as the Old Covenant "vanishes away." (Hebrews 8:13)

CONCLUSION:

The Seven Seals are God's curse upon the nation of Israel for failing to turn from idolatry and sin, resulting in the casting down of the light of Israel, its pomp, pride, and power.

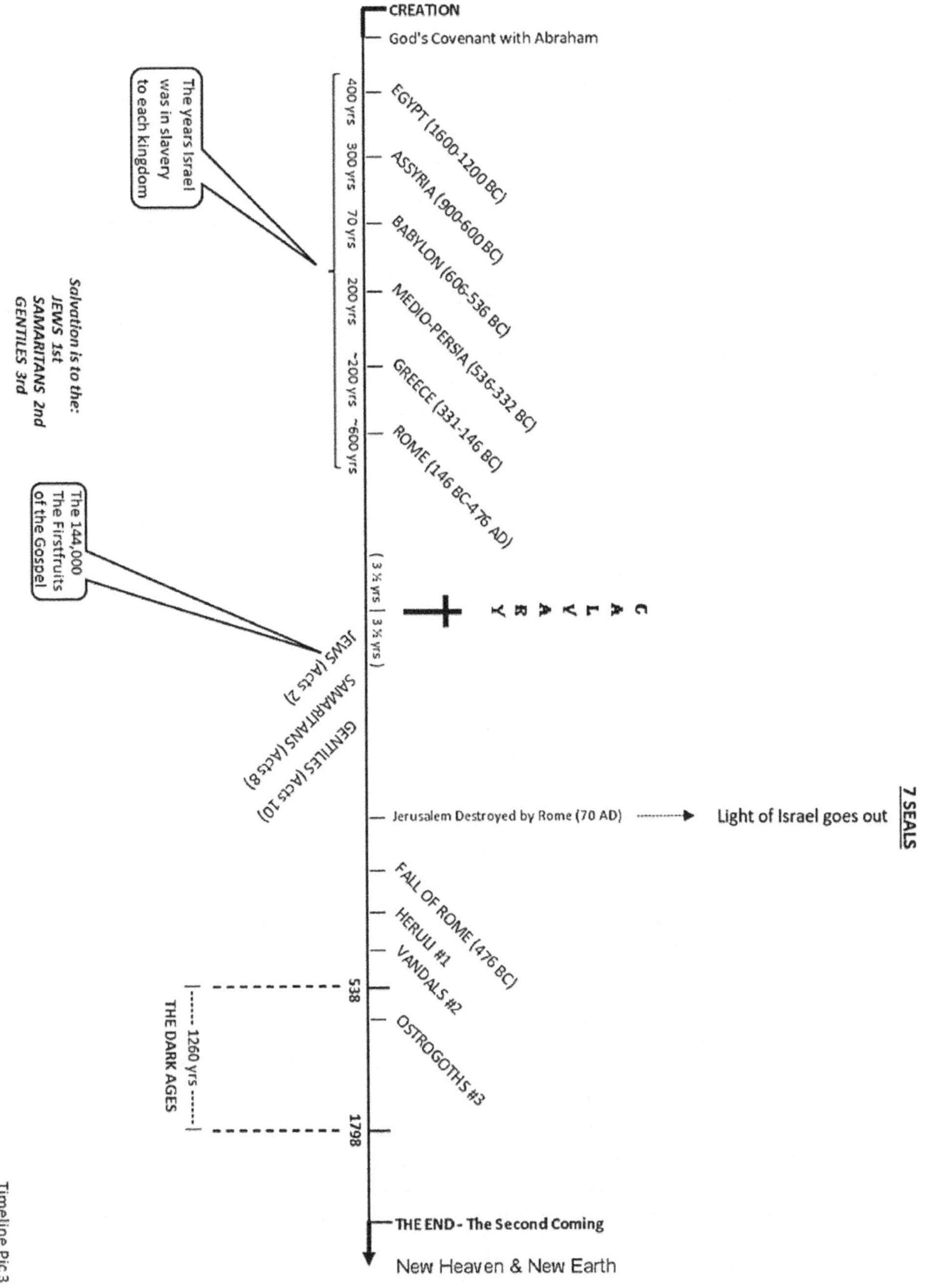
CREATION
God's Covenant with Abraham
EGYPT (1600-1200 BC)
ASSYRIA (900-600 BC)
BABYLON (606-536 BC)
MEDIO-PERSIA (536-332 BC)
GREECE (331-146 BC)
ROME (146 BC-476 AD)
400 yrs
300 yrs
70 yrs
200 yrs
~200 yrs
~600 yrs
The years Israel was in slavery to each kingdom
Salvation is to the:
JEWS 1st
SAMARITANS 2nd
GENTILES 3rd
The 144,000 The Firstfruits of the Gospel
3 ½ yrs | 3 ½ yrs
CALVARY
JEWS (Acts 2)
SAMARITANS (Acts 8)
GENTILES (Acts 10)
Jerusalem Destroyed by Rome (70 AD)
Light of Israel goes out
7 SEALS
FALL OF ROME (476 BC)
HERULI #1
VANDALS #2
OSTROGOTHS #3
538
1798
1260 yrs
THE DARK AGES
THE END - The Second Coming
New Heaven & New Earth
Timeline Pic 3

CHAPTER 9

THE SEVEN TRUMPETS

Revelation 8-11

THE PREMISE:

The Seven Trumpets are God's judgment upon Rome for persecuting "The Church," resulting in the casting down of the light of the Roman Empire as a dominant world power. The rise of Arabian and Turkish Mohammedanism was twofold. It came about primarily as a judgment upon a religious world professing Christianity but steeped in idolatry. It was also used in the overthrow of Rome.

NOTE: "The Church" shall refer to the body of believers that have been *Born Again* according to Acts 2, 8, 10, and 19 through repentance, water baptism in the name of Jesus Christ, and Spirit baptism in the Holy Ghost.

SCRIPTURE TEXT:

Revelation 8:2-13 *And I saw the **seven angels** which stood before God; and to them were given **seven trumpets**. And another angel came and stood at the altar, having a golden censer; and there was given unto him much incense, that he should offer with the prayers of all saints upon the golden altar which was before the throne. And the smoke of the incense, which came with the prayers of the saints, ascended up before God out of the angel's hand. And the angel took the censer, and filled it with fire of the altar, and cast it* *into the earth: and there were voices, and thunderings, and lightnings, and an earthquake. And the seven angels which had the seven trumpets prepared themselves to sound. The* ***first angel sounded****, and there followed hail and fire mingled with blood, and they were cast upon the earth: and the third part of trees was burnt up, and all green grass was burnt up. And the* ***second angel sounded****, and as it were a great mountain burning with fire was cast into the sea: and the third part of the sea became as blood; And the third part of the creatures which were in the sea and had life, died; and the third part of the ships were destroyed. And the* ***third angel sounded****, and there fell a great star from heaven, burning as it were a lamp, and it fell upon the third part of the rivers, and upon the fountains of waters; And the name of the star is called Wormwood: and the third part of the waters became wormwood; and many men died of the waters, because they were made bitter. And the* ***fourth angel sounded****, and the third part of the sun was smitten, and the third part of the moon, and the third part of the stars; so as the third part of them was darkened, and the day shone not for a third part of it, and the night likewise. And I beheld, and heard an angel flying through the midst of heaven, saying with a loud voice, Woe, woe, woe, to the inhabiters of the earth by reason of the other voices of the trumpet of the three angels, which are yet to sound.*

Revelation 9:1-21 *And the* ***fifth angel sounded****, and I saw a star fall from heaven unto the earth: and to him was given the key of the bottomless pit. And he opened the bottomless pit; and there arose a smoke out of the pit, as the smoke of a great furnace; and the sun and the air were darkened by reason of the smoke of the pit. And there came out of the smoke locusts upon the earth: and unto them was given power, as the scorpions of the earth have power. And it was commanded them that they should not hurt the grass of the earth, neither any green thing, neither any tree; but only those men which have not the seal of God in their foreheads. [men and women who do not have the seal of the New Birth] And to them it was given that they should not kill them, but that they should be tormented five months: and their torment was as the torment of a scorpion, when he striketh a man. And in those days shall men seek death, and shall not find it; and shall desire to die, and death shall flee from them. And the shapes of the locusts were like unto horses prepared unto battle; and on their heads were as it were crowns like gold, and their faces were as the faces of men. And they had hair as the hair of women, and their teeth* *were as the teeth of lions. And they had breastplates, as it were breastplates of iron; and the sound of their wings was as the sound of chariots of many horses running to battle. And they had tails like unto scorpions, and there were stings in their tails: and their power was to hurt men five months. And they had a king over them, which is the angel of the bottomless pit, whose name in the Hebrew tongue is Abaddon, but in the Greek hath his name Apollyon. One woe is past; and, behold, there come two woes more hereafter. And the* ***sixth angel sounded****, and I heard a voice from the four horns of the altar which is before God, Saying to the sixth angel which had the trumpet, Loose the four angels which are bound in the great river Euphrates. And the four angels were loosed, which were prepared for an hour, and a day, and a month, and a year, for to slay the third part of men. And the number of the army of the horsemen were two hundred thousand thousand: and I heard the number of them. And thus I saw the horses in the vision, and them that sat on them, having breastplates of fire, and of jacinth, and brimstone: and the heads of the horses were as the heads of lions; and out of their mouths issued fire and smoke and brimstone. By these three was the third part of men killed, by the fire, and by the smoke, and by the brimstone, which issued out of their mouths. For their power is in their mouth, and in their tails: for their tails were like unto serpents, and had heads, and with them they do hurt. And the rest of the men which were not killed by these plagues yet repented not of the works of their hands, that they should not worship devils, and idols of gold, and silver, and brass, and stone, and of wood: which neither can see, nor hear, nor walk: Neither repented they of their murders, nor of their sorceries, nor of their fornication, nor of their thefts.*

But in the days of the voice of the ***seventh angel****, when he shall begin to sound, the mystery of God should be finished, as he hath declared to his servants the prophets.*

REVELATION 10:7

The second woe is past; and, behold, the third woe cometh quickly. And the ***seventh angel sounded****; and there were great voices in heaven, saying, the kingdoms of this world are become the kingdoms of our Lord, and of his Christ; and he shall reign for ever and ever.*

REVELATION 11:14-15

THE SEVEN TRUMPETS AT GLANCE

1st Trumpet	Hail, fire, and blood cast into the earth; a third of trees and grass burnt up
2nd Trumpet	Great burning mountain cast into the sea; the third part of the sea becomes blood
3rd Trumpet	Great burning star falls upon the third part of the rivers and fountains, making them bitter; the star's name is Wormwood
4th Trumpet	Third part of the sun, moon, and stars smitten
5th Trumpet	Star falls from heaven to earth with the key to open the bottomless pit releasing smoke that darkens the sun and air; locusts come out of the smoke with the power to hurt those that do not have the seal of God
6th Trumpet	Army of 200,000,000 horsemen loosed; a third of the men were killed by the fire, smoke, and brimstone that came out of the mouth of the horsemen
7th Trumpet	Mystery of God accomplished

THE SETTING, ROME IN HISTORY

World history can be divided into three periods:

Ancient History:	Egypt, Assyria, Babylon, Persia, Greece, Rome
Medieval History:	Fall of Rome to the discovery of America
Modern History:	15th century to present

Rome was founded in 753 B.C. and grew in strength, reaching its zenith of power from 46 B.C.–A.D. 180. The decline and fall of the Roman Empire lasted from A.D. 180–476.

EMPERORS AND EVENTS DURING THE ZENITH OF ROMAN POWER:

- Julius Caesar	46–44 B.C.	Lord of the Roman World
- Augustus	31 B.C.–A.D. 14	In his reign, Christ was born
- Tiberius	A.D 12–37	In his reign, Christ was crucified; Stephen stoned to death
- Caligula	A.D. 37–41	
- Claudius	A.D. 41–54	
- Nero	A.D. 54–68	Persecuted Christians, Paul executed, Peter crucified, James (brother of Jesus) stoned
- Galba	A.D. 68–69	
- Otho	A.D 69	
- Vitellius	A.D. 69	
- Vespasian	A.D. 69–79	Destruction of Jerusalem
- Titus	A.D. 79–81	
- Domitian	A.D. 81–96	Persecuted Christians, banished John
- Nerva	A.D 96–98	
- Trajan	A.D. 98–117	
- Hadrian	A.D. 117–138	Persecuted Christians
- Antoninus Pius	A.D. 138–161	Persecuted Christians, Polycarp martyred
- Marcus Aurelius	A.D. 161–180	Persecuted Christians

THE FALL OF THE ROMAN EMPIRE

The **Third Part** of the earth, sea, rivers, heavenly bodies, and men were smitten as if destruction were only partial. These events appear to represent God's judgments upon the Roman Empire for its persecution of "The Church." Halley's Bible Handbook quotes the following historical events paralleling the scripture in amazing detail.

1ST TRUMPET (REVELATION 8:7): HAIL, FIRE & BLOOD CAST UPON THE EARTH.

The **Goths** (**AD 409**) descended upon Italy in savage fury and left behind burning cities and scorched, bloody, and desolate lands.

2ND TRUMPET (REVELATION 8:8-9): GREAT BURNING MOUNTAIN CAST IN THE SEA.

The **Vandals** (**AD 422–AD 452**) swept across Gaul and Spain into Africa, built a Navy, and fought against the Roman Navy, who for 600 years controlled the Mediterranean and drove it from the Sea.

3RD TRUMPET (REVELATION 8:10-11): GREAT BURNING STAR FELL UPON THE RIVERS.

Atilla the Hun (**AD 440**), from the depth of Central Asia, appeared on the banks of the Danube at the head of 800,000 fighting men. Pushing westward, they met the Roman armies. They successfully defeated them with awful slaughter on the River Marne, the River Rhone, and the River Po so that the rivers ran with **blood.** When Atilla the Hun died, the river Tisza was turned aside, and his body was buried beneath its bed. The waters still flow over his grave. He was indeed a scourge of the rivers.

4TH TRUMPET (REVELATION 8:12-13): THIRD PART OF THE SUN, MOON, AND STARS DARKENED.

Odoacer (**AD 476**), at the head of another horde of Barbarians, besieged and took the city of Rome, and the light of the Roman Civilization went out. Nevertheless, **the Third Part** of the Earth, Sea, Rivers, and Heavenly Bodies were smitten, indicating that the destruction was only partial.

FOUR SUCCESSIVE BLOWS

1. The Gothic invasion of Italy (AD 409) - **Earth**
2. The Vandal's destruction of the Roman Navy (AD 422) - **Sea**
3. Atilla the Hun's slaughter on the rivers of Central Europe (AD 440) - **Rivers**
4. Odoacer's seizure of Rome, headquarters of power – **Heavenly Bodies**

Under these disasters, the mighty Roman Empire, which had ruled the world for over 500 years, was cast down. The light of the Roman Civilization went out, making way for the **Dark Ages**. Physical Rome was being stamped out but would soon come back to life in more of a spiritual sense.

5TH TRUMPET (REVELATION 9:1-3): ARMY OF DEMON LOCUST – ARABIAN MOHAMMEDANISM

"Locust" - Arabia, pre-eminently, was a land of locusts. It was in Arabia that Mohammedanism originated.

The shapes of locusts were like war horses, with scorpion-like tails, crowns of gold, faces like men's faces, hair like women's hair, teeth like lion's teeth, breastplates as of iron, and wings that sounded like chariots and horses rushing to war, as described in Revelation 9:7-10. This is an excellent description of the Mohammedan Armies, composed of fierce, relentless horsemen famous for their beards with long hair, like women. In addition, the Mohammedan warriors wore iron coats of armor, along with yellow turbans on their heads that looked like golden crowns.

Smoke from the Abyss (Revelation 9:2-3): It was out of this smoke that the locust came. The smoke that had darkened the sun and the air refers to the idolatry and false teachings which had clouded and corrupted the church of Mohammed's day in its worship of images, relics, and saints. The IDOLATRY of a degenerate and apostate church gave Mohammed his chance. "Destruction of Idols" was his slogan.

Hurt not the grass, nor any green thing (Revelation 9:4): Mohammedans spared trees, grass, and all vegetation because Mohammed had so commanded. Trees and vegetation were a blessing for those living in the wastelands of the Arabian desert.

Torment men five months (Revelation 9:5): Five months, the typical stay of locusts (May-September) is approximately **150 days.** Using the year-for-a-day interpretation method of Ezekiel 4:6, this would be **150 years.** That was roughly the period (AD 630–AD 780) when the Mohammedans continued their effort for world conquest.

And they had a king over them, which is the angel of the bottomless pit, whose name in the Hebrew tongue is Abaddon, but in the Greek tongue hath his name Apollyon.
REVELATION 9:11

Now notice the two scriptural names given to the leader of the Mohammedan movement. The first is **Abaddon, Hebrew** for **"a destroying angel or messenger."** The second is **Apollyon,** which is **Greek** for **"a destroyer."** This aptly fits because Mohammed went forth with a sword to kill, destroy, and force all to be Muslim.

6TH TRUMPET (REVELATION 9:13: ARMY OF TWO HUNDRED THOUSAND THOUSAND

Euphratean Horsemen – Turkish Mohammedanism

This army was comprised of horrible-looking monsters, with a complex appearance of men, horses, lions, serpents, belching fire, smoke, and brimstone. This is also a predictive picture of Mohammedanism but in a different setting. The **Arabians** ruled the Mohammedan World for 400 years (AD 630–AD 1058). The **Turks** then took over and have been in control almost until now. A vast horde of Turks from Central Asia appeared on the banks of the Euphrates, and, in their westward march, they replaced the Arabians as rulers of Mohammedan lands.

Out of the horses' mouths proceeded fire, smoke, and brimstone (Revelation 9:17). The Eastern Roman Empire, with Constantinople as its capital, had been a bulwark of Europe against Mohammedanism for centuries. But, in AD 1453, it fell to the Turks. At the Battle of Constantinople, **artillery** with **gunpowder** was first used, which gave victory to the Turks.

This lasted for **an hour, a day, a month, and a year.** This totals 396 days; therefore, for 396 years (AD 1057–AD 1453), the Turks slaughtered and butchered millions, even more brutal than the Arabians. (Revelation 9:15).

7TH TRUMPET (REVELATION 11:15): VOICES IN HEAVEN DECLARING THE LORD'S VICTORY OVER THE KINGDOMS OF THIS WORLD AND THE ETERNAL REIGN OF JESUS CHRIST

*And the **seventh angel sounded;** and there were great voices in heaven, saying, the **kingdoms of this world are become the kingdoms of our Lord, and of his Christ;** and he shall reign for ever and ever.*

REVELATION 11:15

TWO VIEWS ON THE 7TH TRUMPET, THE 7TH VIAL, AND THE 7TH THUNDER

One view is that between the 6th and 7th Trumpet, the 7 Vials are poured out. Then, between the 6th and 7th Vial, the 7 Thunders utter their voices. Therefore, the 7th Trumpet, the 7th Vial, and the 7th Thunder sound simultaneously in one accord declaring the ultimate victory and the eternal reign of the Lord and the words "It is Done!"

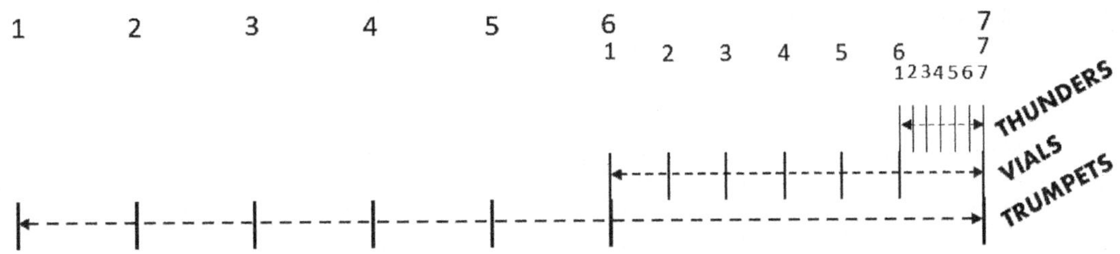

The Second view is that the 7th Trumpet, the 7th Vial, and the 7th Thunder are endings of God's vengeance upon whatever current system was persecuting the church. And, by and by, the Lord declares that He is sovereign, and the kingdoms of the world are under His authority until the end of the world, where God heralds, "It is Done!"

I tend to favor the Second view as the most likely of the two. However, both have possibilities worthy of thought.

THE ROMAN EMPIRE FELL INTO THREE SECTIONS

The Western Part (AD 476) – By the Goths, Vandals, and the Huns
The Asiatic & African Parts (7th Century) – Overrun by Arabian Mohammedans
The Eastern European Part (AD 1453) – Overrun by Turkish Mohammedans

CONCLUSION:

The Seven Trumpets are primarily God's judgment upon Rome for persecuting The Church resulting in the casting down of the light of the Roman Empire as a dominant world power. However, it also appears that God allowed the spread of Arabian and Turkish Mohammedanism as a judgment upon a religious world professing Christianity but steeped in idolatry, as well as Rome.

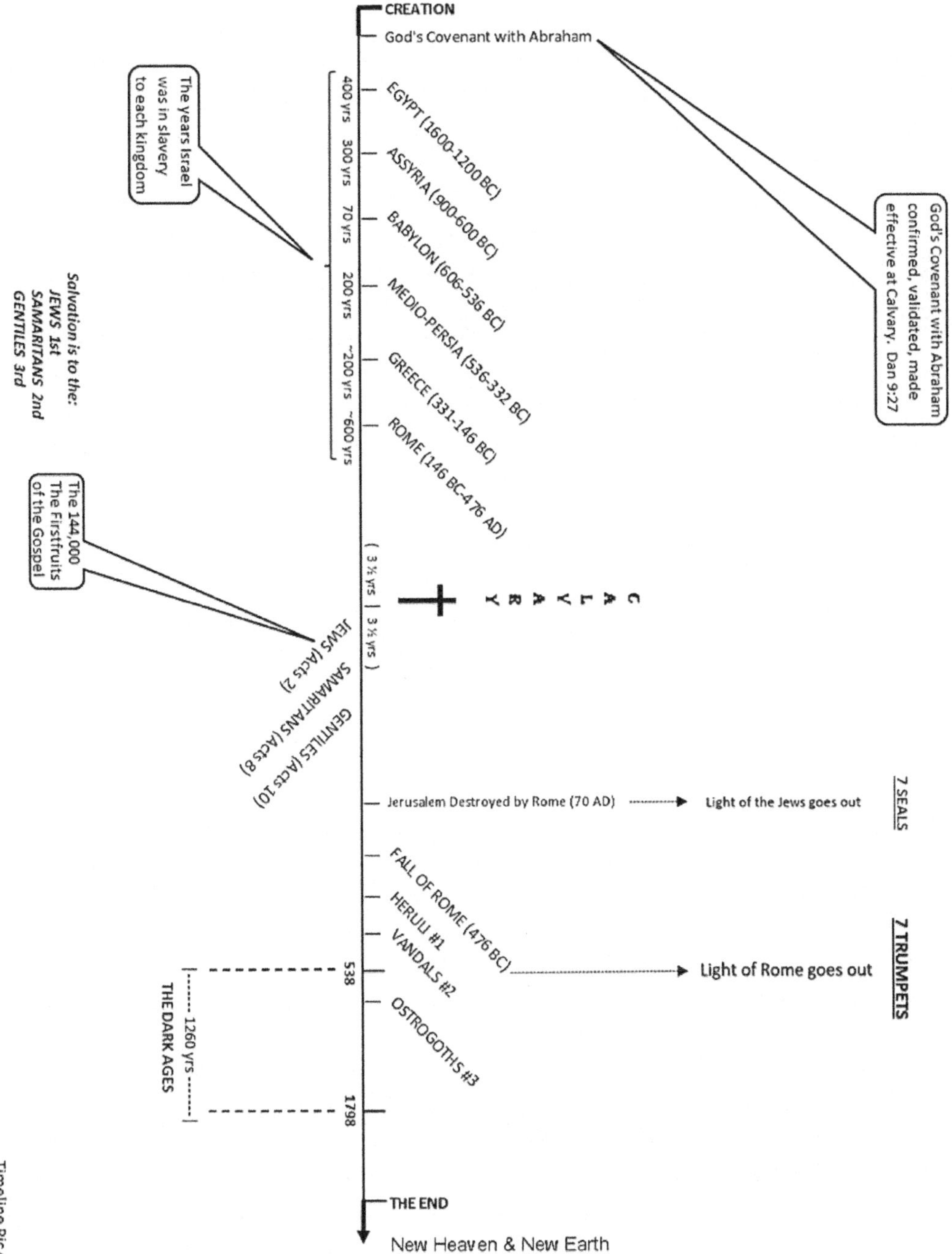
CREATION
God's Covenant with Abraham
God's Covenant with Abraham confirmed, validated, made effective at Calvary. Dan 9:27
EGYPT (1600-1200 BC)
ASSYRIA (900-600 BC)
BABYLON (606-536 BC)
MEDIO-PERSIA (536-332 BC)
GREECE (331-146 BC)
ROME (146 BC-476 AD)
400 yrs 300 yrs 70 yrs 200 yrs ~200 yrs ~600 yrs
The years Israel was in slavery to each kingdom
Salvation is to the:
JEWS 1st
SAMARITANS 2nd
GENTILES 3rd
(3 ½ yrs | 3 ½ yrs)
CALVARY
The 144,000 The Firstfruits of the Gospel
JEWS (Acts 2)
SAMARITANS (Acts 8)
GENTILES (Acts 10)
Jerusalem Destroyed by Rome (70 AD)
Light of the Jews goes out
7 SEALS
FALL OF ROME (476 BC)
HERULI #1
VANDALS #2
OSTROGOTHS #3
Light of Rome goes out
7 TRUMPETS
538
1798
1260 yrs
THE DARK AGES
THE END
New Heaven & New Earth
Timeline Pic 4

CHAPTER 10

THE SEVEN VIALS

Revelation 15-16

THE PREMISE:

The Seven Vials are God's wrath and judgment upon the Roman Papacy for persecuting The Church. The Seven Vials, also called the Seven Last Plagues, were poured out upon the Roman Papacy, forcing her into ruin and decay. However, three unclean spirits emerge from the dragon, the beast, and the false prophet to surround The Church, warring against the souls of the redeemed. Vengeance belongs to God, and He will fight for us and win!

NOTE: The Church shall refer to the body of believers that have been Born Again according to Acts 2, 8, 10, and 19 through repentance, water baptism in the name of Jesus Christ, and Spirit baptism in the Holy Ghost.

SCRIPTURE TEXT:

Revelation 15:1; 7-8 *And I saw another sign in heaven, great and marvelous,* ***seven angels having the seven last plagues****; for in them is filled up the wrath of God. And one of the four beasts gave unto the seven angels seven golden vials full of the wrath of God, who liveth for ever and ever. And the temple was filled with smoke from the glory of God, and from his power, and no man was able to enter into the temple, till the seven plagues of the seven angels were fulfilled.*

Revelation 16:1-21 *And I heard a great voice out of the temple saying to the seven angels. Go your ways, and pour out the vials of the wrath of God upon the earth. And the* ***first*** *went, and poured out his* ***vial*** *upon the earth; and there fell a noisome and grievous sore upon the men which had the mark of the beast, and upon them which worshipped his image. And the* **second** *angel poured out his* ***vial*** *upon the sea; and it became as the blood of a dead man: and every living soul died in the sea. And the* **third** *angel poured out his* ***vial*** *upon the rivers and fountains of waters; and they became blood. And I heard the angel of the waters say, Thou art righteous, O Lord, which art, and wast, and shalt be, because thou hast judged thus. For they have shed the blood of the saints and prophets, and thou hast given them blood to drink; for they are worthy. And I heard another out of the altar say, Even so, Lord God Almighty, true and righteous are thy judgments. And the* **fourth** *angel poured out his* **vial** *upon the sun; and power was given unto him to scorch men with fire. And men were scorched with great heat, and blasphemed the name of God, which hath power over these plagues: and they repented not to give him glory. And the* ***fifth*** *angel poured out his* ***vial*** *upon the seat of the beast; and his kingdom was full of darkness; and they gnawed their tongues for pain. And blasphemed the God of heaven because of their pains and their sores, and repented not of their deeds. And the* **sixth** *angel poured out his* ***vial*** *upon the great river Euphrates; and the water thereof was dried up, that the kings of the east might be prepared. And I saw three unclean spirits like frogs come out of the mouth of the dragon, and out of the mouth of the beast, and out of the mouth of the false prophet. For they are the spirits of devils, working miracles, which go forth unto the kings of the earth and of the whole world, to gather them to the battle of that great day of God Almighty. Behold, I come as a thief. Blessed is he that watcheth, and keepeth his garments, lest he walk naked, and they see his shame. And he gathered them together into a place called in the Hebrew tongue Armageddon. And the* **seventh** *angel poured out his* ***vial*** *into the air; and there came a great voice out of the temple of heaven, from the throne, saying, It is done. And there were voices, and thunders, and lightnings; and there was a great earthquake, such as was not since men were upon the earth, so mighty an earthquake, and so great. And the great city was divided into three parts, and the cities of the nations fell: and great Babylon came in remembrance before God, to give unto her the cup of the wine of the fierceness of his wrath. And* *every island fled away, and the mountains were not found. And there fell upon men a great hail out of heaven, every stone about the weight of a talent: and men blasphemed God because of the plague of the hail; for the plague thereof was exceeding great.*

The **Seven Vials of Wrath** are poured out upon the **Empire of the Beast**. The following is a brief outline of the subsequent chain of events. Although the book is written in a cyclical style, a pattern is evident. The various kingdoms that persecute The Church fall with astounding predictive accuracy concluding with the light of each kingdom going out, never to shine again as it once did.

THE SEVEN VIALS AT A GLANCE

1st Vial	Noisome and grievous sore fell on those with the mark of the beast
2nd Vial	Sea became blood, and every soul in the sea died
3rd Vial	Rivers and fountains of water became blood
4th Vial	Sun was given the power to scorch with fire
5th Vial	Kingdom of the Beast is darkened
6th Vial	Euphrates dried up that the way the kings of the east might be prepared; three unclean spirits come out of the mouth of the dragon, the mouth of the beast, and the mouth of the false prophet and go forth to deceive.
7th Vial	God says, "It is done!"

DOMINATE KINGDOMS THROUGHOUT HISTORY

Before the modern era in which we live, eight world powers towered above and largely dominated the course of history. These powers seem to represent the spirit of one evil power manifesting itself in various forms and to various degrees in various ages. Each of these afflicted and persecuted God's people.

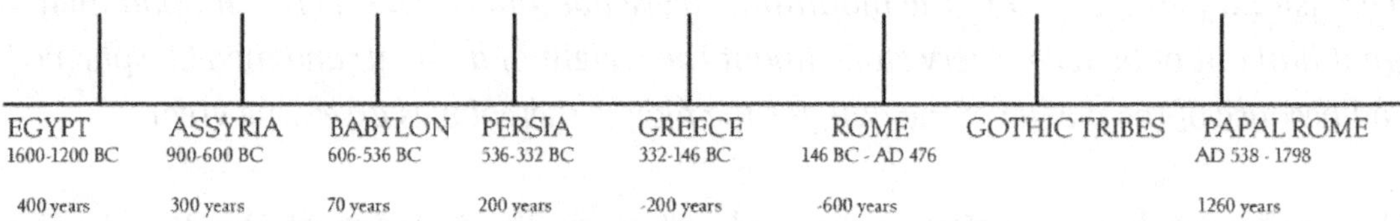

FROM ROME TO PAPAL ROME

And there are seven kings: five are fallen, and one is, and the other is not yet come; and when he cometh, he must continue a short space. And the beast that was, and is not, even he is the eighth, and is of the seven, and goeth into perdition.

REVELATION 17:10-11

The angel tells John that there are **seven kings**, ***five are fallen*** (Egypt, Assyria, Babylon, Persia, Greece), ***one is*** (Rome), and ***the other is not yet come*** (The Gothic Tribes). And the *beast that was*, and *is not*, and yet is, *he is the eighth*. **Rome** "was" and then it "was not" because it fell to the Gothic Tribes, but "yet it was" because it returned as **Papal Rome**. Papal Rome is another name for the **Papacy**. The Papacy is the office and the jurisdiction of the Pope, the presiding bishop of Rome, operating from Vatican City. The office of the Pope is also called the **Holy See** and serves as the governing body of the Roman Catholic Church.

THE EIGHTH KINGDOM

In a vision, Daniel saw that, from Babylon forward, there would be four world powers in the natural. It would be five world powers if the Ten Gothic Tribes or the ten toes of Daniel's vision are taken into consideration. Several hundred years later, the apostle John saw a composite sea beast of these four (Babylon, Persia, Greece, and Rome). Again it would be five if the Ten Gothic Tribes or the ten horns of John's vision are considered.

John's vision of this embodiment into one conglomerate testifies to the severity of this empire. The empire of this beast was the Roman Papacy. It is also referred to as

The Little Horn in Daniel, Chapter 7. The Roman Papacy dominated the world for some 1260 years. This era is also known as The Dark Ages.

After the resurrection of Jesus Christ, early Christians were persecuted first by the Jews for a few years and then by the Roman Empire for a few hundred years. But the Papacy tortured Christians in the most horrible and gruesome ways imaginable for centuries. It is estimated that some 50,000,000 or more died at the hands of the Roman Catholic Church's directive. No wonder this period which covers over twelve and a half centuries, is called The Dark Ages!

THE OBJECTIVE OF THE SEVEN VIALS OF WRATH

The Seven Vials of The Lord's wrath were poured out upon the Empire of the Beast for its persecution of Christians. How ironic that the most horrible, severe, and lengthy persecution of true Christians was carried out at the hands of an institution under the label of "Christian."

Like the plagues of the first Four Trumpets (Revelation 8:7-12), the first Four Vials fell successively on the Earth, Sea, Rivers, and Sun. The Seven Vials' objective was to bring God's judgment upon the Papacy and cast down her power and dominance.

FIRST VIAL: POURED OUT UPON THE EARTH

Albigenses or Cathari, a religious movement in Southern France, Northern Spain, and Northern Italy, criticized the Papacy and its practices. By the late 1100's they embraced a substantial portion of South France and North Italy. But Pope Innocent III ordered a crusade in 1208, and a bloody war of extermination followed. Within 100 years, the Albigenses were utterly rooted out.

The Waldenses of Southern France and Northern Italy, similar to the Albigenses but not identical, taught the Bible and criticized the Papacy's practice. As a result, the Waldenses were gradually repressed except in the Alpine Valleys southwest of Turin. Nevertheless, they became the leading Protestant body in Italy.

All of this stirred the people of the Earth to desire more freedom from the Papacy that so had them bound. Thus, they could aptly be called the **Forerunners of the Reformation.**

SECOND VIAL: POURED OUT UPON THE SEA (PEOPLE)

The Papacy had just finished its victorious 200-year struggle with Germany. Pope Boniface received the Papacy at its height but met his match with the King of France, Philip the Fair. Philip the Fair humbled the Papacy to the dust, beginning its Era of Decline. France had always worked hand in hand with the Papacy to do its bidding and keep it in power, but now, Philip the Fair had taken up the struggle with the Papacy. It started with the taxation of the clergy and ended with the Papacy being brought into complete submission to the French state.

THIRD VIAL: POURED OUT UPON THE RIVERS (THE RIVERS WERE THE LIFE-GIVING WATERS)

Another way of putting this is the rivers were the tributaries feeding the Papal Empire. With this plague, even the clergy were going to rise and preach against the Papacy. Men who rose against the Papacy were:

- John Wyclif (1324-1384) aka, "The Morning Star of the Reformation"
- John Huss (1369-1415)
- Savonarola (1452-1498)
- Erasmus (1466-1536)

Many others preached against the cruelties and evil practices of the Roman Catholic Church. Most were martyred for their stand.

FOURTH VIAL: POURED OUT UPON THE SUN

Martin Luther (1483-1546) became one of the most influential men in church history. He led the world in its break for freedom from the most oppressive institution in history. Martin Luther was born to poor parents at Eisleben, entered the University of Erfurt (1501) to study law, then later (1505) entered a monastery and became an exemplary monk.

One day, in 1508, while reading his Bible, Martin Luther's enlightenment and peace came suddenly as he read in Galatians (3:11), "*the just shall live by faith*." This passage changed his whole life and the entire course of history. The Reformation was now in full swing. In 1511, he went to Rome and was appalled at the corruption and vice of the church.

On October 31, 1517, he posted his thesis on the church door in Wittenberg. He, of course, was excommunicated by the church in 1520. On December 10, 1520, Luther burned the Bill of Excommunication, and a whole new age in history began. At the sounding of the Lutheran Trumpet, many nations were startled and, like giants awakening out of their sleep, began to move for more freedom and break ties with the Papacy.

FIFTH VIAL: POURED OUT UPON THE SEAT OF THE BEAST (HIS THRONE)

The Fifth Vial was poured out upon the Throne of the Beast, whose realm had already suffered terribly from the first four Vials. While these five Vials may have other meanings, they seem, prophetically, to parallel the colossal convulsions of the 18th century by which the Papacy ceased to be a world power. Under Napoleon of France, the Papacy was dethroned, and statehood was removed.

No longer was the Papacy in such a position of world power and prestige as in its former days. The Papacy, the Roman Catholic Church, was the dominating power in the world from the 6th to the 18th century, some 1260 years in all.

SIXTH VIAL: POURED OUT UPON THE GREAT RIVER EUPHRATES

This scripture references the fall of Babylon in the Old Testament. The Euphrates River was the water supply that fed Babylon. Cyrus, king of Persia, diverted the river that ran under the Babylon wall into a channel used to irrigate the Babylonian crops outside the city walls. Cyrus then marched his army into the city on the dry riverbed.

The water supply of the Papacy (the nations and peoples that gave life and power to the Papacy) was dried up. As a result, a way was made for the *kings of the east* (unclean spirits of devils).

And I saw **three unclean spirits** *like frogs come out of the mouth of the dragon, and out of the mouth of the beast, and out of the mouth of the false prophet. For they are the* ***spirits of devils, working miracles, which go forth unto the kings of the earth and of the whole world****, to gather them to the battle of that great day of God Almighty.*
REVELATION 16:13-14

Just as the Fall of Rome gave way to the Ten Gothic Tribes, the decay of the Roman Papacy gave way to various means by which unclean devils work to deceive the world and persecute God's people.

The dragon (Satan) gave power to the beast (the Roman Catholic Church), whose visible head was the false prophet (the Papacy or office of the Pope).

THREE UNCLEAN SPIRITS, LIKE FROGS, COME OUT OF THE MOUTH:

- of the **dragon** (Satan)
- of the **beast** (the Roman Catholic Church)
- of the **false prophet** (the Papacy or office of the Pope)

Interestingly, each entity (the dragon, the beast, and the false prophet) decayed into three parts. They are:

- **The Dragon** who reemerged as the three city-states that control the world:
    1. City of London
    2. City of Washington, DC
    3. Vatican City
- **The Beast** who birthed the three main branches of Christianity (aka, "the mother of harlots"):
    1. Eastern Orthodox
    2. Catholic
    3. Protestant
- **The False Prophet** who vomited three heretical doctrines:
    1. Doctrine of the Trinity (Three divine beings in the Godhead)

2. Baptism in the titles "Father, Son, and Holy Ghost" (Not in the name of Jesus)
3. The Baptism of the Holy Ghost is not necessary for Salvation (Note: Speaking in tongues is not the initial evidence of Spirit Baptism)

THE THREE UNCLEAN SPIRITS OUT OF THE MOUTH OF THE DRAGON

- **London City** rules over the world through financial control.
- **Washington, D.C.** rules over the world through military control.
- **Vatican City** rules over the world through religious control.

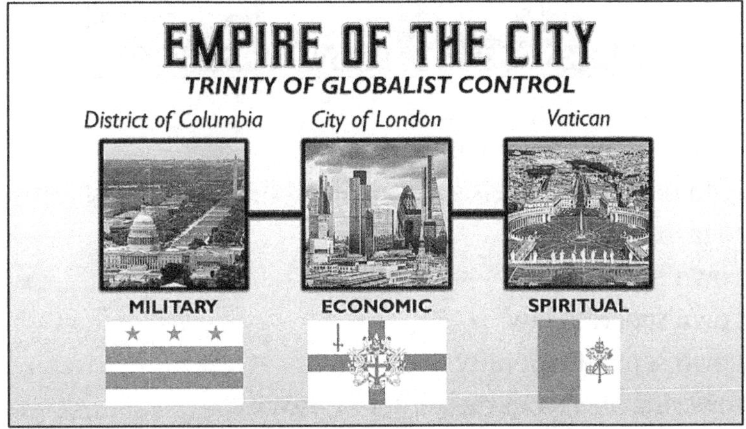

The photo on this page and the next were taken from *The Trinity of Globalist Control: Vatican City—City of London—Washington, D.C*
Ghislainbiblestudent.blogspot.com

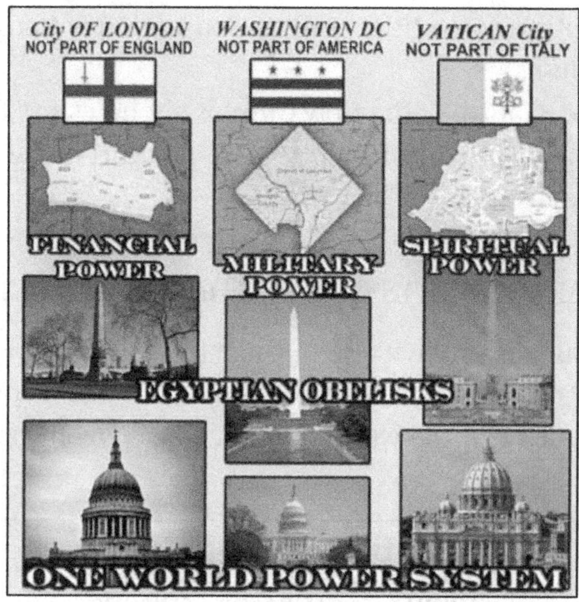

Each city associated with the three unclean spirits:

1. belongs to no nation (i.e., is sovereign and independent of its own country)
2. pays no taxes
3. has its own flag
4. has its own separate law
5. has its own separate identity
6. has a towering obelisk in the center of the city.

Vatican City was established in 1929 and has numerous services, including its own postal service, newspaper, radio and television station, army, and prison. As the biggest wealth accumulator and landowner in the world, Vatican City controls two billion of the six billion world population.

London City became a sovereign state in 1694 when King William privatized and turned its control over to the bankers. In 1812 Nathan Rothschild crashed the English stock market and gained control over the Bank of England. Today it is the world's financial power center and the wealthiest square mile on the earth. It houses the central banks of the world and is the headquarters for worldwide overseas freemasonry, as well as the worldwide money cartel known as "The Crown."

The Crown is not associated with the royal family or the British monarch but is the private City of London Corporation. The Crown is run by thirteen of the most powerful families in the world and their descendants. The Crown Corporation holds title to worldwide Crown land and Crown colonies like Canada, Australia, and New Zealand.

Washington, D.C., was founded in 1790. The Act of 1871 created a separate corporate government for the District of Columbia. It operates as a corporation outside the U.S. constitution. Washington, D.C. controls the Pentagon, the headquarters for the United States Military.

THE 3 UNCLEAN SPIRITS OUT OF THE MOUTH OF THE BEAST

The decay of the Roman Papacy (the Roman Catholic Church) through the Protestant Reformation gave way to three main branches of Christianity:

- **Eastern Orthodox**
- **Catholic**
- **Protestant**

MAIN BRANCHES OF CHRISTIANITY

The following is an excerpt directly taken from an article compiled by Felix Just, S.J., Ph.D., titled "Who Are Christians?" According to Dr. Just, three main branches of Christianity proceeded out of Roman Catholicism:

- **Orthodox**
- **Catholic**
- **Protestant**

And potentially **Anglican or** Anglo-Catholic, which is halfway between Catholic & Protestant.

Some schemes suggest five, six, or even more main branches, including Nestorian, Monophysite, Orthodox, Catholic, Protestant, Anglican, Restorationist, Independent, Marginal, etc. Subdivisions of the Main Branches (*here in overview; see the next section for more details*):

- **Eastern Christians** are mostly Eastern Orthodox, but some are Nestorians (Church of the East) or Monophysites (Oriental Orthodox).

The divisions among these Eastern Churches go back almost 1500 years, stemming from disagreements in the fifth century CE. Long after the East/West divisions of 1054, some Eastern Churches reunited with the Roman Catholic Church (thus called Uniate Churches).

- **Catholic Christians** are mostly Roman Catholic, yet some groups still call themselves Catholic but are no longer united with Rome.

The Old Catholic Church broke away in 1870, disagreeing with the decrees from the First Vatican Council about papal infallibility.

Various groups of Traditionalist Catholics or Tridentine Catholics broke after 1965, disagreeing with reforms of the Second Vatican Council. Other groups of Progressive Catholics broke in 1965, thinking the reforms instituted by Vatican II did not go far enough.

- **Protestant Christians** are subdivided into thousands of different denominations, as well as independent or non-denominational groups.

The historically earliest was founded in the 16th century by Martin Luther (Lutherans) and by John Calvin (Reformed or Calvinist Christians). The Anglicans, or the Church of England, separated from the Roman Catholic Church for political, not theological, reasons; thus, Anglo-Catholic beliefs and practices are similar to Roman Catholics, but Anglicans don't acknowledge the leadership role of the Bishop of Rome (the Pope).

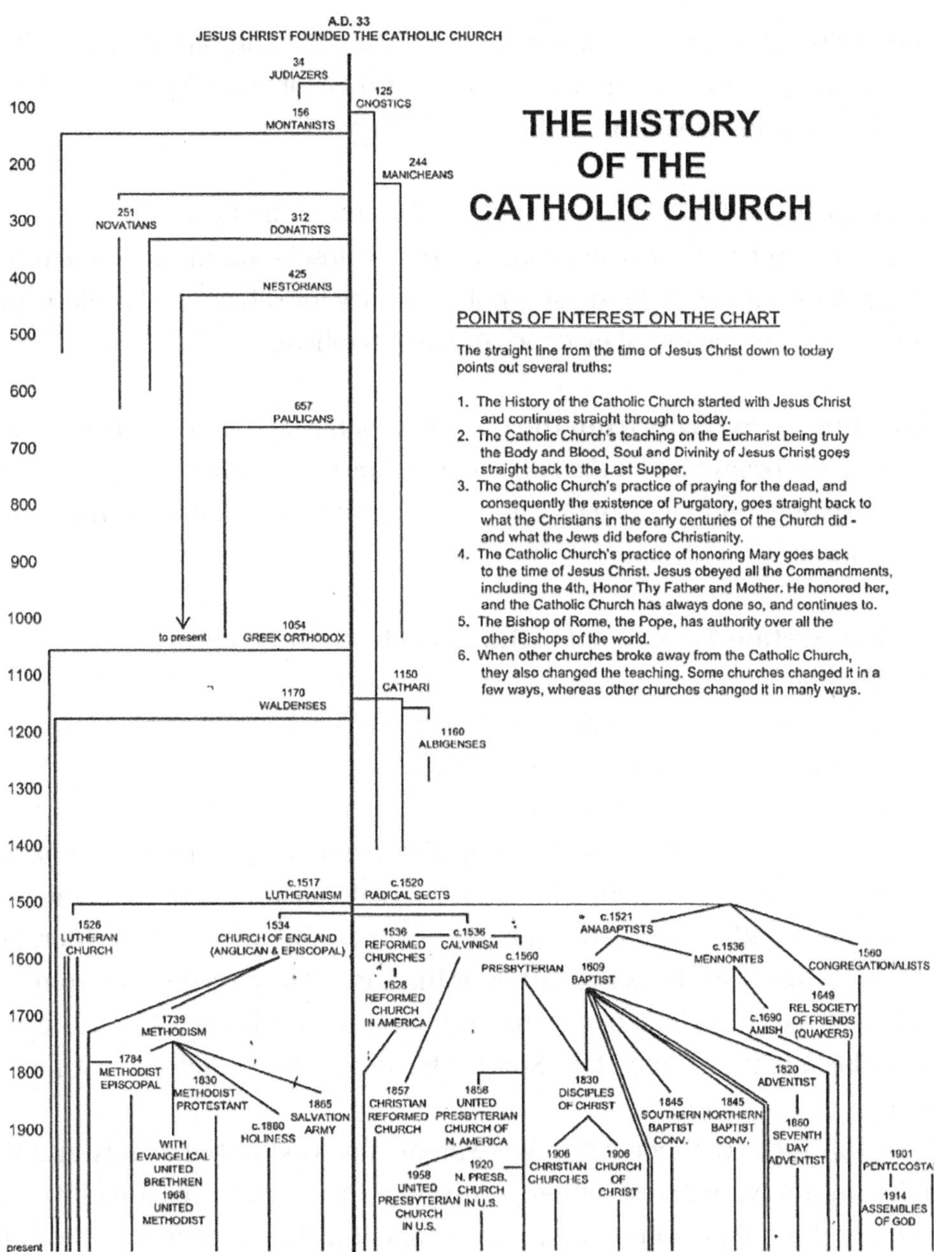

The illustration is taken from *The History of the Catholic Church* as compiled by Felix, S.J., Ph.D.

THE 3 UNCLEAN SPIRITS OUT OF THE MOUTH OF THE FALSE PROPHET

It is interesting that the Greek Orthodox, Catholics, and Protestants, although different in many ways, still agree at the core of their philosophy. It is in their core doctrine that they all agree. And in these three, they all agree:

1. Doctrine of the Trinity - three divine beings in the Godhead
2. Baptism in the titles "Father, Son, and Holy Ghost" - Not in the Name of Jesus
3. The Baptism of the Holy Ghost is not necessary for salvation - Speaking in tongues is not the initial evidence of Spirit Baptism

The following are excerpts from the *Catechism of the Catholic Church,* the *Apostolic Constitution Fidei Depositum on the Publication of the Catechism of the Catholic Church* English translation (Copyright 1997) United States Catholic Conference, Inc. – Libreria Editrice Vaticana.

Part One, Section Two, Chapter One, Article 1, Paragraph

III. The Holy Trinity in the Teaching of the Faith

From the beginning, the revealed truth of the Holy Trinity has been at the very root of the Church's living faith, principally through Baptism.

The divine persons are really distinct from one another. "God is one but not solitary." "Father," "Son," and "Holy Spirit" do not simply name designating modalities of the divine being, for they are really distinct from one another: "He is not the Father who is the Son, nor is the Son he who is the Father, nor is the Holy Spirit he who is the Father or the Son." They are distinct from one another in their relations of origin: "It is the Father who generates, the Son who is begotten, and the Holy Spirit who proceeds." The divine Unity is Triune.

Now, this is the Catholic faith: We worship one God in the Trinity and the Trinity in unity, without either confusing the persons or dividing the substance; for the person of the Father is one, the Son's is another, the Holy Spirit's another; but the Godhead of the Father, Son, and Holy Spirit is one, their glory equal, their majesty coeternal" (Athanasian Creed; DS 75; ND 16).

Part One, Section Two, Chapter Three, Article 9, Paragraph 3

III. The Church is Catholic

"The Church knows that she is joined in many ways to the baptized who are honored by the name of Christian, but do not profess the Catholic faith in its entirety or have not preserved unity or communion under the successor of Peter." Those "who believe in Christ and have been properly baptized are put in a certain, although imperfect, communion with the Catholic Church.

Part Three, Section One, Chapter Three, Article 2

II. Grace

Grace is, first and foremost, the gift of the Spirit who justifies and sanctifies us. But grace also includes the gifts that the Spirit grants us to associate us with his work, to enable us to collaborate in the salvation of others and in the growth of the Body of Christ, the Church. There are sacramental graces and gifts proper to the different sacraments. There are furthermore special graces, also called charisms after the Greek term used by St. Paul and meaning "favor," "gratuitous gift," and "benefit." Whatever their character—sometimes it is extraordinary, such as the gift of miracles or of tongues—charisms are oriented toward sanctifying grace and are intended for the common good of the Church. They are at the service of charity which builds up the Church.

To teach God is a coming together of three persons that are each coequal and coeternal is to teach three separate divine beings. To teach three separate divine beings is to teach three Gods. This is in Direct Opposition and Contradiction to God's First and Greatest Commandment.

Hear, O Israel: The LORD, our God, is one LORD:

DEUTERONOMY 6:4

The Doctrine of One God is the core of the Jewish faith.

THE APOSTLES TAUGHT ONE GOD, NOT A TRIUNE GOD

For in him [Jesus] dwelleth all the fullness of the Godhead bodily.

COLOSSIANS 2:9

To wit, that God was in Christ, reconciling the world unto himself…

II CORINTHIANS 5:19A

And without controversy great is the mystery of godliness: ***God was manifest in the flesh*** *…*

I TIMOTHY 3:16A

One *Lord,* ***one*** *faith,* ***one*** *baptism, …*

EPHESIANS 4:5

Furthermore, whenever anyone was baptized in the Book of Acts to fulfill being Born of Water, it was always in the name of JESUS. It was never in the titles Father, Son, or Holy Spirit.

And whatsoever ye do in word or deed, do ***ALL*** *in the name of the* ***LORD JESUS****.*

COLOSSIANS 3:17A

Baptism in the Name of Jesus Christ is the identity of the early Apostolic Church. Baptism is the titles Father, Son, and Holy Spirit is the identity of the Catholic Church. To minimalize the importance of "Born of Spirit," evidenced by speaking in an unknown tongue, is to further deny Jesus access and control of our hearts. Although the gift of tongues and the interpretation of tongues **as taught** in I Corinthians 14 is indeed one of the gifts of the Spirit, every reference to speaking in tongues in the Book of Acts was given for **confirmation** of our initial Spirit Baptism. Whenever anyone in the Book of Acts was baptized in the Holy Ghost (Born of Spirit), the sign was always speaking in an unknown tongue. Water Baptism is a physical event we can see. Holy Ghost Baptism is a spiritual event we must hear.

They went out from us, but they were not of us; for if they had been of us, they would no doubt have continued with us: but they went out, that they might be made manifest that they were not all of us.

I JOHN 2:19

According to the above scripture, they (false Christians) were part of the original Book of Acts Church. Still, they left because they were not complete in the unity of faith and doctrine. The sad part of the story is these judgments brought no pleasure to the Lord. The Lord is merciful and long-suffering, and His desire was for these judgments to cause sinners to repent. The Lord plagued Rome for a few hundred years, and now the Papacy for several hundred years—but neither found a place of repentance. Oh, let us never frustrate the mercy and grace of Almighty God!

And the rest of the men which were not killed by these plagues yet repented not of the works of their hands; that they should not worship devils, and idols of gold, and silver, and brass, and stone, and of wood: which neither can see, nor hear, nor walk; Neither repented they of their murders, nor of their sorceries, nor of their fornication, nor of their thefts.

REVELATION 9:20-21

CONCLUSION:

The Seven Vials are God's wrath and judgment upon the Roman Papacy for persecuting "The Church." The Seven Vials, also called the Seven Last Plagues, were poured out upon the Roman Papacy, forcing her into ruin and decay. However, three unclean spirits come out of the dragon, the beast, and the false prophet to surround "The Church" and battle for the souls of the redeemed. Vengeance belongs to God, and He will fight for us and win!

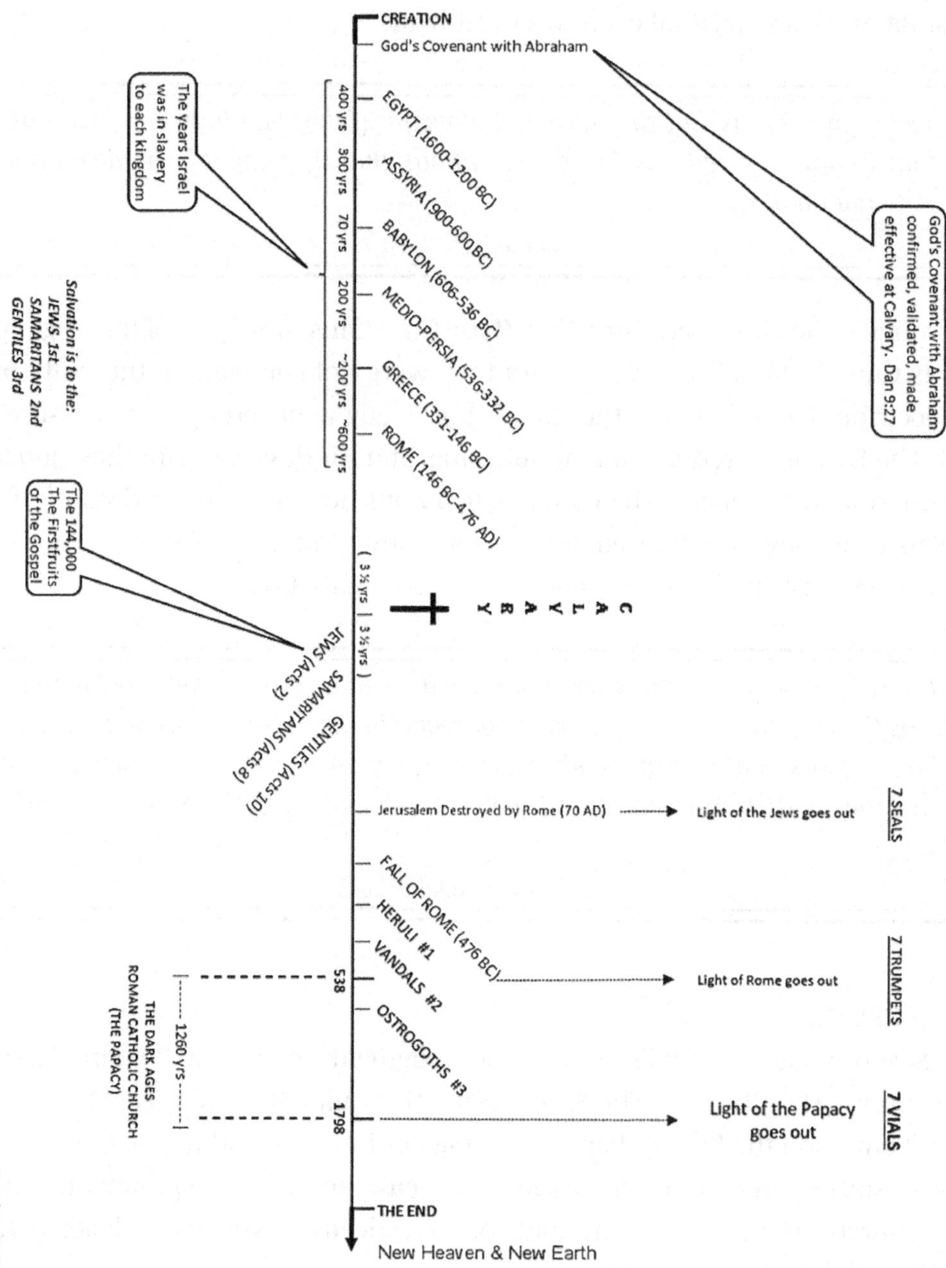
CREATION
God's Covenant with Abraham
God's Covenant with Abraham confirmed, validated, made effective at Calvary. Dan 9:27
The years Israel was in slavery to each kingdom
400 yrs
300 yrs
70 yrs
200 yrs
~200 yrs
~600 yrs
EGYPT (1600-1200 BC)
ASSYRIA (900-600 BC)
BABYLON (606-536 BC)
MEDIO-PERSIA (536-332 BC)
GREECE (331-146 BC)
ROME (146 BC-476 AD)
Salvation is to the:
JEWS 1st
SAMARITANS 2nd
GENTILES 3rd
(3 ½ yrs | 3 ½ yrs)
CALVARY
The 144,000
The Firstfruits
of the Gospel
JEWS (Acts 2)
SAMARITANS (Acts 8)
GENTILES (Acts 10)
Jerusalem Destroyed by Rome (70 AD)
Light of the Jews goes out
7 SEALS
FALL OF ROME (476 BC)
HERULI #1
VANDALS #2
OSTROGOTHS #3
538
Light of Rome goes out
7 TRUMPETS
1260 yrs
THE DARK AGES
ROMAN CATHOLIC CHURCH
(THE PAPACY)
1798
Light of the Papacy goes out
7 VIALS
THE END
New Heaven & New Earth
Timeline Pic 5

CHAPTER 11

THE SEVEN THUNDERS

Revelation 15-16

THE PREMISE:

It is not for us to know what the Seven Thunders uttered except that they do follow a pattern and are the final culmination of God's judgment.

SCRIPTURE TEXT:

Revelation 10: 1-7 *And I saw another mighty angel come down from heaven, clothed with a cloud: and a rainbow was upon his head, and his face was as it were the sun, and his feet as pillars of fire: And he had in his hand a little book open: and he set his right foot upon the sea, and his left foot on the earth, And cried with a loud voice, as when a lion roareth; and when he had cried,* ***seven thunders uttered their voices.*** *And when the seven thunders had uttered their voices, I was about to write: and I heard a voice from heaven saying unto me, Seal up those things which the seven thunders uttered, and write them not. And the angel which I saw stand upon the sea and upon the earth lifted up his hand to heaven, And sware by him that liveth for ever and ever, who created heaven, and the things that therein are, and the earth, and the things that therein are, and the sea, and the things which are therein, that there should be time no longer: But in the days of* *the voice of the seventh angel, when he shall begin to sound, the mystery of God should be finished, as he hath declared to his servants the prophets.*

THE SEVEN THUNDERS AT A GLANCE

1st Thunder	Not revealed
2nd Thunder	Not revealed
3rd Thunder	Not revealed
4th Thunder	Not revealed
5th Thunder	Not revealed
6th Thunder	Not revealed
7th Thunder	Mystery of God finished

Clearly, God did not want us to know what the Seven Thunders uttered; however, He did want us to know that there were seven utterances. The explicit details given in such highly figurative language under the Seven Seals, the Seven Trumpets, and the Seven Vials let us know two things. First, understanding is available to those who desire to know. Second, the Seals, Trumpets, and Vials all follow a similar divine pattern. Therefore, it is likely the same pattern would continue under the Seven Thunders, but John was the only one that ever heard what the Seven Thunders uttered.

So why was only John able to hear what was uttered and then be commanded not to write it down? It is my opinion, but if, perhaps, we were to know what was uttered, then we could, with much accuracy, predict the future and the end of the world. Although we may attempt to speculate upon whom God's wrath will fall next, it is not for us to know. *But of that day and hour knoweth no man* (Matthew 24:36). We are simply admonished to keep our lamps trimmed and ready.

Even so, it is now high time to awake out of sleep and be vigilant, for the kingdom of God truly is at hand and the hour draweth nigh. Oh, how close we really must be to the coming of the Lord! There will be *no* second chance! When it is over, it is over! But to the blood-bought saints of God, it is a day of Great Anticipation!

CONCLUSION:

It is not for us to know what the Seven Thunders uttered except that they do follow a pattern and are the final culmination of God's judgment.

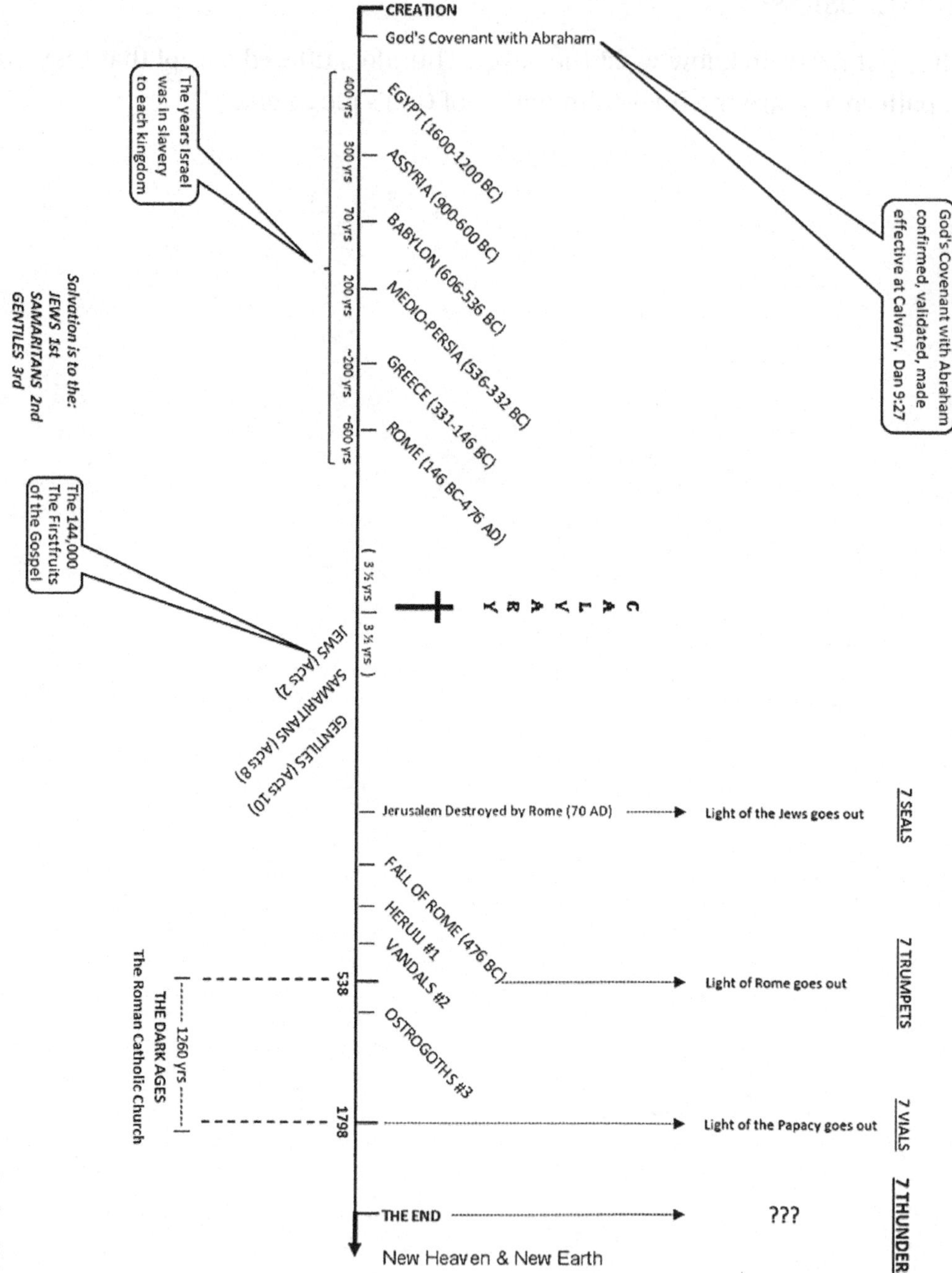
CREATION
God's Covenant with Abraham
God's Covenant with Abraham confirmed, validated, made effective at Calvary. Dan 9:27
The years Israel was in slavery to each kingdom
400 yrs
300 yrs
70 yrs
200 yrs
~200 yrs
~600 yrs
EGYPT (1600-1200 BC)
ASSYRIA (900-600 BC)
BABYLON (606-536 BC)
MEDIO-PERSIA (536-332 BC)
GREECE (331-146 BC)
ROME (146 BC-476 AD)
Salvation is to the:
JEWS 1st
SAMARITANS 2nd
GENTILES 3rd
The 144,000
The Firstfruits of the Gospel
(3 ½ yrs | 3 ½ yrs)
CALVARY
JEWS (Acts 2)
SAMARITANS (Acts 8)
GENTILES (Acts 10)
Jerusalem Destroyed by Rome (70 AD)
Light of the Jews goes out
7 SEALS
FALL OF ROME (476 BC)
HERULI #1
VANDALS #2
OSTROGOTHS #3
538
Light of Rome goes out
7 TRUMPETS
1260 yrs
THE DARK AGES
The Roman Catholic Church
1798
Light of the Papacy goes out
7 VIALS
THE END
???
7 THUNDERS
New Heaven & New Earth

Timeline Pic 6

CHAPTER 12

MYSTERY BABYLON

Revelation 13, 17, 18

THE PREMISE:

The Little Horn, the Man of Sin, the Sea Beast, the Woman on the Beast, Mystery Babylon, and the Mother of Harlots are all depictions of what is commonly referred to as the Beast or the Antichrist. The Beast is the Roman Papacy (the office of the Pope, Bishop of Rome), and the Image of the Beast is whoever occupies that office. The Mark of the Beast is its baptismal formula.

TRUTH IS OBSCURED BY DRAMATIC MISREPRESENTATION

Please consider that popular opinion is seldom ever the truth, especially so in spiritual matters. However, those who desire to know the truth will find many times, the truth has been there all along, hidden in plain sight, obscured by worldly distractions.

We have heard many tall tales of this horrible beast in Revelation 13, referred to as the Antichrist. Dramatic and scary stories have been told about how the government wants to tattoo our foreheads or inject a computer chip into our hands so we cannot buy or sell anything. Many presidents and world leaders have been charged with being the Antichrist. Even Hollywood has jumped on the fear-mongering campaign to leave us feeling fearful and anxious. Hopefully, this lesson will dispel that fear and obscurity.

SCRIPTURE TEXT:

I John 2:18-22 *Little children, it is the last time: and as ye have heard that* ***antichrist*** *shall come, even now are there many* ***antichrists;*** *whereby we know that it is the last time. They went out from us, but they were not of us: for if they had been of us, they would no doubt have continued with us: but they went out, that they might be made manifest that they were not all of us. But ye have an unction from the Holy One, and ye know all things. I have not written unto you because ye know not the truth, but because ye know it, and that no lie is of the truth. Who is a liar but he that denieth that Jesus is the Christ? He is the antichrist, that denieth the Father and the Son.*
II Thessalonians 2:3 *Let no man deceive you by any means: for that day shall not come, except there come a falling away first, and that* ***man of sin*** *be revealed, the son of perdition.*
Revelation 12:3-4 *And there appeared another wonder in heaven; and behold a great red dragon, having seven heads and ten horns, and seven crowns upon his heads. And his tail drew the third part of the stars of heaven, and did cast them to the earth: and the dragon stood before the woman which was ready to be delivered, for to devour her child as soon as it was born.*
Revelation 13:1-18 *And I stood upon the sand of the sea, and saw a* ***beast*** *rise up out of the sea, having seven heads and ten horns, and upon his horns ten crowns, and upon his heads the name of blasphemy. And the* ***beast*** *which I saw was like unto a leopard, and his feet were as the feet of a bear, and his mouth as the mouth of a lion: and the dragon gave him his power, and his seat, and great authority. And I saw one of his heads as it were wounded to death; and his deadly wound was healed: and all the world wondered after the* ***beast****. And they worshipped the dragon which gave power unto the* ***beast****: and they worshipped the* ***beast,*** *saying, Who is like unto the* ***beast?*** *Who is able to make war with him? And there was given unto him a mouth speaking great things and blasphemies; and power was given unto him to continue forty and two months. And he opened his mouth in blasphemy against God, to blaspheme his name, and his tabernacle, and them that dwell in heaven. And it was given unto him to make war with the saints, and to*

overcome them: and power was given him over all kindreds, and tongues, and nations. And all that dwell upon the earth shall worship him, whose names are not written in the book of life of the Lamb slain from the foundation of the world. If any man have an ear, let him hear. He that leadeth into captivity shall go into captivity: he that killeth with the sword must be killed with the sword. Here is the patience and the faith of the saints. And I beheld another beast coming up out of the earth; and he had two horns like a lamb, and he spake as a dragon. And he exerciseth all the power of the first beast before him, and causeth the earth and them which dwell therein to worship the first beast, whose deadly wound was healed. And he doeth great wonders, so that he maketh fire come down from heaven on the earth in the sight of men. And deceiveth them that dwell on the earth by the means of those miracles which he had power to do in the sight of the beast; saying to them that dwell on the earth, that they should make an image to the beast, which had the wound by a sword, and did live. And he had power to give life unto the image of the beast, that the image of the beast should both speak, and cause that as many as would not worship the image of the beast should be killed. And he causeth all, both small and great, rich and poor, free and bond, to receive a mark in their right hand, or in their foreheads: And that no man might buy or sell, save he that had the mark, or the name of the beast, or the number of his name. Here is wisdom. Let him that hath understanding count the number of the beast: for it is the number of a man; and his number is Six hundred threescore and six.

Revelation 17:3-6 *So he carried me away in the spirit into the wilderness: and I saw a* ***woman*** *sit upon a scarlet coloured beast, full of names of blasphemy, having seven heads and ten horns. And the* ***woman*** *was arrayed in purple and scarlet colour, and decked with gold and precious stones and pearls, having a golden cup in her hand full of abominations and filthiness of her fornication: And upon her forehead was a name written, MYSTERY, BABYLON THE GREAT, THE MOTHER OF HARLOTS AND ABOMINATIONS OF THE EARTH. And I saw the* ***woman*** *drunken with the blood of the saints, and with the blood of the martyrs of Jesus: and when I saw her, I wondered with great admiration.*

THE SEVEN HEADS AND TEN HORNS

The Dragon (Revelation 12:3), the Sea Beast (Revelation 13:1), and the Scarlet-Colored Beast of Babylon (Revelation 17:3) all had *seven heads and ten horns*. All three represent the same thing, the Beast we refer to as the Antichrist.

HISTORICAL WORLD POWERS THAT PERSECUTED GOD'S PEOPLE

Prior to the Dark Ages, seven world powers towered above and dominated the course of history and enslaved or persecuted God's people.

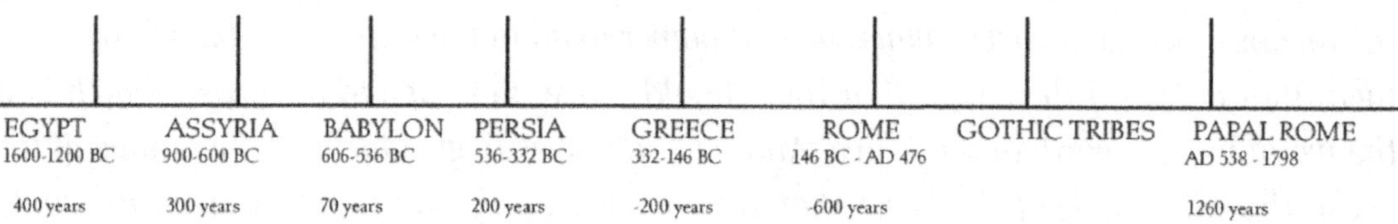

THE SEA BEAST - REVELATION 13:1-10

This composite Leopard-Bear-Lion Beast is the same Beast that kills the **Two Witnesses** in Revelation 11:7 and is still more fully described in Revelation chapter 17. *Upon his heads the name of blasphemy* is a hint to an apostate religious ruling system. Both John and Daniel saw the same thing but from different views. Daniel was at Babylon looking forward toward the end of time, while John was at the end of time looking backward toward the past. This explains the order in which each animal appeared in each respective vision. Refer to Chapter 5.

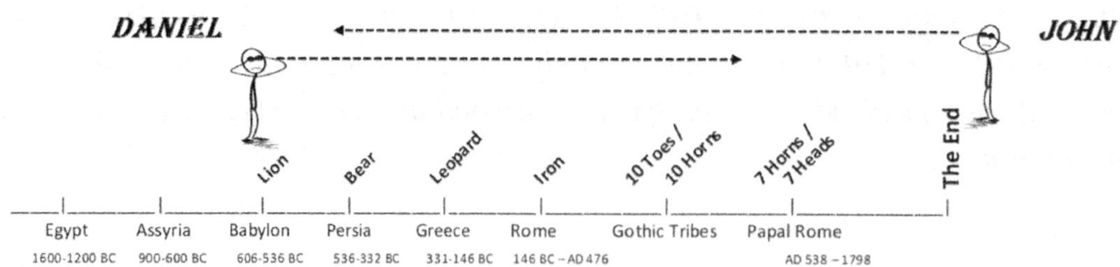

NEBUCHADNEZZAR AND DANIEL DREAM OF THE FUTURE

In Daniel, Chapter 2, Nebuchadnezzar saw **Four Solid Metals: Gold, Silver, Brass,** and **Iron.** These were the Babylonian Empire, the Medo-Persian Empire, the Grecian Empire, and the Roman Empire. The **legs of Iron** are the Roman Empire that fell into decay to the **Ten Toes** or the **Ten Gothic Tribes.** The feet and toes were part iron and part clay to denote that this kingdom is divided into ten smaller kingdoms, but they *shall not cleave one to another* (Daniel 2:43). Note that there were four and *only* four One World Powers or One World Governments, as we like to call it. There is no mention of another One World Government in the physical sense of the word.

In Daniel, Chapter 7, Daniel saw **four great beasts**. The **Lion** was the Babylonian Empire. The **Two Eagle's Wings** that carried it were Nebuchadnezzar and Belshazzar, its two rulers.

The **Bear** that raised itself up on **one side** was the Medo-Persian Empire that came into being because on the one side, Cyrus, ruler of Persia, conquered the land and gave part of the kingdom to his Uncle Darius the Mede to rule. The **three ribs** in its mouth were the three provinces of Babylon that it conquered: Babylon, Lydia, and Egypt.

The **Leopard** was the Grecian Empire that Alexander the Great set up. The **Four Wings** were the four generals Alexander used to conquer, and the **Four Heads** were the sections that the four generals split the Grecian Empire into:

- **Cassander over Greece**
- **Ptolemy over Egypt**
- **Lysimachus over Asia Minor**
- **Seleucus over Syria and Babylon**

The **Last** or **4th Beast** was extraordinarily strong and took away the influence of the kingdoms before it. It was diverse from the ones before it and had **Ten Horns** and **Teeth of Iron**, denoting that it was **Roman.** History states that the Roman Empire fell in decay, and the **Ten Gothic Tribes** took dominion.

These **Ten horns** (same as the Ten Toes) were:

1. Heruli
2. Suevi
3. Burgundians
4. Huns
5. Ostrogoths
6. Visigoths
7. Vandals
8. Lombards
9. Franks
10. Anglo-Saxons

These are spoken of in history as the **Ten Kings** that arose out of the **Roman Empire.**

THE LITTLE HORN

> *I considered the horns, and, behold, there came up among them another* ***little horn****, before whom there were three of the first horns plucked up by the roots: and, behold, in this horn were eyes like the eyes of man, and a mouth speaking great things.*
>
> DANIEL 7:8

Out of this Roman Empire also arose another **Little Horn** that did away entirely with **three** of the **Gothic Tribes**. It is this **Little Horn** who is proposed to be the **Antichrist,** that **Beastial Empire.**

Now, if we can identify who it was that destroyed three of the Ten Kings, we will have identified the **Little Horn.**

CHARACTERISTICS OF THE LITTLE HORN

1. The horn on the beast grows out of the beast. The Beast is Roman; therefore, the Horn is Roman.

2. The Little Horn was to be revealed in power among the ten kingdoms after the Fall of the Roman Empire, sometime after 476 A.D.
3. The Little Horn was to **pluck up 3** of the other horns, kings, or kingdoms.
4. It would be **diverse** from the other kingdoms.
5. It had a **mouth** speaking great things.
6. It had **eyes,** and his look was more **stout.**
7. It would make **war with the saints** and **wear out the saints.**
8. It would think to **change times and laws.**

The Papacy fits these descriptions, which follow exactly!

Definition of the papacy:

i. the office of the Pope
ii. a succession or line of popes
iii. the term of a pope's reign
iv. *capitalized*: the system of government of the Roman Catholic Church, of which the Pope is the supreme head

THE PAPACY AND THE LITTLE HORN

1. The **Papacy** is **Roman** and is known as the **Roman Catholic Church.**
2. The **Papacy** did rise to power in Rome and among the **Ten Gothic Tribes.**
3. The **Papacy** did eradicate **3** of the **Ten Gothic Tribes:** The **Heruli** in **493 A.D.**, the **Vandals** in **534 A.D.**, and the **Ostrogoths** in **553 A.D.**
4. The **Little Horn** would rise among the **Ten Horns** or kingdoms but would be **"diverse"** from the other kingdoms out of the Roman Empire. Other kingdoms have claimed temporal power, but the **Papacy** rose up, claiming **Spiritual Power** as well as **Temporal Power. Diverse!**

   Henry Grattan Guinness, in his book *Romanism and The Reformation,* writes: "Is not the Papacy sufficiently diverse from all the rest of the kingdoms of Western Europe to identify it as the Little Horn? What other ruling monarch of Christendom ever pretended to have Apostolic authority or ruled men in the name of God? Does the Pope dress in royal robes? Nay, but in priestly garments. Does he wear a crown? Nay, but a triple tiara, to show that he reigns in heaven, earth, and hell! Does he wield a scepter? Nay, but a crosier or crook, to show that he is the good shepherd of the church. Do his subjects kiss his hand? Nay, but his toe! Verily this power is 'diverse' from the rest, both in great things and little. It is small in size, gigantic in its pretensions."

5. With pride and arrogance, the Papacy teaches corrupt and unscriptural doctrines. The sentences of the Pope are considered final. His utterances are declared infallible, and his decrees irreformable.
6. The Pope, or whoever fills the office, claims to be the overseer of the whole earth and the whole church. Hence, Vatican City is given the name Holy See. He also claims to possess the keys to the Kingdom of Heaven!
7. For a few years, Early Christians were persecuted by the Jews and then by the Roman Empire for a few hundred years. But for centuries, the Papacy tortured Christians who would not profess the Papacy as the god of this earth. Christians were stretched and torn apart on the rack, crushed and stabbed in the Iron Virgin, nailed to trees, burned to death, and scalded with oil. They had melted lead poured into the eyes, ears, and mouths. They had their heads twisted off, fingers thumb-screwed off, legs and feet crushed with Spanish Boots, and many other horrible acts done to them. It is estimated that some 50,000,000 or more died at the hands of the Roman Catholic Church's directives. No wonder this period is called the **Dark Ages**—some **1260 years** in all!
8. The **Little Horn** would think to **change times and laws**. Politicians always do this, but the Little Horn speaks against God; therefore, these are "Divine Laws." The Papacy, when in supreme power, canceled the decrees of kings. In religion, the Pope claims infallibility. The Papacy instituted the observance of saint days and other days for which we have no scripture. The Papacy also instituted rituals and rites from paganism and set itself up as the authority in place of the Bible.

In the Catholic mass, you do not bring your Bible. You read from a missalette, a short periodical for congregational use. In 325 A.D., it changed baptism from the name of Jesus Christ to the titles Father, Son, and Holy Spirit. In 1312 A.D., it changed baptism to sprinkling, and so on and so on.

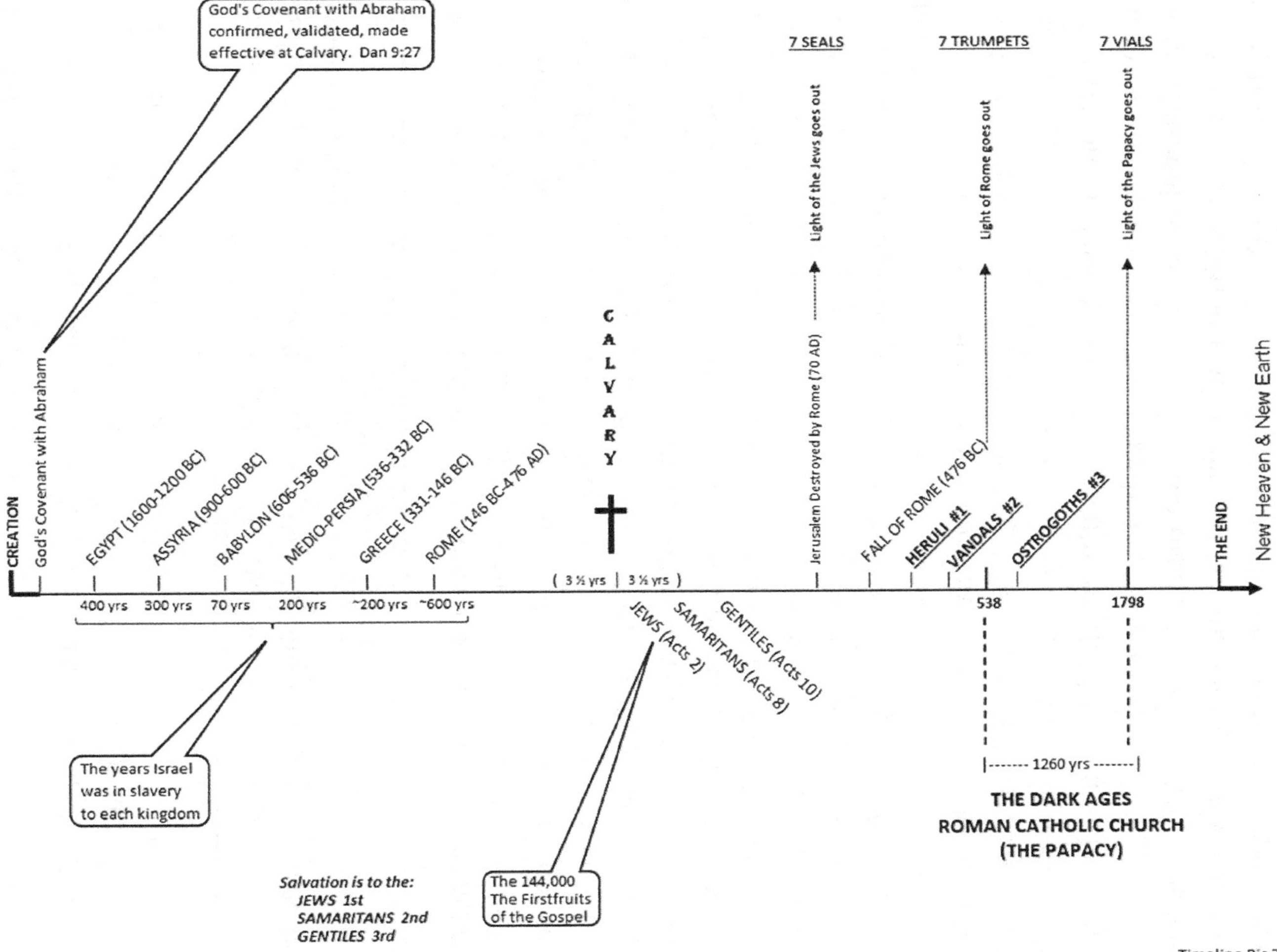

God's Covenant with Abraham confirmed, validated, made effective at Calvary. Dan 9:27
7 SEALS
7 TRUMPETS
7 VIALS
Light of the Jews goes out
Light of Rome goes out
Light of the Papacy goes out
CREATION
God's Covenant with Abraham
EGYPT (1600-1200 BC)
ASSYRIA (900-600 BC)
BABYLON (606-536 BC)
MEDIO-PERSIA (536-332 BC)
GREECE (331-146 BC)
ROME (146 BC-476 AD)
CALVARY
Jerusalem Destroyed by Rome (70 AD)
FALL OF ROME (476 BC)
HERULI #1
VANDALS #2
OSTROGOTHS #3
THE END
New Heaven & New Earth
400 yrs
300 yrs
70 yrs
200 yrs
~200 yrs
~600 yrs
(3 ½ yrs | 3 ½ yrs)
JEWS (Acts 2)
SAMARITANS (Acts 8)
GENTILES (Acts 10)
538
1798
1260 yrs
The years Israel was in slavery to each kingdom
THE DARK AGES
ROMAN CATHOLIC CHURCH
(THE PAPACY)
Salvation is to the:
JEWS 1st
SAMARITANS 2nd
GENTILES 3rd
The 144,000
The Firstfruits
of the Gospel

Timeline Pic 7

SHORT HISTORY OF THE EARLY CHURCH

Around 100 A.D., the first Apostolic organization was formulated and called "The Catholic Church." The word "catholic" means universal. Over the next 250 years, it went from being a Monotheistic organization to a predominantly Trinitarian one.

> *They went out from us, but they were not of us: for if they had been of us, they would no doubt have continued with us: but they went out, that they might be made manifest that they were not all of us.*
>
> I JOHN 2:19

Since about 100 A.D., many ideas and teachings concerning the Godhead have been injected into the mainstream of religion. Some contain elements of truth but not full scriptural truth about the Godhead. Many of these teachings resulted from such factors as lack of communication, limited access to scripture, education and cultural backgrounds, language barriers, limited travel, and lack of freedom of worship. Political leaders embraced religion to gain popularity. Paganistic practices were incorporated into church services, then taught and practiced as though they were scriptural. Such setting and climate fostered false doctrine, deviations from the truth, and error that became so entrenched in the minds and writings of men until they influenced not only their day but ours as well. Perhaps this will stir us up to search out the Truth and *earnestly contend for the faith which was once delivered unto the saints*. Jude 1:3.

One of the earliest uses of the word Trinity is found by **Theophilus of Antioch (180 A.D.).** He wrote Autolycus, an epistle defending his own Christianity. He said, "In like manner also the three days which were before the luminaries, are types of the trinity of God, and His Word, and His Wisdom." **Theophilus of Antioch** seems to be the first to denote the relation of three divine persons by the term "triad."

Gregorius Thaumaturgus, whose last name means "wonderworker," was born around A.D. 213 to a wealthy pagan family and became Bishop of Neo-Caesarea. Sometime between 260 A.D. and 270 A.D., he wrote *Ekthesis tes pisteos* (Exposition of the Faith) about the Trinity. He was a pupil of **Origen,** who was also a proponent of the **Triad Theory.**

Many great names of history are linked to this period, apparently, each one trying to define with more flair and flamboyancy than his predecessor who God is. Controversies surrounding the Godhead raged on in these early years, with lines finally drawn between the teachings of two men: **Arius** and **Athanasius.** Both men were prominent in their time, Arius being a priest and Athanasius a deacon. Debate raged so hotly between the beliefs of these men until **Constantine, Emperor of Rome,** called the **Council of Nicaea.**

The council met in the city of Nicaea in 325 A.D., with 318 Bishops and the Pope's legate, forming the First General or Ecumenical Council. In reality, neither Arius nor Athanasius believed in the Oneness of God as the Bible teaches. Arius was nearer to the truth than Athanasius but still didn't understand or biblically explain the Godhead. At this council, baptism was changed from being performed "in the name of Jesus Christ" to the titles "Father, Son, and Holy Spirit," establishing the foundation and identity of the Roman Catholic Church.

As long as there was a Roman government in the city of Rome, it was illegal to have any other type of governing body there. Therefore, Constantine moved the capital from Rome to Constantinople. This move allowed the Roman Catholic Church to move its headquarters to the most popular city of the empire, Rome. It has remained there to this day, the Vatican.

DEFINITION OF "ANTICHRIST"

The scripture text says He is **antichrist**, that **denieth** the Father and the Son. What does this mean? The word **"Anti"** according to Strong's Concordance word 473 in the Greek dictionary is often used to denote **substitution**:

> **anti**, an-tee, a prim. Particle. Apposite, i.e., instead or because of (rarely in addition to): in the room of. Often used in composition to denote contrast, requital, substitution, correspondence, etc.

Thus, the word "Antichrist" can be correctly interpreted as someone who substitutes or appoints himself in place of Jesus Christ. The Papacy fits the description in every detail.

The Catholic Dictionary, edited by Peter M. J. Stravinskas, states that Vicarius Christi (Vicar of Christ) is the "title used almost exclusively of the Bishop of Rome as the successor of Peter and, therefore, the one in the Church who particularly takes the place of Christ, but also used of bishops in general and even of priests." It goes on to say that "All bishops are vicars of Christ for their local churches in their ministerial function as priest, prophet, and king, as the Pope is for the universal church. The title further denotes they exercise their authority in the Church not by delegation from any other person, but from Christ himself!"

DEFINITION OF "DENY"

The word "deny," according to Strong's concordance #720, comes from the Greek word **arneomai**, meaning: to contradict.

Thayer's Greek Lexicon: arneomai

- to deny, to deny someone, to deny one's self
- to disregard his own interests or to Proverbs false to himself
- act entirely unlike himself
- to deny, abnegate, renounce or reject (something desired or valuable), abjure
- not to accept, to reject, to refuse something offered

To deny the Father and the Son is to disavow that One God manifested himself as the Father, the Son, and the Holy Ghost. It is to reject the notion of One God revealing himself in different offices and/or relationships and instead declare that three totally separate divine entities, beings, or persons with three separate centers of consciousness are coming together to create God.

Furthermore, to be baptized while having the words "Father, Son, and Holy Ghost" spoken over an individual, as they are immersed in water, instead of the actual name "Jesus Christ," is to deny Jesus. The command in Matthew 22:18 is to go and baptize *in the name of the Father, and of the Son, and of the Holy Ghost.* But obedience to the command is to baptize in the *name* which is *Jesus Christ*! This logic agrees with Acts 4:12 and Colossians 3:17, which admonishes us to do ***all*** things in the name of the Lord Jesus Christ.

So, if we are going to pray for the sick, bless our food, command the devil to flee, etc., *in the name of Jesus Christ,* then why would we not be baptized *in the name of Jesus Christ?* Again, we are to do ***all*** things in the name of the Lord Jesus Christ.

It may seem trivial, but baptizing *in the name of Jesus Christ,* which is exactly how all the examples of Acts played out, is to acknowledge the Father and the Son. Not only are we acknowledging that the Father and Son are one, but we are taking on the name of Jesus as our identifying spiritual mark of ownership. The following diagram shows the correct versus the incorrect view of God. One's mode of baptism identifies the individual to the acknowledgment of one of these views.

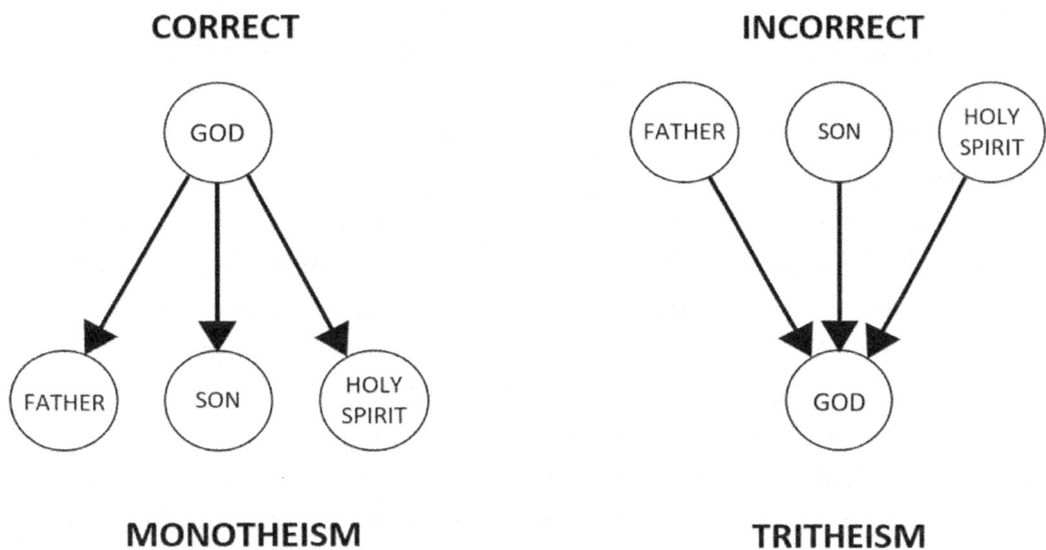

THE BISHOP OF ROME, VICARIUS CHRISTI

According to the Webster Handy College Dictionary, **vicarious** is a Latin word meaning: substituting for or filling in place of another. It is the root word for **vicar.** The New Riverside Desk Dictionary states that the word **vicar** means:

- a parish priest in the Church of England
- a cleric in the Episcopal Church in charge of a chapel
- one who serves as a substitute for another

The Papal title of **Vicar of Christ,** which in Latin is **Vicarius Christi,** literally means a **Substitute for Christ,** synonymous with **Antichrist** (assuming the power of Christ, the Son of God on earth). This blasphemous claim is repeatedly made by various popes and is the very foundation of Roman Catholicism.

The foundational teaching of the Roman Catholic Church instructs that Jesus was the visible head of the whole Church who handed the "keys" of authority to Peter by succession. Peter then passed his authority on to the next Bishop of Rome. Whoever occupies the office of the Bishop of Rome, the Pope, known officially as the Vicar of Christ, is considered the visible head and supreme authority over the whole Church of the world and can exercise his power *unhindered*.

Here is an excerpt from the *Catechism of the Catholic Church,* the *Apostolic Constitution Fidei Depositum on the Publication of the Catechism of the Catholic Church.*

Section Two, Chapter Three, Article 9, Paragraph 3

I. The Church is Catholic

The Lord made Simon alone, whom he named Peter, the "rock" of his Church. He gave him the keys of his Church and instituted him as shepherd of the whole flock. "The office of binding and loosing which was given to Peter was also assigned to the college of apostles united to its head." This pastoral office of Peter and the other apostles belongs to the Church's very foundation and continues by the bishops under the primacy of the Pope.

The *Pope*, Bishop of Rome, and Peter's successor "is the perpetual and visible source and foundation of the unity both of the bishops and of the whole company of the faithful." "For the Roman Pontiff, by reason of his office as Vicar of Christ, and as pastor of the entire Church, has full, supreme, and universal power over the whole Church, a power which he can always exercise unhindered."

Author's Note: Peter was ***not*** the rock. The rock upon which The Lord built His Church was the *Revelation of Jesus Christ*. It was the revelation that *God was in Christ reconciling the world unto himself*, II Corinthians 5:19. Peter was just the first to have this divine revelation.

Vicarius Filii Dei, Latin for **Vicar of the Son of God**, are the letters inscribed in the Pope's miter. Catholics hold that the church, which is a visible society, must have a visible head. Christ, before His ascension into heaven, appointed St. Peter to act as His representative. Upon the death of Peter, the man who succeeded in the office of Peter as Bishop of Rome was recognized as the head of the Church. Hence, the Bishop of Rome, as head of the Church, was given the title **Vicar of Christ.**

So, as the **Vicar of Christ,** the Pope speaks from **Peter's Chair** in the Cathedral of God, declaring himself to be infallible in defining and declaring doctrines that are not biblical which he claims to be essential to salvation as though he were God. The Beast in Revelation is the Roman Papacy, and the image of the Beast is the one who sits in Peter's Chair or, rather, the one who carries the title Vicarius Christi, the Pope. Note what great religious and political power rests upon the office of the Pope.

How ironic that the Roman Catholic Church regards Peter as the 1st bishop of Rome, yet it does not follow Peter's instruction in Acts, Chapter 2, where he commanded everyone to repent, be baptized in the NAME of Jesus Christ, and receive the gift of the Holy Ghost.

THREE CHARACTERISTICS THAT DISTINGUISH THE BEAST

1. The Mark
2. The Name
3. The Number of his name (666)

And that no man might buy or sell, save he that had the mark, or the name of the beast, or the number of his name. Here is wisdom. Let him that hath understanding count the number of the beast: for it is the number of a man; and his number is Six hundred threescore and six.

REVELATION 13:17-18

THE MARK OF THE BEAST – IDENTIFICATION THRU BAPTISM

The Mark of Identity of the Catholic Church is Baptism in the Trinitarian Formula. I refer once again to the *Catechism of the Catholic Church, the Apostolic Constitution Fidei Depositum on the Publication of the Catechism of the Catholic Church.*

> **Section Two, Chapter Three, Article 9, Paragraph 3**
> III. The Church is Catholic
> The Church knows that she is joined in many ways to the baptized who are honored by the name of Christian but do not profess the Catholic faith in its entirety or have not preserved unity or communion under the successor of Peter. Those "who believe in Christ and have been properly baptized are put in a certain, although imperfect, communion with the Catholic Church.

To be baptized in the titles Father, Son, and Holy Spirit instead of the name of Jesus Christ "joins" a person and puts a person in "communion with the Catholic Church!" Baptism is important, insomuch that in Acts, Chapter 10, Peter commanded them to *be baptized in the name of the Lord Jesus Christ* (NIV). It is not a mere ceremonial public exhibition of our belief, but it is our identity with Jesus Christ, whereby we receive remission of sins through the power of His Name.

THE NAME OF THE BEAST – "SUBSTITUTE FOR JESUS CHRIST"

The Latin title for the Pope is VICARIUS FILII DEI. The definition of the words are:

- VICARIUS – substituting for, or in the place of,
- FILII – son
- DEI – God

Vicarius Filii Dei literally means "substitute for or in the place of the Son of God."

THE NUMBER OF THE BEAST – 666

The Roman Empire was the beast that suffered the deadly head wound but came back to life—not in the physical but in the spiritual, as the Roman Papacy. Since the Beast is of Roman origin, it follows that we would use Rome's Numerical System.

THE ROMAN NUMERAL SYSTEM

I	=	1
V	=	5
X	=	10
L	=	50
C	=	100
D	=	500
Total	=	666

Even the Roman Numeral System adds up to 666. Please note that the "M" was not an original numeric character and did not become a part of the numeral system until later.

VICARIUS FILII DEI – "V" AND "U" ARE USED INTERCHANGEABLY

V = 5
I = 1
C = 100
A = no value I = 1
R = no value I = 1
I = 1
V = 5
S = no value
112

F = no value
I = 1
L = 50
I = 1
I = 1
53

D = 500
E = no value
I = 50
501

112 + 53 + 501 = 666

DUX CLERI – TRANSLATED MEANS CAPTAIN OF THE CLERGY (A TITLE)

D = 500
U = 5
X = 10

C = 100
L = 50
E = no value
R = no value
I = 1

515 + 151 = 666

LUDOVICUS - TRANSLATED MEANS VICAR OF THE COURT (ALSO A TITLE)

L = 50
U = 5
D = 500
O = no value
V = 5
I = 1
C = 100
U = 5
S = no value
Total = 666

Not only does **the number of his name** = **666** in Roman Numerals, but his Latin name also adds up to 666 in Greek letters, and his Hebrew name adds up to 666 in Hebrew letters.

Irenaeus, a pupil of **Polycarp** (a pupil of **John**), understood **666** to be the Greek word **Latienos** according to the numeric equivalents of Greek letters. **Latienos** means the **Latin Kingdom.**

NOTE: The numeric equivalent of Greek letters can be found in the Encyclopedia Britannica under Table 8 of the "Languages of the World."

L	=	30	lamba
A	=	1	alpha
T	=	300	tau
I	=	10	iota
E	=	5	epsilon
N	=	50	nu
O	=	70	omicron
S	=	200	sigma
Total	=	666	

Using the numeric equivalents of Hebrew letters, **ROMITH,** which means the **Roman Kingdom** adds up to 666. And **ROMITI,** which means **Roman Man,** also adds up to 666. These are just a few examples. However, the evidence is overwhelming.

With a visual comparison chart of some key features of the Little Horn, the Man of Sin, the Sea Beast, and the Woman on the Beast, we can get an even clearer overview and picture of this entity purported to be the Antichrist.

CHARACTERISTICS CHART: Little Horn / Man of Sin / Sea Beast / Woman on Beast

Characteristics	The Little Horn Daniel 7	The Man of Sin II Thessalonians 2:3	The Sea Beast Revelation 13	Woman on Beast Revelation 17-18
Source	grows out of the head of the ten-horned 4th beast (Rome)	owes his rise to the removal of a hindering power (Rome)	comes from the sea meaning many people (densely-populated Europe)	arises in a city with seven hills (Rome) and rules over many waters (people) and multitudes and nations and tongues
Time of Origin	comes up among ten horns (the divided successors of the Roman Empire)	revealed only after the fall of the hindering Roman Empire	receives power, seat and authority from the Dragon (Satan working through pagan Rome)	arises among the ten horns (divisions of Rome) that will hate her
Religio-Political Church-State Power	diverse in power, blasphemes God, exercises authority over the saints, changes times and laws of the Most High	not mentioned, but demands and receives worship	composite of Daniel's beasts, which are kingdoms, and wears crowns, demands and receives worship	woman is an apostate church and the beast is the power of the state, hence a religio-political power having a priest-king ruler
Blasphemous Presumption	has eyes like the eyes of a man, and a mouth speaking great things and words against the Most High	exalts himself above God	has a mouth speaking great things and blasphemies	full of names of blasphemy
Time of Dominance	given power over the saints for a time, times and a dividing of times (1260 years*)		given power - 42 months (1260 years*)	

Warring against God's People	made war with the saints and prevailed against them		makes war with the saints and overcomes them	woman (apostate church) is drunk with the blood of the saints; in her was found the blood of prophets and saints
Great Power	looks more stout than his fellows	has all power, signs and lying wonders	who is able to make war with Him?	the woman which thou sawest is that great city, which reigneth over the kings of the earth
Demands Divine Homage	sets himself over the saints, times and laws of the Most High	sets himself up as god, above all that is worshipped	causes multitudes to worship him	this woman is the apostate "mother" of harlot churches
End	they shall take away his dominion, to consume and to destroy it unto the end (the Second coming)	The Lord shall consume with the spirit of His mouth and shall destroy with the brightness of His coming	cast into the lake of fire	utterly burned with fire

This chart was created in 2013 by Thomas Sevely for the TerryHomePage: *The Catholic Origins of Futurism and Preterism*

Listing out the above characteristics of the antichrist from the Characteristics Chart, the following becomes readily apparent:

1. It will rise to great power after the fall of the Roman Empire after 476 AD.
2. It will be a geographically small nation, a little horn.
3. It will universally rule over many people, nations, and tongues.
4. Its headquarters will be the city of seven hills, Rome.
5. It will be a religio-political entity ruled by a priest-king having both religious and political power.
6. Its priest-king will make great, blasphemous claims.
7. It will claim authority over all kings.
8. It will seek to change the times and laws of God as its mark of authority.
9. It will be an apostate church causing nations to drink from her cup of apostate doctrine.
10. It will be a persecuting power, killing the faithful saints of Jesus Christ as heretics.
11. It will hold power and authority for 1260 years after the fall of the Roman Empire.
12. It will suffer a deadly wound ending 1260 years of dominance and persecution.

The Papacy fits the description in every detail. Although the Papacy ceased as a dominant world power, her apostate doctrine is still promulgated to this day via her harlot daughters, from whence she has been appointed the name "Mother of Harlots."

THE MARK OF CHRIST VS. THE MARK OF THE BEAST

During the exodus of the children of Israel, the distinguishing characteristic provided for the death angel was the blood on the doorpost. It is and has always been the one defining mark of what belongs to God. The children of God of the New Testament era are marked with the blood via baptism in the name of Jesus Christ.

Likewise, those of the Apostate "Counterfeit" Church or any of her harlot daughter churches are marked with her baptism. And although God honors His Word and faith in Him in these counterfeit churches and miracles, signs and wonders are wrought, the only biblical way to have the blood of Jesus Christ applied is being Born Again of water and spirit, according to Acts, Chapters 2, 8, 10. There is no other way! To deny the New Birth examples found in Acts is to deny Jesus Christ.

Not every one that saith unto me, Lord, Lord, shall enter into the kingdom of heaven; but he that doeth the will of my Father which is in heaven. Many will say to me in that day, Lord, Lord, have we not prophesied in thy name? and in thy name have cast out devils? And in thy name done many wonderful works? And then will I profess unto them, I never knew you: depart from me, ye that work iniquity.

MATTHEW 7:21-23

If we do all these works in the name of Jesus, why would we not be baptized in the name of Jesus?

MYSTERY BABYLON, THE MOTHER OF HARLOTS

This counterfeit religion is called Mystery Babylon because, as stated in Chapter 1, it all began with Nimrod and his mother, Semiramis, in ancient Babylon. It was Nimrod who stirred the people to contempt of God and then his mother/wife Semiramis that fabricated her elaborate lie of how her son Tammuz was the reincarnation of a deceased Nimrod. This was the beginning of a counterfeit religious system that continued to rear its ugly head throughout history to undermine God's true redemptive plan for mankind.

The Roman Catholic Church is called the Mother of Harlots because from her proceeded a multitude of daughter religions called by different names but all in agreement with her core foundational doctrine of a triune God and baptism in the titles Father, Son, Holy Spirit rather than in the name of Jesus.

EVEN THE DEVIL KNOWS WHO BELONGS TO WHO

In the book of Acts, Chapter 19, the seven sons of Sceva attempted the same miracles as Paul and Jesus and were sent away beaten and naked by a man possessed with a devil. Why? Because they attempted to act in authority when they had no authority.

The evil spirit answered and said, 'Jesus I know, and Paul I know; but who are ye?' The identity is the blood.

The Bible states in Matthew 7:21-23 that on Judgment Day, some will say, *"Lord, we have healed the sick in your name, cast out devils in your name,"* to which the Lord replies, *"Depart from me ye workers of iniquity, I never KNEW you!"*

When the Great Harvest comes, the angelic reapers will gather the tares (not marked by the blood of Jesus) to be burned with fire but gather the wheat (marked by the blood of Jesus) into His barn. (Matthew 13:30).

CONCLUSION:

The Little Horn, the Man of Sin, the Sea Beast, the Woman on the Beast, Mystery Babylon, and the Mother of Harlots are all depictions of what is commonly referred to as the Beast or the Antichrist. The Beast is the Roman Papacy (the office of the Pope, Bishop of Rome), and the Image of the Beast is whoever occupies that office. The Mark of the Beast is its baptismal formula.

CHAPTER 13

THE TWO WITNESSES – PART II

Revelation 11

THE PREMISE:

The Two Witnesses of Revelation 11 are the Old Testament and the New Testament and together represent the Word of God, the Holy Bible. Nothing can testify to the validity of Jesus Christ except for the Word of God.

SCRIPTURE TEXT:

Revelation 11:3-14 *And I will give [power] unto my* ***two witnesses****, and they shall prophesy a thousand two hundred [and] threescore days, clothed in sackcloth. These are the two olive trees, and the two candlesticks standing before the God of the earth. And if any man will hurt them, fire proceedeth out of their mouth, and devoureth their enemies: and if any man will hurt them, he must in this manner be killed. These have power to shut heaven, that it rain not in the days of their prophecy: and have power over waters to turn them to blood, and to smite the earth with all plagues, as often as they will. And when they shall have finished their testimony, the beast that ascendeth out of the bottomless pit shall make war against them, and shall overcome them, and kill them. And their dead bodies [shall lie] in the street of the great city, which spiritually is called Sodom* *and Egypt, where also our Lord was crucified. And they of the people and kindreds and tongues and nations shall see their dead bodies three days and an half, and shall not suffer their dead bodies to be put in graves. And they that dwell upon the earth shall rejoice over them, and make merry, and shall send gifts one to another; because these two prophets tormented them that dwelt on the earth. And after three days and an half the Spirit of life from God entered into them, and they stood upon their feet; and great fear fell upon them which saw them. And they heard a great voice from heaven saying unto them, Come up hither. And they ascended up to heaven in a cloud; and their enemies beheld them. And the same hour was there a great earthquake, and the tenth part of the city fell, and in the earthquake were slain of men seven thousand: and the remnant were affrighted, and gave glory to the God of heaven. The second woe is past; and, behold, the third woe cometh quickly.*

In Chapter 3, we identified the **Two Witnesses** as referring to the Old and New Testament, which together represent the Word of God. Only the Word of God holds the credibility to testify that Jesus Christ is the One True God manifested (revealed) in the flesh. In the scripture text, the Two Witnesses prophesied 1260 days clothed in sackcloth. Using the "day for a year" method, 1260 days becomes 1260 years.

It was during the Dark Ages (538 AD–1798 AD) for 1260 years that anyone not in allegiance with the Roman Papacy was severely punished, and owning a translated copy of the Bible was strictly forbidden. The Papacy did not want any thought that encouraged deviations from the organization's "official" teachings. Truly the Word of God was robed in sackcloth.

EXPLOITS OF THE TWO WITNESSES IN THE OLD TESTAMENT

These exploits occur *in the days of their prophecy* (Revelation 11:5-6). It was in the days of the Law and the Prophets—the Old Testament era—that these events occurred.

> *Fire proceedeth out of their mouth and devours their enemies … power to shut heaven that it rain not … power to turn water to blood … power to smite the earth with plagues*
>
> REVELATION 11:5B, 6A

And Elijah answered and said to the captain of fifty, If I be a man of God, then let fire come down from heaven, and consume thee and thy fifty. And there came down fire from heaven, and consumed him and his fifty.

II KINGS 1:10

And Elijah…said unto Ahab, As the Lord God of Israel liveth, before whom I stand, there shall not be dew nor rain these years, but according to my word. And it came to pass after a while, that the brook dried up, because there had been no rain in the land.

I KINGS 17:1,7

And the Lord spake unto Moses, Say unto Aaron, Take thy rod, and stretch out thine hand upon the waters of Egypt, upon their streams, upon their rivers, and upon their ponds, and upon all their pools of water, that they may become blood; and that there may be blood throughout all the land of Egypt, both in vessels of wood, and in vessels of stone.

EXODUS 7:19

In the Book of Exodus, the Lord, through Moses, smote the Egyptians with plagues of frogs, lice, flies, boils, hail, and even death. The Word of God, through the prophets, did such great exploits against the enemies of God.

THE TWO WITNESSES ARE KILLED BY THE BEAST BUT COME BACK TO LIFE.

The culmination of the Dark Ages ended in France. France was the one who gave power to the Roman Catholic Church. This era ended when Napoleon, dictator of France, arrested the pope, placed him in jail, and did away with the temporal (earthly) rule of the Roman Catholic Church. Up until that time, the Roman Catholic Church, or the Papacy, claimed both spiritual and temporal power over the whole earth and ruled accordingly.

At the end of the Dark Ages, during Napoleon's "Reign of Terror," the Two Witnesses were killed in a sense because for three and a half years, the Holy Bible was banned;

it was against the law to even possess one. Mussolini brought back the temporal power of the Papacy. To this day, Vatican City houses ambassadors from around the world. The Papacy eventually fell to the Protestant Reformation as many churches broke ties with the Papacy.

Although these Protestant religions came out from the Roman Catholic Church, they are easily identifiable as "daughters" because they still adhere to the same identifying mark of their mother's core doctrine of a triune deity, expressly through baptism. The Name of Jesus is used freely elsewhere but omitted in baptism.

BAPTISM MUST BE IN THE NAME OF JESUS CHRIST!

These excerpts are noted a second time to magnify the importance of being Born Again according to scripture as exampled multiple times in the Book of Acts. Without the name of Jesus, there is no remission of sin! Without the name of Jesus, the blood is not applied! It is the blood that is the identifying mark of the true Christian!

The following excerpts from the *Catechism of the Catholic Church, the Apostolic Constitution Fidei Depositum* on the Publication of the Catechism of the Catholic Church English translation (Copyright 1997) United States Catholic Conference, Inc. – Libreria Editrice Vaticana:

Section Two, Chapter One, Article 1, Paragraph 1

III. The Holy Trinity in the Teaching of the Faith

From the beginning, the revealed truth of the Holy Trinity has been at the very root of the Church's living faith, principally by means of Baptism.

The divine persons are really distinct from one another. "God is one but not solitary." "Father," "Son," and "Holy Spirit" do not simply name designating modalities of the divine being, for they are really distinct from one another: "He is not the Father who is the Son, nor is the Son he who is the Father, nor is the Holy Spirit he who is the Father or the Son." They are distinct from one another in their relations of origin: "It is the Father who generates, the Son who is begotten, and the Holy Spirit who proceeds." The divine Unity is Triune.

> Now, this is the Catholic faith: We worship one God in the Trinity and the Trinity in unity, without either confusing the persons or dividing the substance; for the person of the Father is one, the Son's is another, the Holy Spirit's another; but the Godhead of the Father, Son, and Holy Spirit is one, their glory equal, their majesty coeternal" (Athanasian Creed; DS 75; ND 16).

Section Two, Chapter Three, Article 9, Paragraph 3

III. The Church is Catholic

> "The Church knows that she is joined in many ways to the baptized who are honored by the name of Christian, but do not profess the Catholic faith in its entirety or have not preserved unity or communion under the successor of Peter." Those "who believe in Christ and have been properly baptized are put in a certain, although imperfect, communion with the Catholic Church.

When one adheres to the doctrine of this Mystery Babylonian religion of three distinct, separate individuals coming together to create God and/or baptism in the *name of the Father, and of the Son, and of the Holy Spirit* (so that one is *not* baptized in the *name of Jesus Christ),* then one is taking upon himself, not the mark of the blood of Jesus Christ, but rather the mark of the Roman Catholic Church. In the Old Testament, the mark of the blood of the lamb during Israel's exodus from Egypt was the identifying mark of the children of God. Likewise, the blood of The Lamb (Jesus) becomes our identifying mark through baptism in the name of Jesus Christ.

CONCLUSION:

The Two Witnesses of Revelation 11 are the Old Testament and the New Testament and together represent the Word of God, the Holy Bible. Nothing can testify to the validity of Jesus Christ except for the Word of God.

CHAPTER 14

ARMAGEDDON

Revelation 16

THE PREMISE:

Armageddon, by interpretation, is “the mount of the congregation.” It is the final gathering place where all the saints are brought together to be with The Lord at the End.

PARAGRAPHS IN THE BIBLE

Since the Bible did not show paragraphs, some KJV Bibles have a pilcrow (symbol ¶) to mark a new paragraph or section of a text. Notice the ¶ at verse 15 in front of the word “Behold.”

This indicates a break in thought between verse 14 and verse 15. In other words, a person should read verses 1-14 of Revelation 16, pause, take a breath, then read 15-18 because the early translators saw this as a new paragraph or section of text.

> 15 ¶ Behold, [v]I come as a thief. Blessed *is* he that watcheth, and keepeth his garments, [w]lest he walk naked, and they see his shame.
>
> 16 And he gathered them together into a place called in the Hebrew tongue Ar-ma-gêd'don.

SCRIPTURE TEXT:

Revelation 16:15-17 *Behold, I come as a thief. Blessed is he that watcheth, and keepeth his garments, lest he walk naked, and they see his shame. And he gathered them together into a place called in the Hebrew tongue* ***Armageddon****. And the seventh angel poured out his vial into the air; and there came a great voice out of the temple of heaven, from the throne, saying, It is done.*

DISSECTING THE WORD ARMAGEDDON

The key to the meaning of the word Armageddon is found in Isaiah 14:13.

> *How art thou fallen from heaven, O Lucifer, son of the morning! How art thou cut down to the ground, which didst weaken the nations! For thou has said in thine heart, I will ascend into heaven, I will exalt my throne above the stars of God: I will sit also upon* ***the mount of the congregation****, in the sides of the north: I will ascend above the heights of the clouds; I will be like the most high.*
>
> ISAIAH 14:12-14

Lucifer declared he would *also sit upon the mount* (**har**) *of the congregation* (**mo'ed**). The phrase ***mount of the congregation*** in Hebrew is ***har mo'ed***

> **H2022. har,** a mountain or range of hills, mountainous region, mount, an elevated geographical region, (sometimes used figuratively), hill (country).
>
> **H4150.** mo'ed, mow'ed, an appointed place of meeting. The meaning of mo'ed is fixed within the context of Israel's religion. First, the prescribed festivals came to be known as the "appointed times" or the set feasts. An appointment; specifically, a festival, conventionally a year; by implication, an assembly (as convened for a definite purpose); technically the congregation; by extension, the place of meeting; also a signal (as appointed beforehand): an appointed (sign, time), (place of, solemn) assembly, congregation, (set solemn) feast, (appointed, due) season, synagogue, (set) time (appointed).

Interestingly, in George Wigram's *Englishman's Hebrew and Chaldee Concordance of the Old Testament* of 1874, the word mow'ed is spelled and pronounced a little differently. He shows it as: **4150: moh-gehd.** Thus, accordingly, ***mount of the congregation*** in Isaiah 14:13 would be: **har moh-gehd.**

BIBLE USAGE OF THE WORDS

H2022 har:

224 as mount
156 as mountains
105 as mountain
36 as hill
37 as hills
1 as hill's

545 total

H4150 mo'ed, mow'ed, moh-gehd

147 as congregation
16 as appointed
8 as solemn feasts
6 as season
5 as set
5 as set feasts
4 as appointed season
3 as seasons
3 as time
3 as solemn
3 as solemnities
2 as assembly
2 as solemn feast
1 as solemnity
1 as feast
1 as congregations
1 as synagogues
1 as assemblies
1 as times
1 as solemn assembly

220 total

ARMAGEDDON IN THE PARABLES OF THE KINGDOM

THE PARABLE OF THE WHEAT AND THE TARES

Another parable put he forth unto them, saying, The kingdom of heaven is likened unto a man which sowed good seed in his field: But while men slept, his enemy came and sowed tares among the wheat, and went his way. But when the blade was sprung up, and brought forth fruit, then appeared the tares also. So the servants of the householder came and said unto him, sir, didst thou sow good seed in thy field? From whence then hath it tares? He said unto them, An enemy hath done this. The servants said unto him, wilt thou then that we go and gather them up? But he said, Nay; lest while ye gather up the tares, ye root up also the wheat with them. Let both grow together until the harvest: and in the time of harvest I will say to the reapers, Gather ye together first the tares, and bind them in bundles to burn them: but ***gather the wheat into my barn.*** *He answered and said unto them, He that soweth the good seed is the Son of man; The field is the world; the good seed are the children of the kingdom; but the tares are the children of the wicked one; The enemy that sowed them is the devil; the harvest is the end of the world; and the reapers are the angels. As therefore the tares are gathered and burned in the fire; so shall it be in the end of this world. The Son of man shall send forth his angels, and they shall gather out of his kingdom all things that offend, and them which do iniquity; And shall cast them into a furnace of fire: there shall be wailing and gnashing of teeth. Then shall the righteous shine forth as the sun in the kingdom of their Father. Who hath ears to hear, let him hear.*

MATTHEW 13:24-43

THE PARABLE OF THE GOOD AND BAD CATCH

Again, the kingdom of heaven is like unto a net, that was cast into the sea, and gathered of every kind: Which, when it was full, they drew to shore, and sat down, and ***gathered the good into vessels****, but cast the bad away. So shall it be at the end of the world: the angels shall come forth, and sever the wicked from among the just, And shall cast them into the furnace of fire, there shall be wailing and gnashing of teeth.*

MATTHEW 13:47-50

In **both** instances, the harvest of souls is done at one and only one singular event at the end of time. Both good and bad were allowed to grow together. There is **no** mention of a secret harvest in which the wheat mysteriously disappears, and the tares are left to carry on for a few more years. In other words, no evidence exists of a secret rapture where automobiles crash, run off the road, people vanish into thin air, and non-Christians are "left behind." **Both** the good and bad were allowed to grow together until the end.

In the end, God sends his reapers, the angels, who harvest the world and separate the harvest into two piles. The evil will be bundled and cast into the fire, and the righteous will be gathered into the His barn. In other words, those that are NOT marked by the blood of Jesus Christ will be cast into Hell, a *furnace of fire*, where *there shall be wailing and gnashing of teeth.* But those who are covered by the blood will be gathered together unto the Lord *into a place called* ***The Mount of the Congregation*** or ***Armageddon*** in Hebrew.

Therefore, at the end of the world, we are *not* gathered atop of the physical mountain of Megiddo. According to Wikipedia, "Mount Tel Megiddo is not actually a mountain at all, but a 'tel' (an artificial mount or hill created by many generations of people living and rebuilding on the same spot) on which ancient forts were built to guard the Via Maris, an ancient trade route linking Egypt with the northern empires of Syria, Anatolia and Mesopotamia." It is a 10-acre summit rising 21.33 meters (approximately seventy feet) above the valley. Some twenty-six layers of settlements have been excavated dating back to the Chalcolithic period" (approximately 4300–3300 BCE). Besides, there is not enough room on top of this hill to fit all the "Born Again" saints over the last 2,000 years, even if it were the case.

WHAT ARMAGEDDON IS NOT

Armageddon is *not* a battle.
Armageddon is *not* the "hill" of Megiddo in Israel.

WHAT ARMAGEDDON IS

An appointed set feast or season where the saints are caught up to meet the Lord in the air. (I Thessalonians 4:17).

CONCLUSION:

Armageddon, by interpretation, is "the mount of the congregation." Armageddon is the final gathering place where all the saints are brought together to be with the Lord at the end.

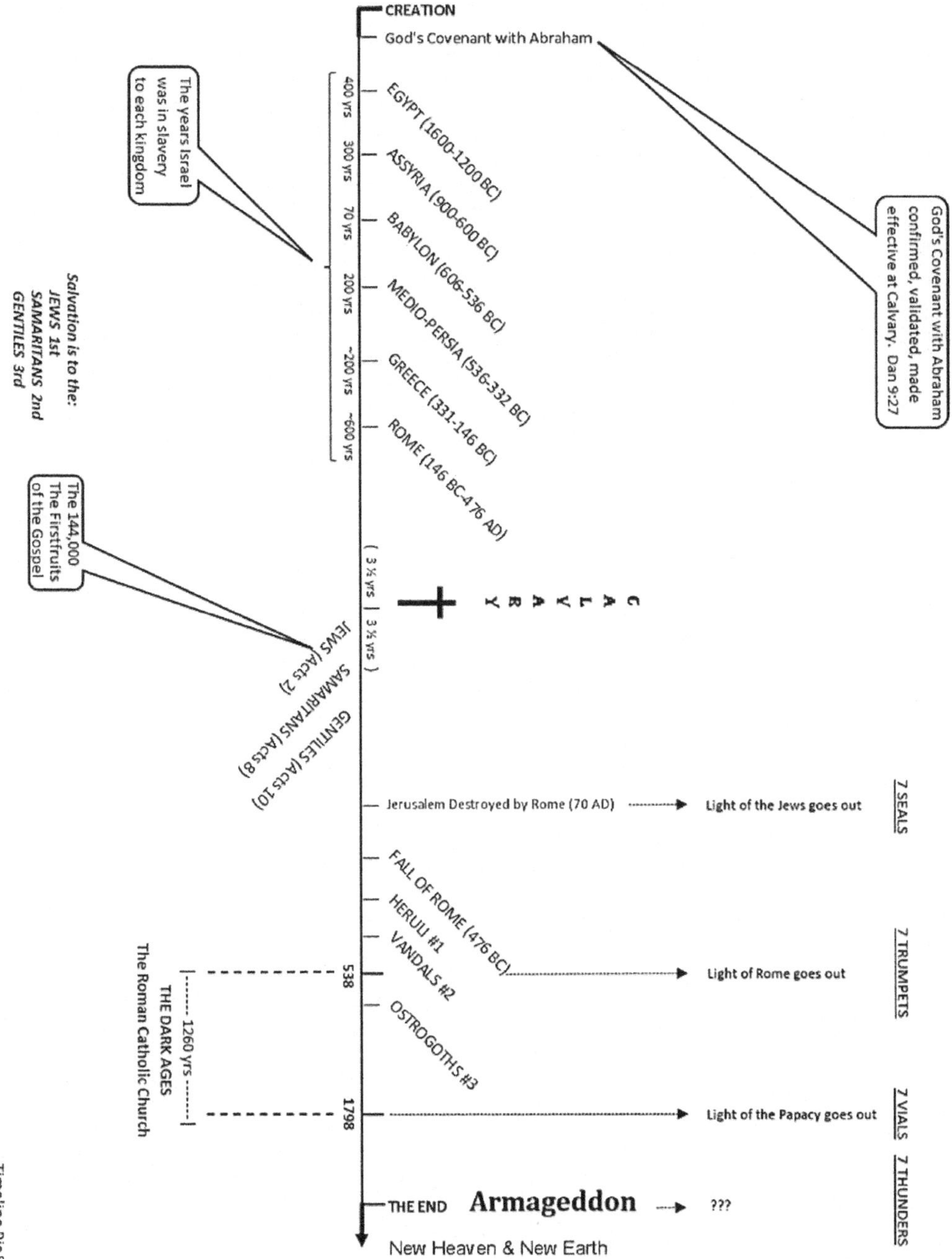
CREATION
God's Covenant with Abraham
God's Covenant with Abraham confirmed, validated, made effective at Calvary. Dan 9:27
The years Israel was in slavery to each kingdom
400 yrs
300 yrs
70 yrs
200 yrs
~200 yrs
~600 yrs
EGYPT (1600-1200 BC)
ASSYRIA (900-600 BC)
BABYLON (606-536 BC)
MEDIO-PERSIA (536-332 BC)
GREECE (331-146 BC)
ROME (146 BC-476 AD)
Salvation is to the:
JEWS 1st
SAMARITANS 2nd
GENTILES 3rd
The 144,000
The Firstfruits
of the Gospel
(3 ½ yrs | 3 ½ yrs)
CALVARY
JEWS (Acts 2)
SAMARITANS (Acts 8)
GENTILES (Acts 10)
Jerusalem Destroyed by Rome (70 AD)
Light of the Jews goes out
7 SEALS
FALL OF ROME (476 BC)
HERULI #1
VANDALS #2
538
OSTROGOTHS #3
Light of Rome goes out
7 TRUMPETS
1260 yrs
THE DARK AGES
The Roman Catholic Church
1798
Light of the Papacy goes out
7 VIALS
7 THUNDERS
THE END
Armageddon
???
New Heaven & New Earth
Timeline Pic 8

CHAPTER 15

THE THOUSAND YEAR REIGN

Revelation 20

THE PREMISE:

The 1000-Year Reign is the church age in which we reign as kings and priests with Christ, provided we have been Born Again, according to the book of Acts.

SCRIPTURE TEXT:

Revelation 20:1-15 *And I saw an angel come down from heaven, having the key of the bottomless pit and a great chain in his hand. And he laid hold on the dragon, that old serpent, which is the Devil, and Satan, and bound him a* ***thousand years****, And cast him into the bottomless pit, and shut him up, and set a seal upon him, that he should deceive the nations no more, till the* ***thousand years*** *should be fulfilled: and after that he must be loosed a little season. And I saw thrones, and they sat upon them, and judgment was given unto them: and I saw the souls of them that were beheaded for the witness of Jesus, and for the word of God, and which had not worshipped the beast, neither his image, neither had received his mark upon their foreheads, or in their hands; and they lived and reigned with Christ a* ***thousand years****. But the rest of the dead lived not again until the* ***thousand years*** *were finished.* ***This is the first resurrection****. [the New Birth] Blessed and* *holy is he that hath part in the first resurrection: on such the second death hath no power, but they shall be priests of God and of Christ, and shall reign with him a* ***thousand years****. And when the* ***thousand years*** *are expired, Satan shall be loosed out of his prison, And shall go out to deceive the nations which are in the four quarters of the earth, Gog and Magog, to gather them together to battle: the number of whom is as the sand of the sea. And they went up on the breadth of the earth, and compassed the camp of the saints about, and the beloved city: and fire came down from God out of heaven, and devoured them. And the devil that deceived them was cast into the lake of fire and brimstone, where the beast and the false prophet are, and shall be tormented day and night for ever and ever. And I saw a great white throne, and him that sat on it, from whose face the earth and the heaven fled away; and there was found no place for them. And I saw the dead, small and great, stand before God; and the books were opened: and another book was opened, which is the book of life: and the dead were judged out of those things which were written in the books, according to their works. And the sea gave up the dead which were in it; and death and hell delivered up the dead which were in them: and they were judged every man according to their works. And death and hell were cast into the lake of fire. This is the second death. And whosoever was not found written in the book of life was cast into the lake of fire.*

CHAPTER HIGHLIGHTS

1. An angel with a key and chain binds Satan for a thousand years.
2. The saints live and reign with Christ for a thousand years.
3. The thousand years is called the First Resurrection.
4. Reigning saints:
    - were beheaded for the witness of Jesus and the Word of God.
    - did not worship the beast or his image.
    - did not receive the mark of the beast.
5. Satan is loosed for a little season at the culmination of the thousand years.
6. God destroys Satan and his army with fire.
7. The earth and heaven flee the face of God.
8. The books are opened, and everyone is judged.

9. Satan, death, hell [Hades], and anyone not written in the book of life are cast into the Lake of Fire [Gehenna].
10. The Lake of Fire [Gehenna] is the second death

Strong's definition of "Hades" is the place (state) of departed souls, namely the grave. "Gehenna" is of Hebrew origin, referring to a place of everlasting punishment. Both are translated into the word hell but have different meanings.

DEFINITIONS

Key [G2807] kleis
A key, since the keeper of the keys has the power to open and to shut
Metaphorically, in the NT denotes power and authority of various kinds
From G2808; a key (as shutting a lock), literally or figuratively:—key.

Bound [G1210] deo
Bind, tie, fasten, impel, compel: declare to be prohibited and unlawful
Properly: an animal, to prevent it from staying around; with the accusative person to bind, to fasten with chains, to throw into chains
Metaphorically: bound or constrained in my spirit, compelled by my convictions, by a Chaldean and rabbinical idiom: to forbid, prohibit, declare to be illicit.

As the usage of the term *bound* in Chaldean and rabbinical idioms suggests, Satan is *bound* in his relation to the church. Satan is forbidden and prohibited from crossing the blood to arbitrarily afflict, oppress, or possess believers at will. Just as in the case of Job, who had a hedge of protection about him, Satan had to obtain permission from God to afflict Job. Once a Believer has been properly "Born Again," Satan is issued a "restraining order" by God.

Only God or the Believer can grant Satan permission and authority in the life of the Believer. Nothing can separate us from the love of God. Nothing can pluck us out of His hand. Only by our own prerogative and willful disobedience can we remove ourselves from the protection of our blood covering in the Kingdom of God.

Bottomless Pit or Deep [G0012] abyssos
Bottomless, unbounded, the abyss, the pit, the immeasurable depth of Orcus, a very deep gulf or chasm in the lowest parts of the earth used as the common receptacle of the dead and especially as the abode of demons

Thousand [G5507] chilioi
Plural of uncertain affinity; a thousand: - thousand.
Affinity has to do with relationships, as in relationship by marriage, according to Merriam-Webster's Dictionary
Thousand (chilioi) seems to have an unknown length of time attached to it or perhaps all-encompassing completeness rather than a literal meaning of time.

Expired [G5055] teleo
To bring to a close

SIMPLY EXPLAINED

Being born into the Kingdom of God (the Church) qualifies us as part of the Bride of Christ. We thereby become heirs to the Kingdom of God. It is in this spiritual kingdom that we reign as kings and priests. God (the true "Opener and Shutter of Doors"), by His Word (the "Key"), binds Satan by constraining, forbidding, and prohibiting him from deceiving the nations until the end of an uncertain affinity of time (a time of a marriage-type relationship). Because we are joint heirs with Jesus Christ in this Kingdom, we, too, have the power to bind and loose in the spirit. We have a God-given authority to exercise this right by the Word of God.

When the "thousand years" (the Church Age) comes to a close, Satan is loosed for a little season and goes out to deceive the nations. Satan and his army encompass the saints only to be destroyed by the fire of God. After this, the books are opened, and everyone is judged. If our name is found written in the book of life, we go to be with The Lord, where He has created a new heaven and a new earth for His chosen. If our name is **not** found written in the book of life, we are cast into the lake of fire along with death, hell, Satan, and his demons.

THE THOUSAND YEARS – LITERAL OR FIGURATIVE

> *Be ye mindful always of his covenant; the word which he commanded to a* ***thousand*** *generations; Even of the covenant which he made with Abraham, and of his oath unto Isaac;*
>
> I CHRONICLES 16:15-16

> *He hath remembered his covenant forever, the word which he commanded to a* ***thousand*** *generations.*
>
> PSALM 105:8

Although the Bible explicitly says a thousand generations, we understand this to be figurative. How could this passage, in any possible way, be taken literally? There are only 42 generations from Abraham to Jesus. Do we then have another 958 literal generations to go? If we interpret "a thousand' literally in this text, and if a generation is 30 to 40 years or more in length, then the Lord's return is not for at least another 30,000 to 40,000 years, conservatively! The point is to discern between what is literal and what is figurative.

Jesus painted many pictures in parables and then expounded them to his disciples later. Even the statement "Jesus painted many pictures" is a metaphor. We use metaphors and figurative language all the time to describe our depth of passion or express something very important. The book of Romans declares that Gentiles are wild olive branches grafted into a holy olive tree. This is another example of figurative language. Obviously, we are not plants.

The New Testament plan of salvation does not end at a "rapture" event, and then "another way" of salvation presents itself! Jesus will not set up an earthly physical kingdom and start a new era with a new way of salvation for the Jews or anyone else who is "left behind." That would contradict the scripture that says there is One Lord, One Faith, and One Baptism. That is blatant false teaching.

THE KINGDOM OF GOD – LITERAL OR FIGURATIVE

Now initially, the disciples believed Jesus would set up a literal earthly kingdom. This caused much contention over who would have the greatest position and/or the most authority in this earthly kingdom. James and John, the sons of Zebedee, were presumptuous enough to request a seat on the right hand and on the left hand of Jesus (Matthew 20:21, Mark 10:37). The disciples all imagined an earthly governmental structure in the physical, with different levels of importance, and authority to rule over people and locales.

They did not understand that citizenship of the Kingdom of God meant having authority in the spirit over sin and the whiles of the devil. They did not understand it to mean having the power of God to live an overcoming life, preach deliverance to the spiritually captive, and pull down strongholds of principalities and spiritual wickedness in high places. Furthermore, the "New Birth" experience was not even available at this point because Jesus had not yet died and risen again. The New Covenant way of salvation remained veiled until Jesus rose from the dead, appeared to his disciples, and opened their understanding.

Jesus taught many parables concerning the Kingdom of God. It is in the Kingdom of God that we shall reign as kings and priests for a thousand years. After his resurrection, Jesus appeared to the disciples, *being seen of them forty days and speaking of the things pertaining to the kingdom of God* (Acts 1:3), and commanded them not to leave Jerusalem until they were baptized with the Holy Ghost. The New Birth is the ONLY method of entry into the Kingdom of God. The disciples were now beginning to understand *the things pertaining to the kingdom of God* and never again asked questions concerning nor spoke of any literal earthly kingdom.

Consequently, the parable of Matthew 20 states that all the workers in the vineyard received the same reward. In Christ, we are all the same. When our Lord returns, we will all receive the same reward of eternal life. To say we shall reign as kings and priests after the coming of The Lord is not to understand the power and authority we have in this life as kings and priests in the realm of the spirit. There will be no hierarchical system in heaven. How can one person be more worthy than the next? How can one individual be more important than another?

I Peter 4:18 declares that, *if the righteous* ***scarcely*** *be saved, where shall the ungodly and the sinner appear?* When this present world passes away, and The Lord creates a new heaven and a new earth, everything will be perfect. There will be no need for a governmental structure to keep order when we all live in perfect harmony.

THE FIRST RESURRECTION IS THE NEW BIRTH

Satan is bound during the thousand. During this period, the souls of the saints who were beheaded for the cause of Christ and who did not worship the beast nor identify themselves with the beast, lived and reigned. Although many saints lost their lives, they lived and reigned in the spirit, and their souls were saved. They were free in spirit! A person can be enslaved or be incarcerated in prison and still be set free from sin and delivered from Satan's snares. Verse 5 refers to this time as the First Resurrection. The First Resurrection *is* the New Birth. When we obey the gospel (the *Death, Burial*, and *Resurrection* of Jesus Christ), we *Repent* by "dying" out to sin, are *Buried* in Baptism in the name of Jesus Christ, and are *Resurrected* in newness of life by the Infilling of the Holy Ghost!

When we obey the apostolic message in the book of Acts, we choose to die out to the flesh. This is the First Death, whereby our obedience frees us from the Second Death, which is spiritual death and eternal punishment. We, by willful choice, die and are Born Again into a spiritual kingdom and become joint heirs with Christ in His kingdom where there is neither Jew nor Greek. We are all the same in the eyes of the Lord. There is one salvation for all, Jew and Gentile alike, which is yet another stumbling block for many eschatologists who teach that there is "another way" for the Jews in addition to Acts 2:38. This is absolute heresy!

LIVING AND REIGNING AS KINGS AND PRIESTS

As part of the church through the New Birth experience, we live and reign as kings and priests with the Lord.

And hath raised us up together, and made us sit together in heavenly places in Christ Jesus:

EPHESIANS 2:6

Ye also, as lively stones, are built up a spiritual house, a holy priesthood …

I PETER 2:5A

Now ye are full, now ye are rich, ye have reigned as kings without us: and I would to God ye did reign, that we also might reign with you.

I CORINTHIANS 4:8

And they sung a new song, saying, Thou art worthy to take the book, and to open the seals thereof: for thou wast slain, and hast redeemed us to God by thy blood out of every kindred, and tongue, and people, and nation; And hast made us unto our God kings and priests: and we shall reign on the earth.

REVELATION 5:9-10

And I will give unto thee the keys of the kingdom of heaven: and whatsoever thou shalt bind on earth shall be bound in heaven: and whatsoever thou shalt loose on earth shall be loosed in heaven.

MATTHEW 16:19

Is not this the fast that I have chosen? To loose the bands of wickedness, to undo the heavy burdens, and to let the oppressed go free, and that ye break every yoke?

ISAIAH 58:6

Notwithstanding in this rejoice not, that the spirits are subject unto you; but rather rejoice, because your names are written in heaven.

LUKE 10:20

Christians sing songs like "bind the devil in Jesus' name" and "the devil is under our feet!" We **absolutely** do have the power to "bind" the devil in the name of Jesus and to "loose" the chains of bondage! Born Again, Holy Ghost-filled saints of God are not under the power of Satan. The blood of Jesus binds Satan! He is rendered powerless by the blood of Jesus. Satan is subject to us and not us to him. Know your rights! Know the Word of God! Just as Satan had to obtain permission from God to afflict Job, he must be allowed permission to have any power in our lives—whether by God or by us. In times past, we walked in bondage. We were not in control. Sin reigned in our mortal bodies. But now, through regeneration, the Spirit works in us to prove what is good and acceptable according to the will of God (Romans 12:2, Ephesians 5:8-10).

Wherein in time past ye walked according to the course of this world, according to the prince of the power of the air, the spirit that now worketh in the children of disobedience; Among whom also we all had our conversation in times past in the lusts of our flesh, fulfilling the desire of the flesh and of the mind; and were by nature the children of wrath, even as others.

EPHESIANS 2:2-3

We are blessed to live in an age where we have the freedom to come and go without fear of persecution unto death. Yes, there are cases of apostolic saints being killed, but it is not the norm. Nevertheless, if the day should so come, so what if we are beheaded, tortured, and murdered as our fellow brethren in times past? Paul said in Romans that our eternal reward could not be compared to any persecution in this present world.

But there is coming a day when Satan will be loosed for a little season. Perhaps it is the age we live in today. The depth of deception, its level and intensity that surrounds us individually and collectively as the church, is astounding. It really seems that Satan has been unleashed. And, because he knows he has but a short time, he is destroying families, individuals, and church bodies, and that is just among the saints, let alone the rest of the world.

We are fighting demons both without and within the church. Churches and organizations are everywhere doing good and notable deeds and even imitating the true church to the point it is difficult to see the dividing line. Yet, ironically, many churches are becoming the greatest enemies of biblical truth. We watch as churches sing familiar songs, worship, have miracles, are blessed, do many honorable deeds, and even allow members to operate in the gifts of the Holy Ghost. They do many great things in the name of Jesus!

So, why do they *refuse* to baptize in the *only name under heaven given among men, whereby we must be saved* as commanded in Acts 4:12, which is the name of Jesus? Therefore, they do not have the blood applied, the mark of Jesus Christ, and He will say on judgment day, "Depart from me; I never knew you."

Not every one that saith unto me. Lord, Lord, shall enter into the kingdom of heaven; but he that doeth the will of my Father which is in heaven. Many will say to me in that day, Lord, Lord, have we not prophesied in thy name? and in thy name have cast out devils? And in thy name done many wonderful works? And then will I profess unto them, I never knew you: depart from me, ye that work iniquity.

MATTHEW 7:21-23

WHAT MARKS THE TRUE CHURCH?

Now, suppose the "mark" or the identity of the true church is:

- Repentance.
- Water Baptism in "the name of Jesus Christ."
- Spirit Baptism in the Holy Ghost, initially evidenced by speaking in an unknown tongue.

Then the mark of the False Church (Mystery Babylon) is any doctrine that teaches otherwise.

EXAMPLES OF FALSE DOCTRINE:

1. Repentance is not necessary.
2. Baptism is only a public display or confession.
3. If baptism is performed, it is done in the titles Father, Son, and Holy Spirit.
4. The Baptism of the Holy Ghost is marginalized.
5. Speaking or praying in tongues is considered taboo.

Let us not forget that according to the bylaws of the Catholic Church, those "who believe in Christ and have been **properly baptized** are put in a certain, although imperfect, communion with the Catholic Church."

Any baptismal formula that **denies** (omits) the name of Jesus is the most obvious clue of a counterfeit daughter church of the Roman Papacy.

Neither is there salvation in any other: for there is none other name under heaven given among men, whereby we must be saved.

ACTS 4:12

And whatsoever ye do in word or deed, do all in the name of the Lord Jesus …

COLOSSIANS 3:17A

Now, if baptism in "the name of Jesus" is the mark of the true church, then the mark of mystery Babylon, the mother of harlots, is none other than a substitute baptismal formula in the titles "Father, Son, and Holy Ghost." How an individual is baptized is the distinguishing spiritual identification as to having the mark of Christ or the mark of the Beast.

The silver lining is that if an individual has not been baptized or has been baptized incorrectly and therefore has the mark of the Beast, one merely needs to be baptized correctly according to scripture. It's that simple!

THE FINAL JUDGEMENT

In Revelation 20:12, all stand before God to be judged. All stand before Him, all that have the blood applied to the doorposts of their hearts, and all those who do not. THEN, the Book of Life is opened. If we have been Born Again, then we are part of the First Resurrection and are found written in the Book of Life because we *live*!

It is called the "Book of Life" because the "Spiritually Alive" are written therein, not the "Spiritually Dead." Our carnal nature died at an altar so that our spirit man may live; therefore, the second death has no power. However, if our carnal nature was not crucified, then our sins will follow and condemn us to eternal death.

Revelation is the greatest book when it comes to the understanding that there truly is only One God, according to Deuteronomy 6:4 and that Jesus is the image and visible manifestation of the invisible God. The first verse declares that it is "The Revelation of Jesus Christ." It is the unveiling of the identity of Jesus Christ. Revelation exemplifies the monotheistic view of God, the New Birth into His Kingdom, and the victorious journey of His Bride through the ages until the grand reward of our future hope. It is a glorious book and not mysterious at all when built upon a sure foundation.

CONCLUSION:

The 1000-Year Reign is the church age in which we reign as kings and priests with Christ, provided we have been born again according to the book of Acts.

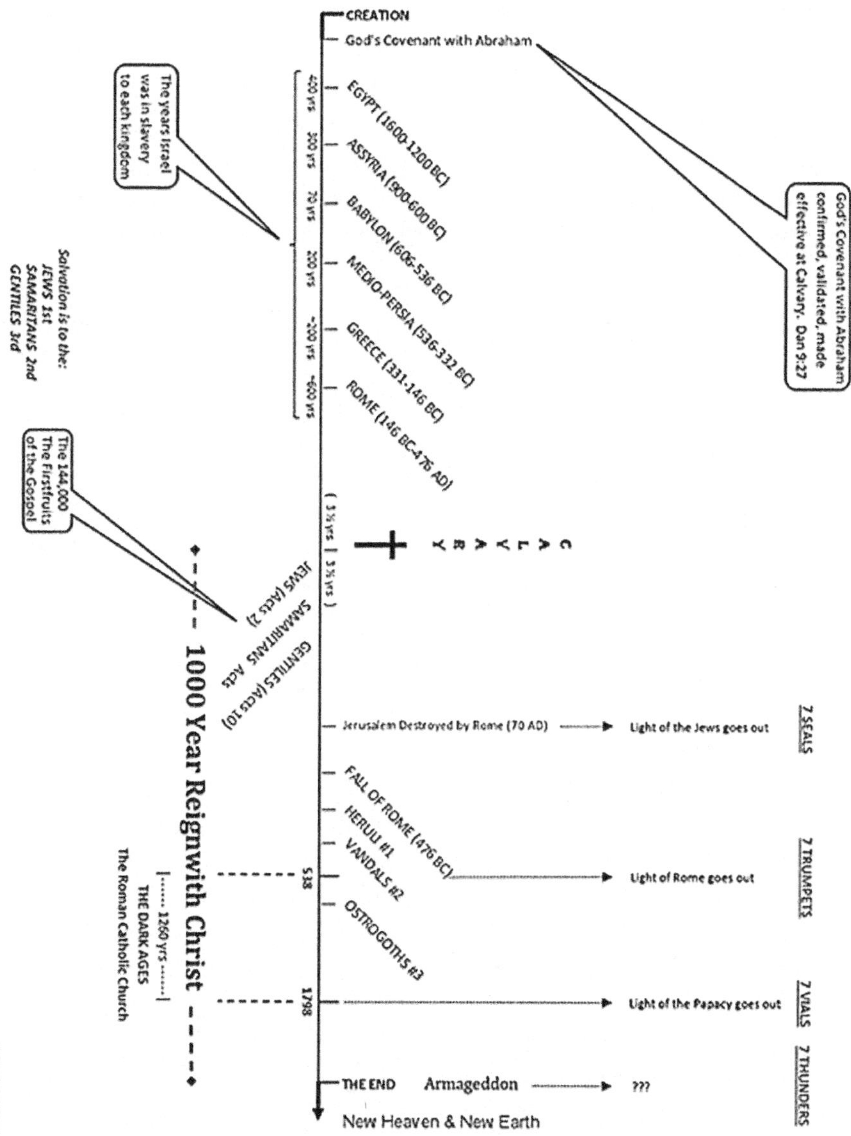

CREATION
God's Covenant with Abraham
God's Covenant with Abraham confirmed, validated, made effective at Calvary. Dan 9:27
EGYPT (1600-1200 BC)
ASSYRIA (900-600 BC)
BABYLON (606-536 BC)
MEDIO-PERSIA (536-332 BC)
GREECE (331-146 BC)
ROME (146 BC-476 AD)
The years Israel was in slavery to each kingdom
Salvation is to the:
JEWS 1st
SAMARITANS 2nd
GENTILES 3rd
C A L V A R Y
The 144,000 The Firstfruits of the Gospel
JEWS (Acts 2)
SAMARITANS Acts
GENTILES (Acts 10)
Jerusalem Destroyed by Rome (70 AD)
Light of the Jews goes out
7 SEALS
FALL OF ROME (476 BC)
HERULI #1
VANDALS #2
OSTROGOTHS #3
538
Light of Rome goes out
7 TRUMPETS
1260 yrs
THE DARK AGES
The Roman Catholic Church
1798
Light of the Papacy goes out
7 VIALS
1000 Year Reignwith Christ
THE END
Armageddon
???
7 THUNDERS
New Heaven & New Earth
Timeline Pic 9

CHAPTER 16

THE NEW JERUSALEM

Revelation 21, 22

THE PREMISE:

The New Jerusalem is the bride, the Lamb's wife, the body of Born Again believers. It is the Church.

SCRIPTURE TEXT:

Revelation 3:12 *Him that overcometh will I make a pillar in the temple of my God, and he shall go no more out: and I will write upon him the name of my God, and the name of the city of my God, which is* ***new Jerusalem****, which cometh down out of heaven from my God: and I will write upon him my new name.*

Revelation 21:1-23 *And I saw a new heaven and a new earth: for the first heaven and the first earth were passed away; and there was no more sea. And I John saw the holy city,* ***new Jerusalem****, coming down from God out of heaven, prepared as a bride adorned for_her husband. And I heard a great voice out of heaven saying, Behold, the tabernacle of God is with men, and he will dwell with them, and they shall be his people, and God himself shall be with them, and be their God. And God shall wipe away all tears from their eyes; and there shall be no more death, neither sorrow, nor crying, neither shall there be any more pain: for the former things are passed away.*

And he that sat upon the throne said, Behold, I make all things new. And he said unto me, Write: for these words are true and faithful. And he said unto me, It is done. I am Alpha and Omega, the beginning and the end. I will give unto him that is athirst of the fountain of the water of life freely. He that overcometh shall inherit all things; and I will be his God, and he shall be my son. But the fearful, and unbelieving, and the abominable, and murderers, and whoremongers, and sorcerers, and idolaters, and all liars, shall have their part in the lake which burneth with fire and brimstone: which is the second death. And there came unto me one of the seven angels which had the seven vials full of the seven last plagues, and talked with me, saying, Come hither, I will shew thee the bride, the Lamb's wife. And he carried me away in the spirit to a great and high mountain, and shewed me that great city, **the holy Jerusalem**, *descending out of heaven from God, Having the glory of God: and her light was like unto a stone most precious, even like a jasper stone, clear as crystal; And had a wall great and high, and had twelve gates, and at the gates twelve angels, and names written thereon, which are the names of the twelve tribes of the children of Israel: On the east three gates; on the north three gates; on the south three gates; and on the west three gates. And the wall of the city had twelve foundations, and in them the names of the twelve apostles of the Lamb. And he that talked with me had a golden reed to measure the city, and the gates thereof, and the wall thereof. And the city lieth foursquare, and the length is as large as the breadth: and he measured the city with the reed, twelve thousand furlongs. The length and the breadth and the height of it are equal. And he measured the wall thereof, an hundred and forty and four cubits, according to the measure of a man, that is, of the angel. And the building of the wall of it was of jasper: and the city was pure gold, like unto clear glass. And the foundations of the wall of the city were garnished with all manner of precious stones. The first foundation was jasper; the second, sapphire; the third, a chalcedony; the fourth, an emerald; The fifth, sardonyx; the sixth, sardius; the seventh, chrysolite; the eighth, beryl; the ninth, a topaz; the tenth, a chrysoprasus; the eleventh, a jacinth; the twelfth, an amethyst. And the twelve gates were twelve pearls; every several gate was of one pearl: and the street of the city was pure gold, as it were transparent glass. And I saw no temple therein: for the Lord God Almighty and the Lamb are the temple of it. And the city had no need of the sun, neither of the moon, to shine in it: for the glory of God did lighten it, and the Lamb is the light thereof.*

Revelation 22:1-21 *And he shewed me a pure river of water of life, clear as crystal, proceeding out of the throne of God and of the Lamb. In the midst of the street of it, and on either side of the river, was there the tree of life, which bare twelve manner of fruits, and yielded her fruit every month: and the leaves of the tree were for the healing of the nations. (Refer to the picture of the Two Witnesses in Chapter 3) And there shall be no more curse: but the throne of God and of the Lamb shall be in it; and his servants shall serve him: And they shall see his face; and his name shall be in their foreheads. And there shall be no night there; and they need no candle, neither light of the sun; for the Lord God giveth them light: and they shall reign for ever and ever. And he said unto me, These sayings are faithful and true: and the Lord God of the holy prophets sent his angel to shew unto his servants the things which must shortly be done. Behold, I come quickly: blessed is he that keepeth the sayings of the prophecy of this book. And I John saw these things, and heard them. And when I had heard and seen, I fell down to worship before the feet of the angel which shewed me these things. Then saith he unto me, See thou do it not: for I am thy fellowservant, and of thy brethren the prophets, and of them which keep the sayings of this book: worship God. And he saith unto me, Seal not the sayings of the prophecy of this book: for the time is at hand. He that is unjust, let him be unjust still: and he which is filthy, let him be filthy still: and he that is righteous, let him be righteous still: and he that is holy, let him be holy still. And, behold, I come quickly; and my reward is with me, to give every man according as his work shall be. I am Alpha and Omega, the beginning and the end, the first and the last. Blessed are they that do his commandments, that they may have right to the tree of life, and may enter in through the gates into the city. For without are dogs, and sorcerers, and whoremongers, and murderers, and idolaters, and whosoever loveth and maketh a lie. I Jesus have sent mine angel to testify unto you these things in the churches. I am the root and the offspring of David, and the bright and morning star. And the Spirit and the bride say, Come. And let him that heareth say, Come. And let him that is athirst come. And whosoever will, let him take the water of life freely. For I testify unto every man that heareth the words of the prophecy of this book, If any man shall add unto these things, God shall add unto him the plagues that are written in this book: And if any man shall take away from the words of the book of this prophecy, God shall take away his part out of the book of life, and out of the holy city, and from the things which are written in this book. He which testifieth these things saith,*

Surely I come quickly. Amen. Even so, come, Lord Jesus. The grace of our Lord Jesus Christ be with you all. Amen.

As Jesus expounded in Matthew 13, the wheat and the tares are harvested together. The wheat is gathered in the master's barn, and the tares are burned with fire. The wheat, the good seed (all the saints, past and present) are caught up to *meet* the Lord in the air. The earth is cleansed by fire, and then that holy city of believers, the new Jerusalem, comes down from that heavenly marriage supper of the Lamb as a bride adorned for her husband to a New Heaven and a New Earth.

THE NEW JERUSALEM, A FIGURATIVE SYMBOL OF THE CHURCH

The angel said he would show John the bride, the Lamb's wife, and then went on to show him in the spirit that holy city, the new Jerusalem. Therefore, it follows that the bride, the Lamb's wife is that holy city, the new Jerusalem! They are one and the same. And thus, the scriptures following describe in highly figurative poetic language the beauty and perfection of the bride and the foundation upon which she stands, and her glorious reward.

When a groom talks of his precious bride, his language is saturated with metaphor and simile. When he is so in love and wants to describe her and how he adores her, he does not simply say she has blue eyes and brown hair and he is fond of her. Oh No! He will embellish her description and speak of inoculating blissfulness and the tingling of electricity shooting through his body. He will tell of the hypnotic effect of her deep blue Caribbean eyes, her silky hair set aglow by the sun and her rose-petal lips that drip with honey. Oh, baby! And is this not how the Lord feels about his bride, The Church?

The Song of Solomon is a romantic masterpiece and beautifully describes the love affair that The Lord has with his church. We find in the Gospels His love for us runs so deep that He took on the form of man to suffer and to be tempted as us but without ever wavering. He even went so far as to be humiliated and crucified to make a way of salvation for us. And, at this very moment, He still desires us just as much! What greater love? God is not in love with a location on a map or a physical city; He is in love with a people.

SCALE MODEL OF A LITERAL NEW JERUSALEM

Now, if we consider the interpretation that the New Jerusalem is a literal city, 1500 miles in width, length, and height, the proportional dimensions would look as pictured:

Adam Clarke wrote concerning John's description of the Holy City: "This description has been most injudiciously applied to heaven; and in some public discourses, for the comfort and edification of the pious, we hear of heaven with its golden walls, golden pavements, gates of pearl, etc., not considering that nothing of this description was ever intended to be literally understood." Instead, he said these descriptions of a city symbolized "the pure and holy Christian church."

THE NEW JERUSALEM IS THE CHURCH

The New Jerusalem represents "The Church." According to the King James Concordance, "church" means "the body of Christ," and according to the Young's Analytical Concordance, "church" means "that which is called out." When Jerusalem is mentioned in the book of Revelation, it refers to "The Church." In fact, the literal city of Jerusalem is never called by name in Revelation but rather called Sodom and Egypt, depicting utter wickedness and bondage (Revelation 11:8).

After a lengthy, detailed description of the New Jerusalem in Revelation, Chapters 21 and 22, John encourages the wicked to be Born Again! What? A call to repentance? Look closely.

For without are dogs, and sorcerers, and whoremongers, and murderers, and idolaters, and whosoever loveth and maketh a lie. And the Spirit and the bride say, ***Come****. And let him that heareth say,* ***Come****. And let him that is athirst come. And whosoever will, let him take the water of life freely.*

REVELATION 22:15, 17

Without the New Jerusalem are *dogs, sorcerers, whoremongers, murderers, idolaters,* etc. If the New Jerusalem is supposed to be a depiction of heaven, why are these wicked people still around? And, why does God tell *him that is athirst* to *take of the water of life freely* if he is speaking of a physical city? This is a call to sinners to Repent, be baptized in the name of Jesus Christ, and receive the Holy Ghost!

The New Jerusalem is the Church! These *dogs, and sorcerers, and whoremongers, and murderers, and idolaters* (and such were some of us!), etc., are outside the body of Christ, the church. But anyone of these can repent and be Born Again into the Church and *partake of the water of life freely.*

Jesus answered and said unto her, If thou knewest the gift of God, and who it is that saith to thee, Give me to drink; thou wouldest have asked of him, and he would have given thee living water. The woman saith unto him, Sir, thou hast nothing to draw with, and the well is deep: from whence then hast thou that living water? But whosoever drinketh of the water that I shall give him shall never thirst; but the water that I shall give him shall be in him a well of water springing up into everlasting life.

JOHN 4:10-11, 14

He that believeth on me, as the scripture hath said, out of his belly shall flow rivers of living water.

JOHN 7:38

MANSIONS IN MY FATHER'S HOUSE

Consider the following conversation between Jesus, Thomas, and Philip in John 14.
Jesus begins by saying:

> ***In my Father's house*** *are* ***many mansions****: if it were not so, I would have told you. I go to prepare a place for you. And if I go and prepare a place for you, I will come again and receive you unto myself; that where I am, there ye may be also. And whither I go ye know, and the way ye know.*

Thomas speaks:

> *Lord, we know not whither thou goest; and how can we know the way?*

Jesus speaks:

> *I am the way, the truth, and the life: no man cometh unto the Father but by me. If ye had known me, ye should have known my Father also: and from henceforth ye know him, and have seen him.*

Now **Philip** speaks:

> *Lord, shew us the Father, and it sufficeth us.*

Jesus speaks:

> *Have I been so long time with you, and yet hast thou not known me, Philip? He that hath seen me hath seen the Father; and how sayest thou then, Shew us the Father?*

Jesus continued His answer to Philip through verse 14, and then, in verse 15, Jesus returned to His discourse from verse 4.

> *If ye love me, keep my commandments. And I will pray to the Father, and he shall give you another Comforter, that he may abide with you forever. Even the Spirit of truth.*

BRIEF SUMMARY

In my Father's house (The Church, the called out, the body of Christ) *are many mansions* (individual saints as temples of God, dwelling places for the Spirit of God (I Corinthians 3:16). *I go* (to the cross to die for you) *to prepare a place for you* (by becoming that perfect sacrificial lamb to atone for your sins so you may now enter the holiest of holy to commune with me personally now and forever). *If ye love me, keep my commandments. And I will pray to the Father, and he shall give you another Comforter* (I will return spiritually in the form of the Holy Ghost, and when you receive the Holy Ghost in Acts, Chapter 2, that will be me living in you to comfort you from within), *that he may abide with you forever* (I, Jesus, will never leave you or forsake you). *I am with you, and shall be in you.* (John14:17)

ONE BODY, ONE BRIDE, ONE CHURCH

In the body of Christ are many members. The members are fitly joined together to comprise one body.

> *For by one Spirit are we all baptized into one body, whether we be Jews or Gentiles, whether we be bond or free; and have been all made to drink into one Spirit. For the body is not one member, but many. But now are they many members, yet but one body. Now ye are the body of Christ, and members in particular.*
>
> I CORINTHIANS 12:13-14, 20, 27

Furthermore, it matters not that we are Jew or Gentile, circumcised or uncircumcised, for circumcision is of the heart, and there is *neither* Jew nor Greek in the kingdom of God according to scripture.

WHAT DOES IT MEAN TO "MEET" THE LORD IN THE AIR?

> *For this we say unto you by the word of the Lord, that we which are alive and remain unto the coming of the Lord shall not prevent them which are asleep. For the Lord himself shall descend from heaven with a shout, with the voice of the archangel, and with the trump of God: and the dead in Christ shall rise first: Then we which are alive and remain shall be caught up together with them in the clouds, to* ***meet*** *the Lord in the air: and so shall we ever be with the Lord.*
>
> I THESSALONIANS 4:15-17

We shall ***meet*** *the Lord in the air*. According to Strong's #G529, the word "meet" in this verse comes from the Greek word ***apnatesis*** and is used to reference a governor, king, or dignitary visiting a city. As the dignitary approached the city or kingdom, the inhabiting citizens would go out to "meet" him and then escort him back to the city or kingdom.

Then shall the kingdom of heaven be likened unto ten virgins, which took their lamps, and went forth to ***meet*** *the bridegroom. And at midnight there was a cry made, Behold, the bridegroom cometh; go ye out to* ***meet*** *him.*

MATTHEW 25:1, 6

The virgins that had their lamps full of oil (the Holy Ghost) were instructed to *go ye out to* ***meet*** *him*. The virgins were going out to "meet" *him* and to usher *him* back to where they had been.

At the end of the world, the saints will **meet** the Lord in the air and usher Him back to a new heaven and a new earth that has been cleansed this time by fire.

Of old hast thou laid the foundation of the earth: and the heavens are the work of thy hands. They shall perish, but thou shalt endure: yea, all of them shall wax old like a garment; as a vesture shalt thou change them, and they shall be changed:

PSALM 102:25-26

But the day of the Lord will come as a thief in the night; in the which the heavens shall pass away with a great noise, and the elements shall melt with fervent heat, the earth also and the works that are therein shall be burned up.

II PETER 3:10

And I saw a new heaven and a new earth: for the first heaven and the first earth were passed away; and there was no more sea.

REVELATION 21:1

SUMMARY:

Salvation came through the Jews, built upon the Apostolic Doctrine of Salvation with the Belief in One God being the chief cornerstone.

Ye worship ye know not what: we know what we worship: for salvation is of the Jews.

JOHN 4:22

Sanctify them [the 12 apostles] through thy truth: thy word is truth. As thou hast sent me into the world, even so have I also sent them [the 12 apostles] into the world. And for their sakes I sanctify myself, that they also might be sanctified through the truth. Neither pray I for these alone, but for them [future believers] also which shall believe on me through their [the 12 apostles] word;

JOHN 17:17-20

We will meet Jesus in the air and usher him back to a new earth under a new heaven. We are members of the Church, citizens of the New Jerusalem. The twelve foundations of the New Jerusalem have the names of the twelve apostles written on the foundation. This is representative of the Church's foundation upon the Apostles' doctrine (the New Birth experience as exampled multiple times in Acts). Jesus Christ is the chief cornerstone (the revelation that Jesus Christ is the express image of God). The twelve gates had the names of the twelve tribes written on them because salvation came through the Jews.

CONCLUSION:

The New Jerusalem is the bride, the Lamb's wife, the body of Born Again believers. It is The Church.

CHAPTER 17

INTERPRETATIONS OF REVELATION

Preterist, Historical, Futurist, Spiritualist

THE PREMISE:

The book of Revelation is given specifically as an in-depth investigation into the identity of Jesus Christ, the doctrine of One God, and the necessity of the New Birth. The various interpretations of the book of Revelation only distract from this crucial point.

INTRODUCTION:

It is interesting when browsing the vast literature surrounding the book of Revelation, the seemingly endless marketing of fear, spookiness, bloodshed, and global government conspiracies. It almost appears as though the book is some sort of scary horror story. The only happy ending is that the overcoming Christians get a giant mansion house in a floating city in the sky. So much is written, and so many put forth their opinions, not as opinions, but as absolutes, with little or no logical support.

Most arguments are philosophical and involve theories on the subject rather than practical applications. Perhaps an open mind with a spirit of reverent humility and the guidance of the Holy Ghost, accompanied by prayer and fasting, is a better way to seek to understand such a book.

THE IMPORTANCE OF REVELATION 1:1

> ***The Revelation of Jesus Christ**, which God gave unto him [John], to shew unto his servants things which must shortly come to pass; and he sent and signified it by his angel unto his servant John:*
>
> REVELATION 1:1A

This scripture is so vitally important! This verse sets the course and tone for the rest of the book.

As we discovered in Chapter Three, **The Two Witnesses – Part I**, all scriptural truths ultimately flow to and from the Golden Candlestick of One God and bear witness of Jesus Christ.

The book of Revelation is a revealing, an unveiling, an exposition of Jesus Christ. It is a book designed to give us a clearer image of Jesus Christ with emphasis on Deuteronomy 6:4. Revelation is without a doubt the most spectacular book on the Oneness of God and the necessity of the New Birth! John was graciously awarded this privilege of seeing Jesus more intimately because it was John who was always closest to Jesus. Satan has in every way attempted to bastardize this beautiful book by surrounding it with so much controversy, more so than any other book.

And why wouldn't he? He does not want us to know who Jesus is! But mention how you enjoy reading the book of Revelation and see the response. Mention any other book, and you are ok. Mention Revelation and beware—especially in "Christian" circles! Or, to really get a myriad of interesting responses, mention that the Lord showed something to you in the book of Revelation or that you understand it and that it is evident to you, and watch the response you get!

THE FOUR PRIMARY INTERPRETATIONS

There are many interpretations of the book of Revelation, all of which have their difficulties—except for the one you are now reading. I'm kidding! It's ok, laugh.

Roughly speaking, according to Halley's Bible Handbook, there are four prominent interpretations, each varying greatly within themselves: Preterist, Historical, Futurist, and Spiritualist.

1. **Preterist Interpretation** (including Partial Preterist) regards the book as referring to its own day. Mainly all prophetic passages are relegated to John's Day.
2. **Historical Interpretation** is that the book was designed to forecast a general view of the whole period of church history from John's time to the end of the world—a sort of Panoramic view of the Church's struggle to final victory.
3. **Futurist Interpretation** centers the book primarily around the time of the Lord's coming and the end of the world. Mainly, all prophetic passages are relegated to the time immediately prior to the Second Coming and afterward. Herein also arises the debate of a Pre-Tribulation, Mid-Tribulation, or Post-Tribulation Rapture.
4. **Spiritualist Interpretation** separates the book's imagery entirely from any reference to historical events (John's day or those at the end of the world). It regards the book as a pictorial representation, in highly figurative language, of the great principles and divine government applicable to all times.

Although both the Preterist and Futurist Interpretations were founded in the late 1500s and promulgated by Jesuit priests (Luis De Alcazar–Preterism and Francisco Ribera–Futurism), the futurist interpretation has maintained a strong following, especially among Protestants over the centuries.

There is such a fantastic parallel between some of the book's imagery and the course of church history that it seems that one of the objects of the book must have been to foretell it. And there is material in the book that so evidently refers to the time of the end that it must be considered regardless of the interpretation.

THE TWO DOMINANT INTERPRETATIONS: PRETERISM AND FUTURISM

Remember that both Preterism and Futurism originated from Roman Catholicism by Jesuit priests!

ROMAN CATHOLIC ORIGIN OF PRETERISM

Luis De Alcazar's interpretation in his commentary "*Investigation of the Hidden Sense of the Apocalypse*" proposed that all of Revelation applied to the era of pagan Rome and the first six centuries of Christianity. He also interpreted the 1260 days, 42 months, and 3 ½ times to be a literal three and a half years. He proposed that:

1. The 3 ½ years are before the destruction of the temple of Jerusalem in 70 A.D.
2. Revelation, Chapters 1–11, describes the rejection of the Jews and the destruction of Jerusalem by the Romans.
3. Revelation, Chapters 12–19, was the overthrow of Roman paganism (the great harlot) and the conversion of the empire to the church, namely, the Catholic Church.
4. Revelation, Chapter 20, describes the final persecutions by the Antichrist who was Cesar Nero.
5. Revelation, Chapters 21–22, describes the triumph of the New Jerusalem.

ROMAN CATHOLIC ORIGIN OF FUTURISM

Francisco Ribera's interpretation proposed that the first few chapters of the Apocalypse applied to ancient Rome. He suggested the remaining chapters were limited to a literal period in the future consisting of three and a half years or immediately before the Second Coming. He then proposed that the Antichrist, a single individual, would:

1. Persecute and blaspheme the saints of God
2. Rebuild the temple in Jerusalem
3. Abolish the Christian religion
4. Deny Jesus Christ
5. Be received by the Jews
6. Pretend to be God
7. Kill the Two Witnesses of Revelation 11
8. Conquer the world.

So, according to Ribera, the 1260 days, 42 months, and 3 ½ times were also a literal 3 ½ years and not 1260 years. Therefore, nothing in the book applied to the Middle Ages when the papacy was at the height of its power, but to the future, hence the name Futurism.

FUTURISM TAKE ROOT

Manuel De Lacunza (1731–1801), a Jesuit from Chile, wrote a manuscript in Spanish entitled "*The Coming of the Messiah in Glory and Majesty*" under the pen name Juan Josafat [Rabbi] Ben-Ezra about 1791. He wrote under an assumed name to obscure the fact that he was Catholic and to give his book better acceptance among Protestants. Also, as an advocate of Futurism, Lacunza's manuscript was published in London, Spain, Mexico, and Paris between 1811 and 1826.

Edward Irving (1792–1834), a Scottish Presbyterian and forerunner of the Pentecostal and Charismatic movements, translated Lacunza's work into English in a book entitled "*Preliminary Discourse to the Work of Ben Ezra–Coming of Messiah in Glory and Majesty*," published in London in 1837 by L.B. Seeley & Sons.

Margaret McDonald, a fifteen-year-old Scottish girl and member of Edward Irving's congregation, had visions in the early 1830s that included a secret rapture of believers before the appearance of the Antichrist. McDonald wrote about her vision in a letter to Irving. He then attended the prophecy conferences in Dublin, Ireland (circa 1830), which were held at Powerscourt Castle. He promoted Futurism and the idea of a secret rapture there.

Samuel Roffey Maitland (1792–1866) was a scholar and librarian to the Archbishop of Canterbury. He further promoted and established Futurism in England after 1826 due to reading the works of Manuel De Lacunza.

John Nelson Darby (1800–1882), a Church of Ireland clergyman, later with the Plymouth Brethren, also promoted Futurism and the idea of a secret rapture. Darby attended these same conferences at Powerscourt, Ireland, that began in 1830, where he apparently learned this theology. Darby soon visited Margaret McDonald at her home in Scotland. Darby visited America several times between 1859 and 1874, where he found that his Futurism theology was widely accepted.

Cyrus Ingerson Scofield (1834–1921), greatly influenced by the writing of Darby, incorporated Futurism into the notes of his Scofield Reference Bible (first printed by Oxford University Press in 1909). In the 20th century, the Scofield Bible established the Jesuit-inspired interpretation in the Protestant Bible schools of the United States.

THE PURPOSE OF PRETERISM AND FUTURISM

The fact these two theologies, Preterism and Futurism, differ greatly matters little. The Papacy, the supposedly divine and infallible scripture interpreter, presented two interpretations that redirected the attention away from the Roman Papacy as fitting any characteristics of the Antichrist. It is interesting to note that the Protestants who broke away from Roman Catholicism have been almost solely responsible for the success and promotion of Jesuit-inspired theology.

In summary, two teachings arose to thwart attention away from the Roman Papacy and prove it was not the Antichrist. One teaching was from a Jesuit Doctor of Theology, born in Spain, Francisco Ribera (1537–1591), and the second from another Spanish Jesuit, Luis De Alcazar (1554–1613). Ribera promoted the Futurist theology, and De Alcazar promoted the Preterist theology.

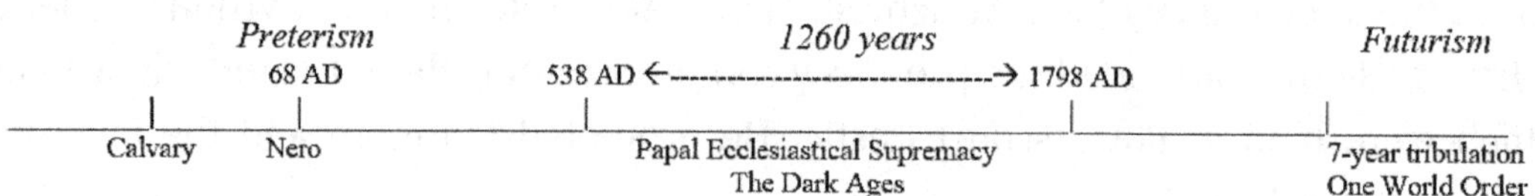

Let us not forget that the doctrine of One God and the New Birth, according to the book of Acts is *not* Protestant doctrine. The doctrine of One God and salvation by repentance, baptism in the name of Jesus Christ, and the baptism of the Holy Ghost evidenced by speaking in an unknown tongue did *not* come out from Roman Catholicism.

It did *not* evolve out of any Protestant movement but began on the day of Pentecost in Acts 2:38. A True Born Again Christian is *not* Protestant! Since the day of Pentecost, the Born Again Christian either grew up in this precious Truth or was converted into it.

CONCLUSION:

Revelation is the greatest book in the Bible regarding revealing and unveiling the identity of Jesus Christ, the doctrine of One God, and the necessity of the New Birth. The various interpretations concerning the book of Revelation are formulated to distract from this crucial point.

GOD'S ULTIMATE PLAN FOR YOUR LIFE

According to God's Holy Word, You Must be Born Again. It is *not* an option.

> *While Peter yet spake these words, the Holy Ghost fell on all them which heard the word. And they of the circumcision which believed were astonished, as many as came with Peter, because that on the Gentiles also was poured out the gift of the Holy Ghost. For they heard them speak with tongues, and magnify God. Then answered Peter, Can any man forbid water, that these should not be baptized, which have received the Holy Ghost as well as we? And he commanded them to be baptized in the name of the Lord.*
>
> ACT 10:44-48

We **must**:

- Repent
- Be born of water (Baptism in the name of Jesus Christ)
- Be born of Spirit (Baptism in the Holy Ghost)

CHAPTER 18

ORIGIN OF THE MUSLIMS

Halley's Bible Handbook, the 24th edition, features some very interesting remarks concerning the Muslim (Mohammedanism) movement:

MOHAMMEDANISM

Mohammed, the grandson of the Governor, was born in Mecca (A.D. 570). In his youth, he visited Syria and came in contact with Christians and Jews. However, he was filled with horror for all the idolatry. In 610, Mohammed declared himself a prophet but was rejected at Mecca and fled to Medina in 622. There he was received and became a warrior and began to propagate his faith by the sword. In 630, he reentered Mecca at the head of an army, destroyed 360 idols, and became filled with enthusiasm for the destruction of idolatry. He died in 632, and his successors were called Caliphs.

The growth was rapid. By 634, Syria was conquered; by 637, Jerusalem; by 638, Egypt; by 640, Persia; by 689, North Africa; and by 711, Spain. Thus, within a short time, the whole of Western Asia and North Africa, the cradle of Christianity, became Mohammedan. Mohammed appeared at a time when the church had become paganized with the worship of images, relics, martyrs, Mary, and the saints. In a sense, Mohammedanism was a revolt against the idolatry of the Christian world and a judgment on a corrupt and degenerate Church. It, however, has proved a worse blight to the nations it conquered. It is a religion of hate, propagated by the sword, and has encouraged slavery, polygamy, and the degradation of womanhood.

The Battle of Tours, France (A.D. 732), was one of the decisive battles of the world. Charles Martel defeated the Muslim army and saved Europe from Mohammedanism. At that time, it was taking over the world like a tidal wave. But for that victory, Christianity may have been completely submerged.

The Arabians dominated the Mohammedan world from 622–1058. The capital was moved to Damascus in 661; to Bagdad in 750, where it remained till 1258. The Turks have ruled the Mohammedan world from 1058 to modern times. They were far more intolerant and crueler than the Arabians. Their brutal treatment of Christians in Palestine ultimately led to the Crusades.

Mongols from central Asia arrested Turkish rule under Genghis Khan (1206–1227), who traversed with the sword at the head of vast armies and torched a great part of Asia. Fifty thousand cities and towns were burned, 5,000,000 people were murdered, and in Asia Minor, 630,000 Christians were butchered. Under Tamerlane (1336–1402), a similar hurricane of destruction left a wake of ruined fields, burned villages, and blood. At the gate of every city, his custom was to build piles of thousands of heads, over 90,000 at Bagdad.

The Fall of Constantinople (1453) to the Turks ended the Eastern Roman Empire. It jarred Europe with the second threat of Mohammedan control, which John Sobieski later stopped in the battle of Vienna (1683). The Papacy was a gradual development, first appearing as a world power in the 6th century A.D., reaching the height of its power in the 13th century, and declining in power from the 13th century to the present.

ROMAN CATHOLICISM EXTENDS CHRISTIAN SALVATION TO MUSLIMS

The following excerpts are from *the Catechism of the Catholic Church, the Apostolic Constitution Fidei Depositum* on the Publication of the Catechism of the Catholic Church English translation (Copyright 1997) United States Catholic Conference, Inc. – Libreria Editrice Vaticana:

> **Section Two, Chapter Three, Article 9, Paragraph 3**
> III. The Church is Catholic
> *The Church's relationship with the Muslims.* "The plan of salvation also includes those who acknowledge the Creator, in the first place amongst whom are the Muslims; these profess to hold the faith of Abraham, and together with us, they adore the one, merciful God, mankind's judge on the last day."

The declaration of salvation extending to the Muslims is quite interesting, considering Muslims do not believe in a Triune God. They are monotheistic. They believe in only One God like the Jews and Oneness Apostolic Christians and despise the idolatry of the Roman Catholic Church. Thus, it appears that they were actually used by God as a judgment against the idolatry found in the early "Christian World."

CHAPTER 19

CONCLUDING REMARKS

So, what is the ultimate goal of all this? What should one really gain from this exhaustive jaunt? Simple! A love for God! A love for the Word of God! A desire to seek truth and an unction to obey the Word of God unto salvation!

But as it is written, Eye hath not seen, nor ear heard. But God hath revealed them unto us by his Spirit: for the Spirit searcheth all things, yea, the deep things of God For what man knoweth the things of a man, save the spirit of man which is in him? Even so the things of God knoweth no man, but the Spirit of God. Now we have received, not the spirit of the world, but the spirit which is of God: that we might know the things that are freely given to us of God.

I CORINTHIANS 2:9-12

My encouragement to you, the reader, is that you *can* understand the Bible! Why would The Lord God Almighty move on holy men of old to pen such wonderful words into the greatest work ever written if only to remain a mystery? Why would He give us an instruction manual that cannot be comprehended?

Yes, the Bible can be complex, but it is *for* us! We are all fully capable of understanding the highly figurative and mysterious book of Revelation. The book of

Revelation is the revelation, the unveiling, of the identity of Jesus Christ and of His glorious church.

It is incredible how reading Revelation from a monotheistic perspective underscores and further supports the doctrine of One God and the New Birth experience by repentance, baptism in the name of Jesus Christ, and the baptism of the Holy Ghost, as found in multiple places in Acts.

Regardless of education level or background, God desires for us to learn of Him and draw nearer to Him. He longs to reveal Himself more fully and intimate to us. Therefore, if you have not been properly "Born Again" according to scripture, do not hesitate. Do not procrastinate. Obey the book of Acts. Experience what it means to truly be Born Again according to scripture as spoken of so many times in this written work. The Holy Ghost is the very Spirit of Jesus Christ that works to lead and guide us into all truth. It is our responsibility to be sensitive to the call.

Be blessed!

APPENDIX

AUTHOR'S COMMENTARY

Treasure maps and treasure hunting have their place in the heart of every red-blooded young boy. It's all part of the adventure. I remember digging for dinosaur bones in my parents' garden at a very early age. Once, I found a small swell in the back of my parents' cow pasture. I contemplated, "Could this be an Indian burial ground?"

For the better part of that day, under the hot Texas sun, I dug deep into the sandy soil, hoping to unearth arrowheads, spears, shields, and all kinds of curious stuff. Although the only thing I found was more dirt, evidence of my excavation still exists today because I was too tired after digging to cover it up.

On other occasions, I would borrow rhinestones that looked like big diamonds from my mother's sewing cabinet and hide them in the house or bury them in the yard. Next, I would draw detailed treasure maps to dig them up later. Some of the treasures I found; some I did not. Sorry, mom!

That little boy still lives inside, looking for a chance to awaken. When I venture into the book of Revelation, or just about any part of the Bible for that matter, I can feel that little treasure hunter come alive in me. The Bible is by far the most incredible treasure map. Growing up Catholic and attending Holy Rosary Catholic School in

Rosenberg, Texas, helped shape my foundation of respect for the house of God and the things of God; I often reminisce about those days.

Out of a curious desire to understand the book of Revelation, I have watched and listened to many preachers, teachers, and scholars, always hoping to glean some critical information to "crack the code." And yes, in elementary school, my friends and I often developed secret codes and exchanged encrypted letters. But now, how could I solve a *real* mystery and crack a *real* code to find *real* treasure? How could I make sense of this mysterious encrypted book of Revelation?

I noticed a commonality among those who taught on Revelation. Each would begin with a scriptural base and then build logically upon it. Everything would follow along orderly and systematically, and then boom! The person teaching would make this giant intuitive leap and leave me wondering, "How in the world did you just go from where you were to where you are now?"

It never seemed to have continuity. It was always ambiguous, and no one seemed to agree. This made it even more interesting. If I asked too many questions, I was told it was not a salvation issue and to be quiet. That only deepened my curiosity and made it even more fascinating.

My dad always told me to go to college so I could learn how to think. I heeded his advice and received a bachelor's degree in mathematics, which now helps tremendously in learning how to think things through in a logical manner. In my college math courses, I had to do many mathematical proofs. That is where you prove how you arrived at your conclusion based on certain given information. This was similar to arguing a legal case step-by-step but with mathematics.

As I began to look at Revelation, I took the same approach, being open and leaving any preconceived views behind. That wasn't easy. Cognitive Dissonance is a compelling thing! I found that in having held a long-accepted belief, whether true or false, my subconscious wanted to reject anything not in harmony with that belief.

I had to go back to what was given. What were the initial building blocks upon which the Word of God stands? First, there is only One God (Deuteronomy 6:4). The doctrine of One God is the first axiom. In mathematics or logic, an **axiom** is an unprovable rule or first principle accepted as accurate because it is self-evident or particularly useful.

The second axiom is there is only one clear plan for salvation, the New Birth experience for the New Testament church (Acts 2, 8, 10, 19). From these two axioms, I began my deductive reasoning. Everything needed to flow logically from these two foundational truths and back to them easily. And it should be on a level easy enough for an adolescent to comprehend. And, because this book is built upon these two fundamental truths, it truly is an Apostolic interpretation.

The Twenty-Four Elders and the Four Beasts was an easy, non-threatening concept and an excellent place to start. It supported and reaffirmed the doctrine of One God. Next, the Two Witnesses neatly overlaid the Twenty-Four Elders and the Four Beasts, further supporting the doctrine of One God. Next, the 144,000 were called Firstfruits. Well, who were the first ones to be *Born Again* in Acts 2?

It was the Jews. The Jews were the Firstfruits and thus the 144,000. Who was *Born Again* after that in Acts 8 and 10? It was all the non-Jews, the "great multitude." The chapter on the 144,000 underscores the plan of salvation so nicely. Then, when all the timelines in Daniel's became clear, they too reaffirmed the New Covenant of repentance, baptism in the name of Jesus, and the infilling of the Holy Ghost. I can't help getting so excited when discussing the book of Revelation from this perspective! It keeps reaffirming One God and the New Birth! It truly is an apostolic perspective!

As Rev. T. F. Tenny said, "keep the main thing the main thing." So, if the main thing is the worship of One God and salvation by the New Birth, then all scripture will ultimately flow to and from the main thing. In doing so, one can clearly distinguish between the true church and the counterfeit church. Again, it all goes back to supporting and further emphasizing One Lord, One Faith, and One Baptism!

More than anything, I want to give glory to God for His mercy, for His sacrifice upon the cross, for forgiving all my horrible sins, for filling me with the Holy Ghost, and for allowing me the unfathomable grace and favor to be a part of the wonderful body of Christ! I sincerely love the Word of God! What a Treasure!

REFERENCES

SOURCES OF INFORMATION

- Henry H Halley. *Halley's Bible Handbook.* Twenty-Fourth Edition, 1965
- Merriam-Webster.com 2011. https://www.merriam-webster.com (8 May 2011)
- *Bible Timeline Chart with World History* https://amazingbibletimeline.com/blog/division-of-west-rome-into-10-tribes
- *Wikipedia*. https://wikipedia.org/wiki/Western_Roman_Empire
- www.wordola.com/wdict/confirm.all.html Source: Wordnet (r) 3.0 2006
- www.wordola.com/wdict/confirm.all.html Source: *Moby Thesaurus II* by Grady Ward
- http://catholic-resources.org/Courses/Christianity-Branches.htm: *The History of the Catholic Church* as compiled by Felix, S.J., Ph.D.
- *Catechism of the Catholic Church*, the *Apostolic Constitution Fidei Depositum on the*
- *Publication of the Catechism of the Catholic Church,* English translation copyright 1997
- United States Catholic Conference, Inc. – Libreria Editrice Vaticana.

- www.history-world.org/persians.htm
- *The Ancient History of the Egyptians, Carthaginians, Assyrians, Babylonians, Medes and Persians, Macedonians and Grecians.* By Charles Rollin, Translated from the French, In Four Volumes. Volume I, 1830
- *Ancient History; Exhibiting a Summary View of Progress, Revolutions, Decline, and Fall, of the States and Nations of Antiquity*. By John Robinson, D. D. 1831
- H. Gratton Guinness. *Romanism and The Reformation.* 1887
- *Catholic Dictionary*, Peter M.J. Stravinskas, Editor, published by Our Sunday Visitor, Inc., Huntington, 1993, pp. 484-485.
- Webster Handy College Dictionary
- Webster's II New Riverside Desk Dictionary
- Strong's Numbers
- George Wigram's *Englishman's Hebrew and Chaldee Concordance of the Old Testament* of 1874, republished by Hendrickson Publishers, Inc., 1996, ISBN 1-56563-208-7
- http://biblehub.com/greek/12.htm
- http://biblehub.com/greek/1210.htm
- *Barnes' Notes*, Electronic Database. Copyright 1997 © by Biblesoft
- *His Truth Is Marching On*, By Ralph Woodrow. Copyright 1977 © Library of Congress Catalog Card Number: 77-84543, ISBN 0-916938-03-4
- *Great Prophecies of The Bible*, By Ralph Woodrow. Copyright 1971 © Third Printing, April 1979, ISBN 0-916938-02-6
- http://biblelight.net/666.htm
- *Babylon Mystery Religion*, By Ralph Woodrow. Copyright 1966 © 1981 Edition, ISBN0-916938-00-X
- *The Wars of the Jews*, by Flavius Josephus

- Newton, *Dissertations on the Prophecies*
- Eusebius, *Ecclesiastical History*, Book 3
- *Clarke's Commentary*, Vol. 1, Matthew-Acts
- *Antiquities of the Jews*, by Flavius Josephus
- http://doctorwoodhead.com/nimrod-the-founder-of-the-occult-and-babylon/
- http://biblelight.net/antichrist.htm
- https://en.wikipedia.org/wiki/Armageddon
- https://www.touristisrael.com/megiddo/9448/
- https://www.bibletools.org/index.cfm/fuseaction/Lexicon.show/ID/G720/arneomai.tm
- http://biblehub.com/str/greek/2807.htm
- http://biblehub.com/str/greek/5507.htm
- http://biblehub.com/str/greek/5055.htm
- https://www.blueletterbible.org/lang/lexicon/lexicon.cfm?Strongs=H3772&t=KJV
- https://en.wikipedia.org/wiki/Will_and_testament
- https://www.blueletterbible.org/lang/lexicon/lexicon.cfm?Strongs=H6944&t=KJV
- https://en.wikipedia.org/wiki/Triple_Goddess_(Neopaganism)
- Green, C.M.C. (2007). *Roman Religion and the Cult of Diana at Aricia*. New York: Cambridge University Press.

ABOUT THE AUTHOR

Born in Houston, TX, **Louis Holub** moved to Rosenberg, TX, with his family in 1969, where he attended Holy Rosary Catholic School. He was an average student interested in the ordinary things of boyhood. Later transferring to public schools, Louis began to excel academically and continued through college, where he studied mathematics and earned a Bachelor of Arts degree in teaching.

His inquisitive mind and logical thinking were balanced by a bold sense of adventure, inspiring him to become a successful entrepreneur. At an early age, he visited several churches with his family until he arrived at a small Pentecostal church. There, he received the Holy Ghost and was baptized in the beautiful name of Jesus Christ.

He remained faithful in church attendance throughout his life, even when he knew he was not walking with God. That faithfulness paid off, and The Lord used his logical and creative ability to teach Bible studies and educate others in the scriptures. Louis began studying the Book of Revelation from a mathematical perspective around 2002. However, he soon found the prevalent views on prophecy were all rooted in Roman Catholicism, leading to more questions and confusion.

Everything seemed overly dramatic, and intuitive theories were presented as absolute facts and were not to be questioned. This was like dumping gasoline on a fire—fueling his inquisitive mind to seek to understand this taboo book from the perspective of the doctrine of One God and the New Birth experience found in the Book of Acts. Two decades later, and voila, you hold this amazing book in your hand.